SECRETS OF THE
TALKING JAGUAR

JEREMY P. TARCHER • PUTNAM
A MEMBER OF
PENGUIN PUTNAM INC.
NEW YORK

SECRETS OF THE TALKING JAGUAR

*Memoirs from
the Living Heart
of a Mayan Village*

Martín Prechtel

Most Tarcher/Putnam books are available at special quantity discounts
for bulk purchases for sales promotions, premiums, fund-raising, and
educational needs. Special books or book excerpts also can be created to
fit specific needs. For details, write Putnam Special Markets,
375 Hudson Street, New York, NY 10014.

JEREMY P. TARCHER/PUTNAM
a member of Penguin Putnam Inc.
375 Hudson Street
New York, NY 10014
www.penguinputnam.com

Library of Congress Cataloging-in-Publication Data

Prechtel, Martín.
Secrets of the talking jaguar : Memoirs from the living heart
of a Mayan village / by Martín Prechtel.
p.   cm.
ISBN 0-87477-970-7 (alk. paper)
1. Prechtel, Martín.   2. Shamans—United States—Biography.
3. Shamans—Guatemala—Santiago Atitlán—Biography.   4. Santiago
Atitlán (Guatemala)—Description and travel.   5. Tzutuhil Indians—
Religion—Miscellanea.   I. Title.
BF1679.8.P74A3   1998
299'.784152'092—dc21   97-48480 CIP
[B]

Book design by DEBORAH KERNER
All interior illustrations by Martín Prechtel

Printed in the United States of America

10

This book is printed on acid-free paper. ∞

ACKNOWLEDGMENTS

Like a strange, spindly tree, my life is rooted in the cultural humus of my ancestors. This book is an odd gathering of fruit from that tree, a fruit of remembrance. Watered into life by the jade tears of the original Tzutujil Maya, this tree was shrouded in a mist hidden from the world.

Robert Bly coaxed my story into public view. Without Don Roberto, this book would have perished with me in the clouds of unflowered possibility.

Secrets of the Talking Jaguar is mostly about keeping the interconnectedness of life alive by remembering. First and foremost I want to remember and thank the Highland Mayan tribes of Chiapas, Yucatan, Campeche, Quintana Roo, Belice, and Guatemala, and indigenous people everywhere.

I remember and thank Robert and Ruth Bly, my best friends of my recent life, without whom I hesitate to ponder how I or my sons might have ended up. But also for their blanket of encouragement that warmed into completing this book when the overwhelming grief and terror of those memories chilled my heart.

I don't forget poet Thomas Smith, and I thank him for his inspired dedication to the project, especially his miraculous ability to read 200,000 English, Spanish, and Mayan words in my legendary illegible handwriting, while typing them into an ornery computer at light speed for a deadline.

I remember my friends, colleagues, and authors Goia Timpanelli, John Lee, Robert Moore, and Malidoma Somé for consistent support and practical suggestions from their personal experiences. They saved me miles of migraines in regards to the business of books and how to survive writing one.

I thank editor Joy Parker for her masterful suggestions and for her patient and sympathetic ear. She will be remembered for defending my writing style and voice.

I am grateful and appreciative to Kerry Graham for her ever-present faith in this book and my work.

I shake the hand, remember, and give thanks to my ex-wife, Dolores Ratzan, from Santiago Atitlán, the mother of my two sons. Like most Tzutujil, she was not an avid fan of the written word, but she has remained a loyal supporter of myself and all Mayan tradition.

I remember and honor Jeremy P. Tarcher for his vision to publish unique works such as mine in an age of homogenization of culture and low-risk marketing. Thank you.

Great thanks to Ned Leavitt and team for letting their big-city ways advocate my old-village way of moving.

With a smile I remember editor Wendy Hubbert, editorial assistant Jocelyn Wright, copyeditor Katherine Pradt, and all the staff at Tarcher Putnam for their willingness to drag and dream this book into the beautiful format it has arrived in.

I thank Dr. Bob Roberts, Rosemary Mum, Christine Westfeldt, Nelson Marks, and all the friends at Project Return in New Orleans who inspire me by example, and whose affection and fine Gumbo helped me finish this book.

I thank my father, George Prechtel, whose admiration, faith, and long conversations have always forced my imagistic ideas into verbal expression.

I want to remember with great honor and gratitude all the men and women, organizers and participants of the various annual conferences, workshops, and institutions where I teach. Their desire for this book and their goodhearted friendship may have been the most powerful force behind this book. Some of these include the Minnesota Men's Conference, Mentone Conferences in Alabama, various California conferences, Utah conferences, The Great Mother Conference, and the Wild Dance events in England, to name just a few.

I remember with gratitude some specific individuals in these conferences such as: Wick Fisher, Tim Young, Miguel Rivera, Orland Bishop, Marylin Bacon, Mark Goodwin, Richard Olivier, and many more.

I want to honor and remember all my Tzutujil teachers and comrades in the struggle to keep *the original flowering earth* alive in Santiago Atitlán. All my sacred house-chiefs, co-chiefs, sub-chiefs, matrons, initiates, principal chiefs, shamans, and all the Tzutujil people of Santiago Atitlán, Chachya, Panabaj, Panaj, Xechivoy, Panul, Xejuyu, especially Nicolas Chivilu, Diego Sisay, Ma Tun Ratzan, Ma Tacaxoy, Ma Sosof, Pascual Mendoza, Ma Slaj, Ma Xuan Chamajay, and thousands more. There is no thanks large enough for them.

I remember any others on this earth whom I may have forgotten, who have helped me, tried to help me, or supported what I do: I don't forget you, I don't abandon you.

Finally I would like to remember and thank my intelligent, overly principled, highly literate, and stubborn Mother. Without her tragic example I would never have taken the courage to wander away from the familiar into the magical destiny whose partial tellings are the *Secrets of the Talking Jaguar.*

Long life
Honey in the heart
No evil
Thirteen thank-yous

This book is dedicated
to my beloved
Johanna Keller,
Lily breathed Sugar water woman

To honor
My sons Jorge and Santiago,
and the youth of all
indigenous people,
that their stories never die

All in fond memory of
Nicolas Chiviliu Tacaxoy,
my friend and teacher.

FOREWORD

I first met Martín Prechtel fourteen years ago, shortly after he arrived from Guatemala. I was visiting a friend in Santa Fe, and he said, "There's an extraordinary man living in a tipi about four miles out of town." I said, "Let's go." It was the middle of winter. We found the tipi. It had no floor, so snow was coming in under the edges; a dark-haired wife, two small children, and a man lived there, who had the Mayan nose and long golden hair. He agreed to see me the next morning, and we spoke a little. At the time he was working as a healer in the Santa Fe area. Eventually we became friends, and remained so, and we have taught hundreds of hours together during the last eight years.

I don't think I've ever known a teacher with so much resilience and joy, so much ability to cope with disturbances in any group he happens to be teaching, with physical illness, with rage, with racism, with rationalism, with shame at being a human being, with the bitterness of the unfathered and unmothered, with so much ability to pull humor out of sober stories.

His father Swiss, his mother a Native American from Canada, Martín is a half-European, half-Huron baby cooked in some darkness he couldn't have imagined. He settled into the famous Mayan village of Santiago Atitlán from the time he was twenty until he was thirty-three. There he received two initiations, one into the village religious tradition and the other into shamanism.

The Mayans call shamans "spirit-lawyers," that is, men or women who go to the spirits and try to argue them into giving a benefit of some sort to human beings. Mayan tradition does not teach that the Gods want people to be sinless or perfect, but they believe that the Gods love beauty, eloquence, fine clothes, great music, fine poems, bravery, high animal spirits, and gratitude. These human qualities taste like honey to the Gods, and the Gods are like bears who have to come into the village whenever they smell that honey. The spirit-lawyers point out all these beauties to the Gods. The Mayan people's main and ancient job is to be beautiful and grateful. Before meeting Martín, I'd never known a representative of such a culture. But I can testify to the integrity, the massive learning, the faithfulness, the lighthearted joy, and the hard-working nature of this representative.

From these metaphors of honey, of Gods crazy about smoke and dancing, we get a scent of the "original flowering earth," that is, the fantastic fragrance that can come into human life when, despite madness and greediness, old women and old men help the young ones to embody beauty and eloquence, and when eight-hundred-year-old rituals of gratitude get a chance to play themselves out. At conferences I've seen men and women weep when Martín Prechtel talks of the complex and rich village life of the Maya. The listeners realize how much more open their lives in youth would have been if their beauty had been honored as the young ones are honored in Santiago Atitlán, and if they'd had a chance to be kissed by the invisible faces "with tongues like puppies." They also weep when they realize how men and women, though they speak separate languages, can fly together like the two wings of a bird.

Several themes or ideas run through Martín Prechtel's account of the Tzutujil Mayan in *Secrets of the Talking Jaguar*. That it's good for each person in the village to be in debt, economically and spiritually, to every other person in the village; that it's wise to give payback to the spirits and to Mother Earth constantly, every morning, every ten minutes; that it's good to weep generously when a human being dies so he or she can make it all the way across to the other side; that it's essential to ask permission for every bit of iron or jade or silver or corn that we steal from the earth. It's enlivening also to understand that the Gods are charmed and fascinated with us as human beings, because we have thumbs—which spirits do not—and so can carve masks, weave cloth, invent musical instruments and play them, whittle sticks, and make paintings. It's good to know that what is needed most in the world, more even than food or warmth, is eloquence; it's good to know that most of life is maintenance—of leaf-roofed huts and our own connections to the spirits—and that it's a disaster to have a metal roof or to be saved once and for all.

Martín Prechtel, whose mother was a teacher in the Indian schools, was brought up in the reservations near Albuquerque. As a boy he was visibly bright; and he was taken into St. John's College at Santa Fe when he was fifteen by the poet and teacher Charles Bell, who had seen one of his poems. He never graduated. Then, after his mother died, he drifted around Mexico with a suitcase holding her dried-out paints. During that time he began to have dreams of a village in a forested mountain area, a landscape he had never experienced. Dreaming always of the same village, he began to recognize the tobacco seller and the houses and even some people whom he'd see walking down the street. Months later, hitchhiking in Guatemala, he was dropped off at a mountain town, and he was shocked to realize it was the same town that he had dreamt about. You can read in the book how all that happened.

It's a precious thing, this book. I've never known another like it. It's a great encyclopedia of beauty that could so easily have been lost if a tree had fallen differently, if a foot had slipped on a rock, if a canoe had sunk in the storm, if the gunman had aimed a little to the left. Like some poems of Neruda's, it is a treasure house of language, in service to life. But it wasn't written by a diplomat. Because Martín Prechtel supported traditional Mayan life, he became a target early in the civil war in Guatemala. After gunmen had made several attempts on his life, a group of old Mayan ladies dressed in traditional clothes appeared at his hut and told him: "You have helped us. We have named our children after you; but you must leave today, within an hour." How did an exile in New Mexico, embittered at the whites who had hit him with two-by-fours as a boy, the whites who hate the indigenous soul, the same ones who had destroyed so much indigenous culture all over the world and had paid for the bullets that killed his friends and collapsed the only home he had ever known, how did this exile overcome the bitterness long enough to write this book?

Three answers are possible. First, the old shaman teacher Nicolas Chiviliu, who had called him down and taught him, told him that the flowering time of the village was over, that soon all the treasures would be broken apart and scattered, the village heart dispersed, and that Martín's task was to carry the teaching north, to the "Land of the Dead." Second, there is the ritual food Martín served others and ate himself during his years in the village, which gave him a vigorous health that survived the move. Third, we could say that despite our own cultural losses, which include a collapse into horizontal materialism, we still have in the United States a community of men and women who want to learn. The gratitude he has received from this community over the last eight years has helped him not to leave the words he knows lying in his throat but to let them flow out.

How can a shaman be developed or created? Old Russian stories provide a metaphor: There's a barrel-boat. The young shaman is enclosed in it with a mother not his own. The boat has no top or bottom, and it is thrown into the ocean. There the two of them remain, floating around for a long time. All is dark inside.

In Martín's case, we could say that the old shaman Nicolas Chiviliu enclosed his initiate in the boat with the Great Mother, with Nature. His aim was to put the student in touch with the feminine, and with a divine force in Nature—perhaps a bear or a jaguar. Such a journey cannot be accomplished in a weekend. Such training, as Martín makes clear in his book, entails months alone with wild things, and it brings maturity of a different kind than we see in the world of technology.

Changing the metaphor slightly, we could say that life itself threw Martín into a stew with the old shaman and Nature and the multigendered spirits. Rumi in one poem lets a chickpea cry out from the stew in which it is cooking: "Why are you doing this to me?" The teacher says:

> Don't you try to jump out.
> You think I'm torturing you,
> I'm giving you flavor,
> So you can mix with spices and rice
> And be the lovely vitality of a human being.

It is hard for us to keep our young ones in the stew long enough for them to turn into adults, let alone the time necessary for them to become cooked adults, that is, to become initiated men and women or healers or elders. In Martín's later years in the village, he arranged and presided over an elaborate initiation ritual for sixty-five young women and sixty-four young men, a long process that we hope he will describe in another book.

Meanwhile we can say that the story told in this book of his own life is a metaphor for a successful initiation and one that did not take place on a distant island three thousand years ago, but in front of our eyes, so to speak, only twenty years ago.

That gives me hope. If the reader can avoid idealizing Martín Prechtel or Santiago Atitlán, if the reader can resist rushing down to find what is left of Nicolas Chiviliu's house, if we can fight off our greed to reexperience what he has experienced, then this book will do us no harm. If we can be quiet, this book will be a bucket that drops down toward the water of our indigenous soul. All the words that Martín writes here amount to a meditation on this soul as a natural force. Whether we are Swiss or Mayan or American, the indigenous soul, threatened all over the globe, still lives inside each of us. We can rejoice in its abundance, its ingenuity, its determination not only to exist but also to continue giving its gifts, if we will turn and meet it.

—ROBERT BLY

CONTENTS

AUTHOR'S NOTE

Never in my entire life did I think I could be convinced to write any kind of book whatsoever—much less a chronicle in English that would include my most treasured and grief-burdened memories of my early days in Guatemala.

Everything I became, both good and bad, I owe to those years. To speak of those times now is like making public the personal secrets of a deep love affair, opening horrific wounds to expose to the world those incredible days I can never have again.

But, too, my life in the village had been immersed in the oral tradition. No notes were ever taken, and no recordings made; one used only one's sheer ability to remember. Mayans know that people write things down, not so much to remember them, but to ensure they don't have to. This gives people a choice to remember things when they feel like it. But to the Tzutujil Maya in the village in which I once lived in Guatemala, to forget something sacred was to dishonor it. We didn't want that choice, so nothing real was permitted to be committed to writing.

Among the pre-European Guatemalan Maya, writing was a ritual activity and never done in a casual way. Writing was not done to communicate or express ideas in the strictest sense, but rather to create a visible "road of words" between the ancestral beings at the beginning of life and the eternal now of our world. This created a sort of sacred diary of sounds made visible, a conduit of writing straight to the Gods and ancestors. Like footprints into the old unseeable past, when read aloud these writings brought magically back into life all the eons of worlds experienced by our forebears and the plants and animals that sustained them, adding our present experience into that sequence. When bundled up and stored, these collective "word paintings" were fed ritually as Deities. This helped keep the road of words viable until they could be read aloud and thus fully brought to life.

The priests in charge of adding daily entries to the living words in accordance with the Mayan Divination Calendar were called *Ajtzib* by the Tzutujil. The position of "Writer-Priest" who fed written words with ritual continued right up to the day when I was a leader in the village of Santiago Atitlán. Another priest, called the *Ajuchan*, read these magically written words aloud in sacred contexts. Nothing written was ever intended to be studied in silence. All writing was made to be read aloud.

Europeans burned, confiscated, or forced these writings into hiding. Others have replaced those lost in some cases, but for the most part, all the rest of such lost writings were kept orally; after all, it was the speaking of words that the Maya held important anyway. Today, writing is still considered both sacred and dangerous by Tzutujil traditionalists.

In my Guatemalan village, my belly was filled to the top with oral histories, mythologies, genealogies, orally told ritual maps of how to get to and back from other worlds. All of this was to be kept secret, used and told only in respectful company, at appointed times in a village context. I would have to defend the secrecy of these writings with my life, as others before me had done. For me to write any of it down would be a flagrant betrayal of the very oral culture that I sought to defend by expressing its beauty in print!

But these are strange and desperate times for anything with a soul, especially what's natural. It's not only indigenous people who are being overrun, sold, twisted, seduced, killed, or trivialized; all peoples are beginning to experience this. My own children were deprived of their culture by the ruling cultures here in the U.S.A. After we fled the warfare and violence of the 1980s in Guatemala, my children were unable to return to that country to live the ceremonial life I'd lived. They were deprived of the benefits of village initiations. They wouldn't see the people, places, and objects described in the stories I told; they could only hear them. We waited for years to be able to go back to Guatemala, only to realize how much had been lost in the interim, killed off and forgotten by the violence and violent proselytizing of businesses, the military, and religious institutions.

For my own children, for your children, and for all that is indigenous in this world, I resorted to this writing, knowing full well how little could really be transmitted on paper—but what's to lose if we stand to lose it all? So, as the Tzutujil people say: "Please receive a little aroma of the Original Flowering Earth." This book-writing became something to remember about where we came from, what I did, and what was done. This way, perhaps, we can all continue this precarious adventure of life in the spirit of those village days. I hope something ancient and indigenous may reawaken inside the modern reader, who may catch a whiff or a glimmer of his or her own ancestral indigenous soul, or a memory of her ancient Celtic ancestral roundhouse, or Dravidian river people, or Polynesian canoe raid. Perhaps the soul could remember a little of its origination, when its people still belonged to the spirit of a place. Possibly my own story will give your stories courage enough to blossom.

INTRODUCTION
GUATEMALA:

A Deep Love Affair

Guatemala is the first country you encounter running out of southern Mexico into Central America. Of the six countries of Central America, Guatemala is the most culturally diverse and geographically varied. There are snow-covered mountains, Sonora-like deserts, high cloud forests, low-land rain forests, two different oceanfronts with two different-colored beach sands, rivers, hot springs, ten-mile-deep caves, blue-eyed German cowboys, West African Garifenos, Hindi jungle dwellers, Mestizos of great beauty, varied cultural modes and speech. In the country's capital of Guatemala City, there are Jewish areas; Italian areas; Lebanese, Spanish, and powerful Chinese clans; and citizens of every country in the world, still speaking their languages, with restaurants to go with each.

It is a land of great magic and incongruity where in Coban, the Quekchi Maya also speak German, and the Germans speak Maya; where in a little high mountain town, a group of Moorish Jews married in with the Mayans three and a half centuries ago. All the people of this town are short, tough, blue-eyed, and light-haired. They wear gold earrings, and dress and talk Quiche Maya while brandishing a Star of David and a menorah, and playing little square tambourines and flageolets.

Delicious, melancholy, lovely, full of flowers, mystery, laughter, and an extraordinary amount of suffering; if Guatemala were a woman, not a man alive wouldn't be lovesick for her. At once the wealthiest and the poorest nation in Central America, she is culturally the richest.

The major population group in the republic is still the indigenous Mayan people, who represent at least six million of the eight million

Guatemalan citizens. These Maya are very much alive and are one of the true living legacies of the Old Maya and Pre-Maya peoples. This makes Guatemala pretty much a Native American country. The Maya of popular history and legend didn't disappear; they just stopped making big buildings.

Today, with a few exceptions, the Maya of Guatemala inhabit many hundreds of hill villages in the country's southwestern highlands. Mostly corn farmers, these Highland Maya live on the fertile slopes and valleys in a range of rolling hills, canyons, and impressive forested volcanoes that stretches from Chiapas, Mexico, to southeastern Guatemala. This range of volcanic peaks runs parallel to the bend of the Pacific Ocean shore, separated from the beach by an eighty-mile-wide strip of coastal plains. This was once the home of the Nahuat Pipil Indians, who are now largely assimilated.

All up and down this Pacific coastline, many archaic cultures once blossomed, becoming the parent peoples to much of Mesoamerica and finally giving birth to the many incarnations of the original Maya people. These first ancestral Mayans lived on the ocean, dependent on fish and on the annual leatherback turtle nesting migrations for food and ritual. This coastline has been forever known as the Coast of Turtles in all the regional tongues. Traditionalist Maya still call it thus.

In this coastal-mountain district alone there are at least thirty language divisions of Mayan speech, many of which are not mutually intelligible. Within these divisions are hundreds of dialects and village variants. Each division of speech has its own indigenous clothing style, handwoven on backstrap looms by the women of that village. Each dialect has a distinct weaving signature and method of wearing the clothing, which reveals where you are from, what language you speak, your marital status, your spiritual position, and so on, all without your speaking a word. For this reason, the Highland Maya classify themselves and their neighboring tribes by speech and by dress. Mayans feel that they wear their speech in their clothing. This is oddly very true, for when a village stops wearing its indigenous outfit, in almost every case it signals the final loss of the village's language as well.

Up in these mountains in Guatemala's south-central region is a great volcanic crater filled with beautiful water over a mile deep and ten miles wide. Surrounded by even more volcanic peaks, this is the famous *Lago Atitlán*, or Lake Atitlán.

On the south shore of the lake, at the base of three forested volcanoes, resides a Highland Maya group known as the Tzutujil. A relatively small tribe, they number less than 50,000. By comparison, their northern Quiche cousins are over a million in number.

Most Tzutujil people live in the enormous village of Santiago Atitlán. The Tzutujil call the town where they live *Chjay* or "At Home." In the 1970s and '80s, this is where I landed. Here I stopped wandering; I lived, loved, married, and served the Tzutujil in native institutions.

A clannish, talkative, proud, spiritual people addicted to laughter, the Tzutujil have always craftily guarded from outsiders all that they are and all that they know. Many studies and articles have been put forth by sociologists, linguists, statisticians, archaeologists, ethnomusicologists, doctors, poets, fiction writers, tourists, developers, churchmen, politicians, journalists, and artists. Dumbfounded and intoxicated by the beauty and dreamlike quality of the land, lake, and people, however, very few of these studies reflect a true understanding of the Tzutujil of Santiago Atitlán. This is mostly because researchers want to learn, write, and then run off without first taking the time it really takes to be trusted by the Tzutujil. None of these researchers ever learned to fully speak the Tzutujil language. And besides all this, the villagers refused to be accurately studied, skirting all questions with courteous, subject-changing replies and even out-and-out fabrications, the subjects of some involved books! These people—university professors, anthropologists, investigators, and import-export people, etc.—were "soft raiders" who thought they were sympathetic with the Mayan people. Most got grants to write books and vacationed in this beautiful country, sort of hunting, gathering, picking, and purchasing information and material culture from people like the Maya in order to keep their tenure or make a living off the Indians, so they could actually live back in the States or Europe when they were finished "mining."

The Tzutujil demand that you "go the route" to learn anything, which means that questions are not answered until they are asked properly, which can only be accomplished by someone who has taken the time to get the Mayan vision of life. This can take years. But by then you are "Mayanized" and don't feel like writing anymore. So you go do something else! This has happened to more than a few. Outsiders who refuse to be Mayanized are coaxed into distributing lots of gifts, and when the gifts stop coming, the people utterly ignore the investigators until they flee in disgust, having learned nothing of what they came for.

My rapid acceptance into this inner sanctum mystified many non-Indian outsiders. They reckoned I was working on some Ph.D. project or compiling a secret study for the government or some other nonsense. These people expressed a lot of jealousy when I became useful to the village in their indigenous societies. Some non-Mayans hated that I corroborated the people's Mayan-ness instead of bringing them into the light of the twentieth century.

During these years, almost all visitors to Santiago Atitlán fell into one of several categories. The first were simple tourists who came, looked, and went. The second were people from big countries who settled in Guatemala to escape the expense of their homelands; they existed on the interest from their investments, employing Guatemalans as their maids, gardeners, and cooks. Unwilling to let anything Indian seep into their souls, they continued to live in the identical pattern of life they had fled. Packed into just a few Spanish colonial towns, they weren't really in Guatemala, but stuck in knots of other rich runaways.

The third kind of visitor to Guatemala came to change the country. These were the developers, Peace Corps people, missionaries, AID officers, and so forth. They were stationed in Guatemala, not visiting or living, not there because they loved the place, but physically there to enforce their code of "developed" reality on the country, to turn Guatemala into a viable business venture or sympathetic political entity.

None of these visitors cared much about Indians, and none of them knew anything about them. None of these people could figure out what I was up to. It was like trying to figure out what a jaguar basking in the sun was up to. Just that; happy to be alive. But people made up stories.

My own involvement in the village of Santiago Atitlán was never as an objective student of the Maya, who planned to leave and publish a book. I was part of the village and very happy and proud of it. In the village, I lived well, the way I'd always dreamed, useful to my people, with no plans to go anywhere else.

To Tzutujil traditionalists in Santiago, I was simply returning to the Center of the Universe: their village, a place a lot of the world had left behind long ago. I was coming home. To them, this was marvelous, but not a mystery. They knew exactly what was going on, and they let me stay.

This is the story of what happened.

JAGUAR BABIES ON THE BEACH OF MIST:

My Early Days

Two furry little heads bounced and turned to survey the tumult of old basaltic walls and village huts rushing by, as they jostled along, safe on Machayal's fast-walking back. Nestled in a simple handspun string bag, two baby jaguars whimpered and mewed, struggling now and then to climb out. But Machayal nudged them back into the tight mesh again with only their big-eyed heads peeking out. The little solidly built man never averted his eyes from his destination, which was my hut off the crowded western shore of the Bay of Santiago, on Lake Atitlán in the Tzutujil Maya village of Santiago Atitlán, Guatemala.

Though he was well known to all his people, most of the village considered him to be a *nicanic*, or simpleton. Some of us, especially the shamans, considered this strange man to be a "child of the wind." The wind was a god to us, the Lord of the Dry Season. Having grown enamored of Machayal's mother while in the forest, the wind had magically impregnated her. When it came time for Machayal to be born, his mother was caught out in the wilds again and gave birth to him under the very trees in the jungle he'd grow to love as an adult. This made him half-human, half-divine. Without village midwives or helpers, his mother had thrown his umbilical cord and afterbirth into a river which, as anybody in the village could tell you, made a child into a restless wanderer, never content to stay in one place.

Machayal did indeed appear to act very clumsy among humans, with no desire for the endless complexities of village life. But in the wilds he excelled, spending most of his days and nights there, vanishing out of the sight of humans just like his father, the wind. About every three weeks, Machayal would return to visit his old mother, but the monkeys and rivers would quickly call him back to the forest-covered volcanoes that form the high, breathtaking walls of Lake Atitlán.

What he did out there, nobody really knew. He had no food, no machete, and no water, and yet time after time he'd return fat and healthy after weeks of absence, loaded down with live animals and flowers.

No animal ever ran from Machayal. He'd simply walk up, touch them, then pick them up and put them in his little bag or carry them in his arms like a little kid with a big puppy, walking fifteen to thirty miles to our village. Then he'd walk into somebody's house and give these wild creatures to the occupants and go back to the bushes. That's how he was.

Once he delivered a pair of spider monkeys to my house. Once he brought an anteater, and another time he left me a pair of supposedly extinct horned guans. I knew people who got giant lizards, kinkajous, trogons, or coatimundis. Some of the creatures he brought were very rare, and some were dangerous to most humans. But all the animals were shy, and nobody knew why they went along with Machayal's plan. There was something divine about it.

On this occasion, Machayal thudded into my compound with a heavy, lumbering gait. With his usual disregard of Mayan village etiquette, he began yelling out in childlike Tzutujil:

"*A Martín Qa'?*" "Martín here?"

"*Jie in kola nen la, naqnawaj lá?*" "I am here. What's your desire, son?" I replied.

Handing me the two solidly built little cats, he gurgled, "*Jie ke a anxin.*" "Here, two of yours!"

And immediately turning, he thumped back up the trail into the bush, heading out of sight for another few weeks. The people at my end of the village poured into and around my in-laws' compound of huts to get a good look at my spotted visitors, as Mayans are very curious and like to bunch up to investigate anything unusual.

When I held the jaguar kits, I felt honored and somehow free, seeing myself as I would like to have always been, with my own spirit, like these twins, friendly in my arms, held close to my heart, heavy and full of play. They had me in a trance of deep admiration, when, coming to my senses, I noticed that there were hardly any teeth showing in the pristine gums of these babies. They were very much still on their mother's milk.

I bolted for the trail, yelling to the villagers up ahead to yell to those farther up the hill to stop Machayal and bring him back to me. In the village, the voice travels much faster than the feet; besides, I was both a chief and a shaman, and in an emergency people often responded quickly to what I asked of them. Some young fellows caught up to the "windman," and he rolled back down the slope to face me and the two magical squirming beasts.

"Have you seen their mother?"

He replied slowly in a sad tone, "Mother?"

"The mother of these two, the 'children of the woman mountain'!" I explained, using the polite form of address for a jaguar in case her spirits were listening.

"I don't know, Father. I just brought them to you; you're the same kind."

"Well, I say we should carry them back to where you found them, because their mother will be coming for them. That could be bad for everything and everyone in between her and us!"

For Machayal, the child of the wind, whose mind served a plan other than the village, this was too complicated. He just shook his head and left for the wilds, melting into the forest unseen and untrackable, just like a breeze.

I waited for word from the surrounding villages of the mother jaguar's whereabouts. An adult jaguar sighting would raise a ripple in any community, and we'd know about it soon enough.

Machayal had brought the little fuzzies to me over the water in a canoe. He'd found them three miles from Chacaya, the bottom of the bay, where the wild meets the water. My guess was the mother would track them to the water using her fine sense of smell and inspired by her fierce loyalty to her little ones. She would get stumped at the water's edge, I figured, and start searching up and down the shore in a desperate rage. If she thought they were in my village, she'd swim the bay, as jaguars prefer fish to all other meat and can therefore swim beautifully. For villagers and cats alike, it would be a dismal and pathetic mess if she made it to the village.

In the meantime, I took care of these two sad little creatures, watching them lap up milk from a rich Mayan cow in the most funny and messiest way. The Lord of the Mountains was said to visit this world as a jaguar, so I prayed on the kits as I'd been taught, placing my prayers on their little bushy heads where their fur made a big M. I asked them to take these gifts and messages to the Lords and Ladies of the other world at the center of the world, hoping that when we released the babies, the Deities would remember us humans in Santiago Atitlán with fondness and allow the powerful force of life of which they had charge to flow into the crops and destinies of the villagers I served.

Finally after a week, word of dead cattle, dogs, and poultry found on the other side of the lake began coming in with the men returning home from their work in the hills. The enraged mother jaguar had been seen depredating up and down the shoreline below Chacaya, that beautiful place at the end of the bay where the wilds ran into the water. So I decided to place the babies in a handwoven sack and row them in a canoe out to the end of the bay by Tuq, and I hung about some two hundred yards off the shore on a humid, windless morning. I let the kits mew and whine, to call the mother's attention.

Suddenly, she let herself into the misting water off to my right from behind a grassy point where a pre-Spanish rock carving of the Serpent of the Southern Wind was hidden. I began rowing frantically through the tules and released the blinking kittens onto the muddy, sparkling black gravel of the shore where the trees meet the water. Her ears wet and laid back, the mother jaguar swam toward them, looking harmless and vulnerable, but I wasn't fooled. I rowed off in my dugout canoe to a safe distance to watch.

Dragging herself to shore, the jaguar shook herself off and ran to her little ones. They jumped around ecstatically, licking her nose and sucking her engorged nipples. She stood tongue out, panting, catching her breath, eyeing me.

I offered my breath to her in prayer, and filled myself with her magic. She turned her head back to her rear and grappled one of the creatures in her mouth, raising her head and pushing stiffly into the green thicket. The other kit followed hard on the nipple right under her, somewhat impeding her long-suffering progress until they'd all disappeared into the forest we called The Flowering Mountain Jade Water Earth: the Kingdom of the Gods.

That night as I lay sleeping, I dreamt a spotted old lady jaguar held me tenderly but inescapably in her grip while she licked my face with her big rasping tongue. In the intervals between great washings of my weeping face, she whispered secrets into my ear in a low rumble like a far-off rainstorm. She filled me with knowledge and the substance of my unopened destiny. I woke up shaking and happy in the middle of one of those washings, knowing the jaguar was my spirit wife, the talker whose secrets from the original earth have kept me alive to this day. These were gifts from the other world for having released my well-treated prisoners, the jaguar babies, back to the Flowering Earth, to the wilds, to the land of dreams. These were the secrets of the talking jaguar.

As a little boy, I could clearly remember that world of eternally merging dreams called life in the womb. It sounded like sand against sand, like friendly whispering. Until I turned nineteen years old, I often dreamt of being a grain of sand. I was one of a billion other souls merged together as beautifully polished jeweled grains. I'd hear the rushing sounds of life as I'd awake, caused by the movement of each sandy soul rubbing against the next. As a teenager I dreamt my body was formed of billions of grains of jade sand. I tried to separate from the beach of sand-souls, to sit up and pull my new form out of the huge sandy matrix. Then every grain of sand began singing its own song. I felt heavy, and could move only by the power of the sand's song. A majestic cacophony of all things in the world sang as I tried to make my own form evident. The world rushed in on me as I awoke from the dream, the sound of the world outside merging with my sand sound. This was not a casual event, for twenty-two years later, the Tzutujil shaman Nicolas Chiviliu Tacaxoy, who became my best friend, confessor, mentor, and initiator, would tell me that his "nature spirit" was sand.

A sad and sickly little child who wept a lot, I walked with a painful limp until I was five or so. Around that time, I started making my famous ball of string, which was formed by tying any loose thread, wire, rope, twine, or fiber to the free end and winding it onto the ball. It grew so immense that I got to pushing it around with two hands, using all my strength, until one day I couldn't budge it anymore. I wanted to be attached to life, and like the threads of dreams and stories one lives out, clothing one's little origination point with one's destiny until one actually begins to appear like what one has learned.

My fascination with fibers and stories may have all come to me from my father's grandparents, who were Swiss cloth weavers. After immigrating to the Americas, in the late 1800s, their centuries-old unmechanized family trade was crushed and scattered on the hard shores of America's industrialized economy. The name Prechtel appears in written form for the first time in records of a trial held in the 1100s in what is now Austria. Assumed to be wizards, a group of aldermen from a remote village in the Alps were being tried by some church tribunal for heretical non-Christian practices. "Prechtel" was the name of the post held by the accused, a magic man, whose leadership abilities were rooted in a pre-Roman relationship with the mountains. The Alps themselves were their ancestors, which is where the name Prechtel is derived.

Like many farm boys after the Depression, my father joined the war effort, ending up stationed in Italy as a bombardier who regularly flew over

Germany. As an undergraduate paleontologist at the University of Wyoming after the war, he found himself fascinated with ancient extinct mammals and the open spaces of the American West, while trying to heal his soul from the horrible crash and fire of the war. The clean, wild air rushing down the mountains and across the badlands and grassy hills slowly sang his shattered spirit back into a life-loving form.

Even then he was changed. He'd been an avid admirer of science and technology, but he couldn't forget the war's nightmare of waste and destruction. He'd participated in it in the name of what he came to call the "absurdity of an abstract idealism." My father watched the friends of his youth, children of immigrant farmers, ground to dust and lost in the machine industry of the crowded cities. Others lost all sense of self and origins, squeezed out and used up in insane corporate competition for the same abstract ideal. This peacetime destruction of human beauty seemed to him a misuse of machines and a subversion of science. It all looked like war.

In the midst of this, I was conceived in a badlands blizzard of great remembrance. My parents were very happy out in the wilds, isolated together with me coming along in the belly. My favorite photograph of my dad shows how hard he tried after the war to make friends again with life. One of his college classmates had shot a mother antelope to help feed the university crew out on a dig in the late 1940s. While sifting and brushing in the Badland clays, my father heard what he thought was a human baby crying. It turned out to be the abandoned child of the mother antelope they'd cooked and eaten.

Someone took a picture of my father bottle-feeding the little orphaned pronghorn (which he later released at the end of the season). The irony of it was that my dad had been disinterring the fossilized remains of a four-horned prehistoric pronghorn when he discovered the very much alive baby. So there he was, a hundred thousand years later, feeding the child of an animal who died to feed him and his friends while digging up the stone memory of both, who died to feed somebody's ancestors.

As the child of a paleontologist, unlike the rest of America's children, when my birthday rolled around I received gifts of gastroliths, petrified hippo teeth, and petrified sponges instead of Tinkertoys or tricycles. But that was perfectly right for me. A shy, sensitive little boy, easily crushed emotionally and not very robust, I did well in nature but not so well with people. I'd see nuances in the tones and flow of life, understanding patterns where others didn't even notice them. More animal than human, I could smell and taste the essential qualities of things, knowing full well what was going on around me just by reading faces and movements.

I'd wander around the Indian reservation in New Mexico where I was raised, catching birds, wild rabbits, mice, snakes, lizards, and turtles. At age five, I found a nest of freshly hatched little snakes, and, worried about their safety, I hauled all fifty writhing beasts into our house, including one uncooperative big one wrapped around my arm, very sure she was the mom. But my own mother was terrified of serpents and wasn't very impressed with my heroic rescue. Anyway, the reservation's cattle dogs killed every last snake in less than five minutes while I screamed and wept and nobody thought to stop them. That's how I learned at an early age to keep some things deeply hidden.

Though both my brother and I were raised on the reservation, I was the only one who became immersed in the Pueblo Indian culture. Speaking the language, I participated—whenever youths were permitted—in the indescribable communal magic of very old secret ways. This gave my fragile soul a lucky friendship with an intact spiritual tradition.

The complete and elegant way in which the Pueblo way of life helped the earth, fed life itself, instead of mining or conquering surroundings, corroborated the belief I'd kept hidden from view: that spirit is everywhere in everything and humans are capable of being part of it; that there are even some humans who do so as tribes.

But we young people on the reservation were forced into schools where this concept was not understood, much less encouraged. Any subtle native understanding of life was patronized as something we should outgrow. American education on the reservation was free, but mandatory. In other words, you could get both your hair cut and your soul pounded at no charge, and you were required to do so by law.

My own mother taught in that very school system. Hated by the school hierarchy, she fought tooth and nail against the insensitive and self-defeatingly anti-native government policies of the day. This got her fired every term, but since she was prized by the Pueblo tribe, she was rehired every new school year. She invariably ended up with the same set of students each year, and, as a result, she walked all her alumni from first to twelfth grade, shielding them from the beatings and racist detours natives ran into in non-native society. She hunted down grants and scholarships for her graduates, most of whom earned their own teaching certificates within the four to six years that followed. While they were doing that, my mother strategically wheedled her way into the much-hated Bureau of Indian Affairs, rising in the ranks of stodgy bureaucrats until she was perched as the Vice Superintendent of the Northern Pueblo Agency, the first woman ever to do such a thing. On her first day in power, she fired thirty child-beating teachers with tenure and replaced them with her certified graduates. She'd dug up an old unenforced New Mexico law that required all the teachers to be fluent in the original language of the children they taught.

Though she herself was of native Indian blood, probably Canadian, her brand of "Indianness" caused anxiety among whites, who generally equated race and color with culture. To those bureaucrats, an Indian was an Indian regardless of tribal origin, and should therefore act like their notion of an Indian. Sending an acculturated Iroquois to teach hard-line traditionalist Zunis was therefore common practice in government schools. This made as much sense as sending a Finn to instruct Tuaregs on their own culture.

My mother was viewed as a danger to the system because she fought hard for Native Pueblo cultural survival while ingeniously using Anglo bureaucratic channels. She achieved this in an environment antipathetic to Indians, women, and cultural integrity. Because of this kind of maneuvering and because she had a French name, spoke French, and was very short, the Old Guard bureaucrats nicknamed her Napoleon. She was proud of her blood, as I am, but outside of some relics and old stories she shared with us, I had no contact with her people at all.

I spent the whole of my very early life in a state of weepy terror about the possibility of the total annihilation of this beautiful world in the hands of a few white men who couldn't understand the beauty we had in this way of life. It was not just a nightmare: That earth-destroying bomb had been invented right there thirty miles away in Los Alamos, and they were proud of it. From the window in my seventh-grade English classroom, I could see Los Alamos laid out flat, ugly, desecrating the Pajarito Plateau and the eastern roots of the magnificent Jemez Mountains. Placed on a hill sacred to at least five local tribes, called the Place of Fog by the Pueblo people, it grinned back at us every day, reminding old Indians of the greater stakes in our lives and how essential their actions and knowledge were to keeping the world alive.

My heart and soul sickened with anxiety and despair; the sight of the bomb city reminded me of the possibility of no future which the atomic bomb represented. I became physically ill, terrorized and emotionally frozen in my powerless position as a child. The spiritual aspect of life began to sprout in me as a result. What utterly confused me and became the most sinister aspect of those days was how everybody else seemed either unaware or unaffected by the fact that this beautiful life might end. For the first time in history, the whole world could be killed, and nobody seemed to care. That lack of concern terrified me more than the bomb itself.

In school we had to duck the "Board of Education." This was a three-foot-long club made of two-by-fours on which the words "Board of Education" were scrawled with fingernail polish or graphite. If you wouldn't respond to a teacher's question or you spoke your native tongue when you answered, you got whacked solidly in the ribs or on the bottom with this weapon. The only thing these teachers taught us successfully was numbness. Don't get me wrong, this was not one of the notorious boarding schools where Native Americans were sent far away from their families. This was a public school, and there were white kids in other places who were treated the same way. But in my young mind, the same people who created and deployed the atomic bomb created and employed these boards. I couldn't tell them apart. These teachers were proud of the bomb.

Some of us Indian boys were considered unteachable, and we'd get ordered into a push-up position. We always laughed to let the teacher know our spirits weren't being conquered. But if you snickered, the "teacher" would walk on your fingers, and if you flinched from that, you got a rib-cracking blow from the Board. Most kids just quit coming to school after a couple of weeks of such treatment. Then they'd get rounded up, dragged back in to get more beatings, then they'd run away again. We were taught to be fugitives in our own land.

Between our terror of the white man with his bomb that was able to blow up our wild ancient world and the constant punishment and terrorism at school for not speaking the language of the terrorizer, most of my generation ended up as drunks, dead, or in prison. Others turned into terrified parodies of white working-class people, pretending, like any recent immigrants, that they understood what went on around them in the cities they had taken jobs in, far away from their loved ones and indigenous identities. A few of the strongest kept their hearts in their chests, and returned to the old ways, heroically trying to reconcile the old and new, some miraculously succeeding.

As I looked out the window of that English classroom one day, trying not to allow the presence of Los Alamos, the "bomb city," to damage my perusal of the otherwise rich natural landscape full of mysterious and mythological happenings, I noticed a small band of newly recruited tiny Pueblo kids, about five or six years old, gathered in front of the school. They were dressed in their one best set of clothes, both thrilled and petrified, away from their mothers and their village for the first time, with no familiar adults around them. Their big pretty black eyes flitted nervously like the deep fearful eyes of weanling calves, penned away from their mothers. They weren't yet numbed and wounded like myself; none of them had even heard English, much less spoken it.

One little girl, while waiting to enter the school building, was dancing around because she had to pee, but her needs went unheeded by her teacher who was herding them with her big Board of Education. The teacher didn't speak the Pueblo tongue, and finally the pretty child, who could hold it no more, stopped dancing, squatted down where she stood, and let out a tiny warm puddle on the concrete sidewalk.

I was in an anti-classroom, self-protective, glaze-eyed trance, so I didn't hear the teacher's words, but up she jumped, raising her club to the side, and without a sound from child or adult she clobbered that girl's head so hard she went down like a head-shot elk, biting her tongue, her eyes rolling back in her bleeding head. Without an argument in my head or a doubt in my heart and knowing I'd be sick for the rest of my life if I didn't get moving, I slithered out the louvered window where I sat, and ran and pounced on the teacher like a clumsy cougar, biting her on the back of the neck. What else could I do? I was not strong, so I bit. It took four grown men to pull me off.

The teacher was acquitted and continued teaching. The little girl recovered, became one of my mother's favorite students, and grew to become New Mexico's first native woman senator. She still shakes a little. But I, on the other hand, refused to speak English for years, in protest, to anyone except my parents, becoming a kind of "fundamentalist" Indian. Half Swiss and half Indian as I was, the teachers called me the white savage.

After that, I didn't get sick all the time, and when I did, I recovered quickly. I spent almost all my time in the Pueblo, hoeing chilis, corn, and melons, watering people's horse herds by taking them to the river, husking corn, watching ceremonies, and making things. The kids called me *Gasha Nushkuni*, "Old White Head," because I stayed around and acted like the old people in the Pueblo.

One day, when I was fifteen or so, my mother asked my little brother and me what we saw ourselves doing by the time we were thirty years old. My brother was going to be an historian, which turned out pretty close. I said I'd become a medicine man, with a lot of silver and turquoise. I'd have a big herd of old-time horses of every color, with old-time saddles and Navajo silver bridles, and I'd be an artist and painter.

My mother believed that a man should be accomplished in many areas. One had to be "well-rounded" and "complete," she'd insist. I'm not sure where her Renaissance standards came from, but they combined elements of medieval Europe and the Old West. I seemed to be the only one required to learn them. It was not unlike the creation myths of my Pueblo Indian upbringing, where the culture hero is encouraged and educated into the "manly arts" under the tutelage of the warrior mothers. While many of her requirements came easily to me and fit into the environment of desert and Indians, others were very foreign, but I've never regretted knowing any of it.

Imagine yourself on a conservative Indian reservation being asked to fence with a foil, play chess, write poems, cook well, eat foods of all nations, read classical books, and play card games (no wild cards!) while still having to be a consummate horseman, painter, archer, fisherman, hunter, and musician. Outside of card-playing and fishing, I'm good at it all, but from this came other talents that my mother approved of as well: silversmithing, horse-breaking, cattle-roping, branding, butchering, tanning hides, making coats and moccasins, saddles and tack.

My mother taught me that a man should be able to speak with every type of person, and listen and empathize with what they had to live under. One should be fair to all. Above all, I was to be courageous and courteous and always stand up for what mattered in life regardless of personal cost or public opinion. I should always negotiate in a civilized way any point or problem, but when all else failed get ready to defend myself and be a good fighter, with words, fists, and strategy. This was like a medieval prince's training.

Taking to wandering, I visited the shrines and sacred places of the Pueblo, praying hard. I'd be gone for days sometimes out in the wilds, causing great worry to my parents and friends. Spirit beings began to visit me in those places, teaching me little lessons, revealing their natures to me. One January night, while watching a series of night dances in the Pueblo, I was conducted by a messenger to a secret meeting of middle-aged Pueblo men. Half-dressed, getting painted amidst piles of fox skins, cornhusks, paints, and mountain tobacco, they were preparing to participate in the night dance. They offered me a thick cornhusk-wrapped cigar, and made me smoke with them.

"You have to choose," said Domingo, an ample, confident man, glistening through the red earth paint. "You know a lot now about our ways, too much really; you know also that you can't stay here unless you go on to learn it all. But if you do, we can't let you leave. We can't let you talk with outsiders. You might teach some white people, some outsiders our ways, and we can't let that happen. So either you dance with us tonight and stay in the village forever, or you leave now, don't come back, and tell no one about this."

There was no good choice, but there was only one. I had to leave. A sixteen-year-old boy has to see the world. But it was a bitter thing to have to choose between such things.

Over the next four years, I made every mistake I could as fast as possible in the interest of living life to the fullest. With no elders or village community to teach me patience, I burned too hot and went too fast into places I wasn't prepared for by my indigenous upbringing. I struggled and starved, took a year of classical college, got married, farmed, and failed at all when my mother died.

Having centered her life on the issues of justice and fair play, my mother's rigidity of principles included a complete detour of her own soul and artistic desires. She had wanted to be a painter, a musician, and an adventurer. But because she was a woman holding a position of bureaucratic power in a white *man*'s world, her soul could never reconcile what she'd become and what she'd sacrificed to get there. So she folded up, withered in the flames of self-resentment. Dead at the age of forty-two, having accomplished some very admirable public coups, she left behind a ghost of unrequited longings and talents that took to haunting me in particular.

After I left the Pueblo, I took up what she never got to do, becoming a clumsy painter at the age of twenty, using my dead mother's unused brushes and paints. Art became foremost in my life as an alternative to a village community. I tried to fill the hollowness of all my losses by wrapping them in music and painting. It became obvious that my immersion in painting and music was my way of mourning. I also had a need to avenge my mother's death and all my losses, and that revenge meant making sure that beauty didn't die.

I equated my mother's untimely death with the destruction of all that was natural in the world: the Great Mother. All the pressures and hard situations that had caused me to lose both my village and my mother stemmed from the same place: the force that built nuclear weapons and beat big-eyed children with boards for speaking their ancestral tongue.

In my thinking, the earth, the wild high-rolling desert and canyon forests of my youth, was like a woman to me. My mother had merged with the natural landscape of the Mother of All, nature and life. I was surrounded by her. And in her, I looked for my own little soul, inside that big rolling earth. I loved her, but that landscape was being cut, mined, subdivided, and desecrated by the same enemy that had terrorized my childhood with its ability to destroy all life and happiness with a bomb and a board. The woman I longed to find, the home I longed to have, the tribe I'd need to survive as a man, had been attacked and denied me by this same power.

This dangerous, beauty-killing power became my enemy. It didn't have a name. The natives called it "white man ways." But it was more than that. Its infectious power had eaten the whites too, which had made them its obvious promoter. This horrible syndrome had no use for the truly natural, the wild nature of all peoples, much less for what was best and strongest in my young self. Many races and cultures would be plagued by this insanity and fall victim to its devouring power, ending up ironically espousing exactly what had destroyed their uniqueness. It was a trance, where a violated woman would marry her rapist. Unthinkable to me.

Like my mother before me, I worked against this ugly force, the force that brought her down. But unlike her, I refused to believe in the status quo. I refused to work in the belly of the monster; I couldn't work within the system. As a result, I became an exile, a renegade of the heart, attempting to keep alive what I knew was culturally valuable. I incorporated this culture into my music, painting, and lifestyle, while rejecting all the rest, even the ways of other modern people in exile.

I headed toward becoming a one-man culture, a lonely young man with a lot of grief, excessive principles, and a mission. I became a renegade. Identifying with the nineteenth-century Apache leaders who had lived just to the south, I began to feel what Victorio or Geronimo must have. After all, I was trying to survive in an ecosystem that had first been disturbed by the predecessors of these same forces of Progress, or Manifest Destiny, that were now killing my life. In those days, Apaches had retaliated against their oppressors by taking the cattle of those who killed the deer their livelihood depended upon. They returned from a major cattle raid, bearing food for their tribe, only to discover the impaled hearts and ruined lives of their people numbed and scattered by these unfeeling forces. Like them, I had no one to bring my "cattle" to, nowhere to give my gifts. When there is no village to hunt for, nothing to come home to, then the self-governing laws of our souls and lives are discarded. That's what makes a person into a careless renegade.

My last winter in the States was endured outside Taos, New Mexico, during a record-breaking blizzard. I stayed huddled close to an adobe fireplace, sleeping and eating, dreaming exactly eleven dreams in eleven days. These unforgettable dreams were both frightening and hopeful. They played out events that later came to pass, involving people and places with whom I was as yet unacquainted. When I later came upon these events over the next fifteen years, I was guided and protected for having remembered them.

With my mother dead, my father having fled the reservation in grief, my brother hidden somewhere and bitter, I was further betrayed by the sight of my wife caressing a wealthy white man. I took five hundred dollars, my guitar, my mother's paints, and what wits I had, and ducked across the Mexican border. I headed south to sort it all out and to practice not being a part of the "Ugliness." I was looking for a home, looking for love, looking for life, and looking for a people to bring my cattle to, to share my gifts. Life never really gets sorted out, but my move south turned out to be a *ruse* of the spirits to push me toward my destiny and get me to the place they wanted me all along. My eleven dreams of the previous winter would be my road map.

I wandered, moneyless but happier, through the towns and villages of Mexico. I experienced many adventures and tight spots, all of which were a preparatory training course purposely laid out for me by the spirits, to groom me for the intense road to becoming a shaman among the Tzutujil Maya of Santiago Atitlán. Without this seemingly arbitrary sequence of magical events in Mexico, I would never have become a true human being, a man, a useful person.

So after nine months I landed in Oaxaca in southern Mexico, in a land of tidy white-washed houses, lots of Indian people, warm rolling hills covered with sharp maguey, and home to a pretty girl named Felicita.

2

THE GODDESS
OF CHOCOLATE

Felicita had a wide, open face with dark skin the texture of a fresh brown egg, glazed with the deep red of a ripe zapote fruit. A Yucatecan Mayan girl of seventeen, smooth and round as all Mayan girls must be, feeling both delicious and powerful, she managed a "smoke in your eyes" eating stall in the west side of the main Oaxaca market.

Her big, active eyes were always hunting for what to do next in such a bustling place, playing like two dolphins of black jade, leaping and diving beneath her eyelids. I made a habit of arriving early in the day to ensure myself a seat at the only bench in front of her counter. Every morning, I'd crowd in with seven or more hungry men. Our breakfasts were all the same: a gourdful of hot chocolate and a cake of sweet Oaxacan bread.

Minute dewdrops of sweat formed on the visible area of her breasts as they rhythmically churned along with the back and forth of her hairless arms and smooth copper arms and hands, rotating the long wooden hot chocolate whisk in her palms, expertly raising a froth up over the edge of her bulging pottery jar, nestled in the blue flames of oak charcoal. Each of us received a full gourd of the sumptuous beverage. She would hand them to each of us in turn, spilling nothing, but conceding to me a new, unused, elongated gourd from her big clacking basket full of chocolate gourds.

Like thirsty horses at a shallow spring, all eight of us noisily and tenderly sucked in the cinnamon-spiced foam from the breastlike gourds, heavy and warm with chocolate. I think we all knew Felicita herself was in that liquid; we drank her in with finesse and a glazed look on our faces, and it was good. After a few days of this, I caught Felicita watching us out of the corner of her eye, studying how each of us negotiated our breakfasts, slyly assessing which of us would make the best husband by the way we approached the bread and chocolate. Women did this sort of thing, but I thought she was flirting.

At some point I learned that if I asked for one of the bigger breads shaped like a pregnant belly in miniature, topped with brown sugar and glaze, I could tarry longer and legitimately outwait my competitors, who would eventually flee to their jobs and errands. One day as I was dipping the last of the big bread into the last of the chocolate in my gourd, Felicita really did begin to flirt. This became a thrilling daily ritual for which I was not prepared, and I fell utterly in love with this Mother of Chocolate.

She would sit in front of me, her face cocked to one side, her eyelids lowered as she looked toward the gourd. Then she'd give a pained, affected smile showing a little of her fine white teeth, drenching my defenseless, uncooked heart with a devastating onslaught of beauty, hope, and wonder. Flirted into a corner of words, completely outmatched, I knew I had to flee when the smiles and good feelings reached their peak. I didn't want to risk coming back to normal but wanted to stay in the painful lusciousness of her smile's spell. So I invented places to go, and pretended to go there.

One morning to show off, I paid a wandering music group to serenade us as I consumed my frothy gourdful. There was a saxophone, a standup bass, and two fellows on a portable gourd marimba. After that, the little group, Flor de Oaxaca, was waiting by Felicita's stall every day, and the music became part of our courtship.

I was a puppy-like nomadic bandit prince. I had my own music, erotically prepared breakfasts, and a beautiful girl with whom to play the courting game in an ancient bubbling market packed with a million aromas and mysterious necessities of Oaxacan life.

After several weeks had passed, I became aware of a gradual increase in the number of Felicita's family in her stall each day. First only her mother came to the stall, then her aunts, then her aunts and uncles, then her mother, aunts, uncles, some pretty sisters and little brothers, until one day most of the market stood privy to our chocolate ritual. A young man seated next to me couldn't take it anymore. Venting his jealousy on me, he threw me up against a post. Felicita's relatives responded by charging down on the poor fellow, driving him completely out of the marketplace like angry blackbirds mobbing a hawk.

The next morning I bought Felicita a handful of yellow orchids, which she neatly arrayed in her long black hair off to one side. That deep yellow, together with her moist red-chocolate skin, smooth lowered eyelids, noble stance, and elegant hands, gave her the look of a Mayan Goddess. By then everybody knew that we were engaged to be married. Everyone, of course, except myself.

The local women saw love in a practical way, and as women do, they wanted to bring it all to its logical conclusion. I, on the other hand, wanted only to be drinking in the moment with Felicita's radiance, oblivious to any thoughts of its permanence. To me her beauty and acceptance of my longing was heaven in itself. This moment was some kind of arrival for me, a destination achieved. Whereas for these ladies it was all simply the flimsy and flowery beginning of a long, arduous journey into child rearing and economic survival. For me an end in itself, for them an anxiety unresolved.

One morning Felicita asked me to take her out that evening. I felt an earthquake in my knees, and swelled up so big that in my puffed-up state I hardly fit through the market gates on my way out to round up some cash to take her God knew where. Little did I suspect in my entranced state ' that, to her, this would seal an unspoken contract of betrothal. I was more than willing to comply to her desires, as I sought simply to maintain the favor of my Chocolate Goddess.

Unbeknownst to Felicita, I was broke. I lived in a towel room off the servants' quarters in a high-class hotel left over from the eighteenth century. That five-by-ten room cost me a dollar a night, and I only slept there by night. The daytime was off limits because the maids were in and out all the time. But to all appearances, it looked like I was living at a fancy colonial hotel!

That day, on my way to my room, I met an American tourist importer who offered me fifty dollars a day to translate for her and to carry her purchases on her buying trip through the district. She needed me as badly as I needed her cash, especially now to impress my Mayan princess. So off I went to villages, stores, translating and bargaining for black pottery in Ocotlan, blankets in Teotitlán, Trique gowns, and so on. By the time I'd lugged all this back with this white woman, it was late at night, and Felicita was nowhere to be found.

Despondent and angry at my poverty, furious at all the world's patronizing tourists, I slept, bound and determined that at dawn I would beg and charm things back into accord with Felicita for not having shown up at the appointed hour. When I arrived, she was smoldering. Felicita had seen me in the dark entering into the hotel with the white woman and our purchases. She could have started the cooking fires with her blazing stare.

Meanwhile, like a cow-eyed fool, I took my place on the little bench with six other pretenders waiting patiently for her to make our accustomed frothy breakfast. But . . . Felicita had her back to us, and was furiously killing the hot chocolate with the whisk, glaring at the fire. She embarked upon an endless, louder than usual, accusatory tirade about how I was a traitor to go out with a white lady, how I was a two- or three-timer, a bum, a piece of trash, etc., and how I obviously just wanted to ruin rich women and was playing her humble Indian status for a fool.

I tried and tried to get a word in edgewise, but I couldn't explain my poverty and the room without showing how I'd misled Felicita in other ways. And the white lady—no way would she believe that I was carrying her purchases for money, and if I was being paid, then that meant I was a gigolo, and so forth and so on. As I dug myself deeper and deeper, the truth seemed more pathetic than my alleged crime, and so no matter what, I was already sentenced.

While I pleaded and Felicita shouted, the marimba band lined up behind me as usual, and started pumping the *umpa, pa umpa umpa, um* of a fast bolero played on a sick sax and plinky marimba by four skinny, grinning musicians. Felicita had had enough. She was boiling over. She spun around with the hot pot in her lovely grip and drenched all of us boys across our chests with several gallons of scalding hot chocolate. The bench toppled over and all of us rolled on the ground, scrambling to avoid the barrage. I did a pretty good somersault and stood up, while the band kept chugging away, keeping well out of range. But when we noticed Felicita still yelling, climbing over the counter, scaling it like a cat and brandishing the chocolate whisk, we all began a retreat to the market entrance with the band in tow.

Her mother and a flood of female cronies appeared out of nowhere, cackling behind us, pelting us with whatever was handy. By now we were all running, the musicians playing pretty well on the run. Guilty by association, they fled the premises with us. The market was full of people running to get a look at our defeat. Laughter and shrieks almost drowned out the screaming group of women, who were now slinging guavas, avocados, oranges, rocks, cups, and so forth. We made it to the street along with the band still chugging away. They wanted to be sure of getting paid, after all that.

After Felicita's enraged chocolate blessing, the other boys had dispersed, leaving me to smoke away my sorrow and hunger alone. That feeling parent birds feel when scared off the nest and they abandon their eggs came over me, and I knew it was time to move on. Seventeen hours later, under cover of darkness, with my only two possessions, my guitar and a suitcase full of my mother's dried oil paints, I struggled to the hardest part of Oaxaca to await a Grade B bus. It would haul me away from Oaxaca, away from my failure with Felicita, into the very hot, untouristed Tehuantepec coast.

My old flamenco guitar was my faithful companion throughout my journeys. She repeated my feelings in her more beautiful sounds, converting the pain and confusing irony of such a day into an inspired creation. If all things in life interfaced like rain into a great river, then my little flamenco gurgled her rage and beauty into something bigger, giving me a feeling of belonging again to some mysterious whole.

I sat with a few Zapotec families, waiting for a one A.M. bus, strumming my guitar, my chest blistered, my heart broken, misunderstood, my legs dangling over a wall just above a street full of garbage, human feces, a dead spotted dog, and the usual accumulation of chicken feathers and pale dried corn husks. Then, out of the foggy darkness, a road-sweeping man came limping. He hobbled out of the mist, scratching and kicking the trash into lines and piles, both hands firm on a cumbersome sweeping device. It was a long, homemade affair that looked like a demented giant's hockey stick bristling at the crook with a trembling bundle of tough switches.

You could see how precious trash was to this man; it was a kind of peculiar livestock disguised as garbage, and his goal was to gradually herd his flock of corn husks, piss, and paper into his "trash corral" located in the alley up against an old stone wall of an unused, burned-out building. He didn't just clean the streets for the public, he was concerned with the welfare of the trash. He worried about it. I'd say he was a trash shepherd! Both feet were bare; his left leg was clubfooted, and ironically this was his stable side, while the other "good" foot struggled to keep up.

The old man, mostly skin and bones, worked his way past us. His taut face looked like a skull with old tobacco-colored skin stretched over it. Something had cut away most of his nose, and it had healed in a sort of flat, triangular way, making his breathing somewhat horselike.

I kept playing my sad guitar, trying to disguise what began as pity and grew into amazement at what I deemed this man's hard life, when he looked straight at me and started dancing to my waltz. His clubbed foot remained stationary while the rest of him pumped and swayed around it, circumscribing a ring in his herd of thick trash like a human protractor, more gracefully than one would have imagined. He grinned as he danced, revealing some crooked, horselike teeth and the fact that he had no tongue at all and could not speak.

All of a sudden he stopped, stiffened, and looked at me hard with eyes so generous I almost fell into them. Then he rocked back and forth, imitating my guitar postures and indicated with gestures and head-bobbing that I should keep playing. I obeyed, while he swept and danced his herd of trash to its safe nest in the alley. I thought he'd drifted off to some other street in the fog, but he limped back empty-handed to my place at the wall and began pulling at my shirt pocket, pointing toward his trash pen. Eventually I followed this strange, small, limping bony being across the street, away from the bus office.

In the breezeless, muggy fog of a March Oaxacan night, I found myself watching the road-sweeper dig through his treasured junk heap until he pulled out the object of his search: a large deck of cards in a filthy plastic sack, so entirely soaked through with urine that the warped deck looked like a dwarf's accordian. He reached into this awful, stinking bag and retrieved a card without looking, put it in my shirt pocket and poked at it, indicating by pointing that this card was me.

When I took the card out and looked at it, I realized it was a tarot card, the Prince of Wands. Then he handed me the Queen of Swords and then the Burning Tower, and so on and so on. I was impressed. I knew very little about the Tarot, but the old man made signs on my cheeks like tears when the dark-haired Queen of Swords appeared, and he was right. My heart was a heavy sack of tears that I toted around, all I had left from the scorched and smoking landscape of my mother's untimely death and my just-ruined marriage.

The bus had pulled in and was blasting its horn for everyone to board. I began returning the man's cards, of which he accepted all but the Prince of Wands, gesturing for me to keep him as a gift. I wanted to give him something in return, and I wanted to stay and figure out this whole strange event, but I had to get on the departing bus. I shook hands with the old guy and began running toward the transport, dragging my mother's suitcase full of paints and my guitar over my head, with the skull man hobbling hard on my heels.

The bus driver's helper was delighted to get one more fare, as the bus had already started to depart. The driver slowed up and the *ayudante* stepped outside to grab my dead mother's suitcase and my guitar to toss them on top as is the custom. Just as I began to step into the moving vehicle, my little trash-sweeping friend grabbed my arm with a powerful grip like a monkey and pulled me back to the street. Reasoning kindly with him, I escaped and began to enter the bus again when the little skull-face fellow tackled me solidly, grappling his skinny arms around my knees, knocking both of us onto the ground.

The young *ayudante* let out some heavy oaths when the old man refused to release me from his viselike, bony grip. Since he was unable to speak back to explain what he was up to, the unsympathetic *ayudante* commenced to kicking his ribs and kidneys. Then I began cursing the *ayudante* for trying to hurt an old, sick man just for a two-dollar fare.

I talked off the angry bus man, and as the vehicle spun out in a furious blue cloud of diesel fumes, my friend released his grip. Standing and turning to reason with him, I found myself talking alone. He had disappeared into the smoke, vanished like the honking bus into the fog. Alone I stood in the night, not even positive it had all happened. I felt my shirt pocket, and the acrid-smelling card was snug in its place over my heart on my blistered chest.

After this incident, I was obliged to take the next transport out or wait another twenty-four hours for a cheaper one.

The next bus came at dawn. It was brand-new, nonstop, and expensive. The dawn bus ate up miles and miles of tight curves, winding us down the bristling maguey-studded hill country between Oaxaca and the Pacific coast. Lurching and rolling, the big bus knocked me conscious every mile or so, out of a half-smiling, luscious, back-of-the-bus dream state where my soul churned fantasies to the heavy-geared hum of the engine.

I'd grown to love riding the crazy little pig-faced converted Bluebird school buses that entered every hamlet, plantation, and village within three miles of the highway, taking five times as long to get anywhere, but which tried to make up for the indirect route by going the speed of light when they did finally hit the highway. These worn-out, brightly painted old wrecks filled up and emptied every two miles with the most beautiful native people of the land. Only here while riding them could you eat what the Indians ate, which is impossible to buy. You could find out what life was really about in these places. Tourists feared even to board these old deathtraps, but I rode them whenever possible.

The precarious hand-to-mouth budget under which these brave bus owners operated was due to the fact that they served the more humble people of the region, both Indian and Meztizo, who could not afford to ride an expensive transport and would otherwise have to walk. So to counter the impossible expense of repairing burned rings, shot bearings, wobbly steering gears, and worn-out brakes, the drivers heavily relied on the spirit realm to guide their wits, hands, and feet through a great many unorthodox mechanical maneuvers necessary to bring such a rattling heap of bolts safely home. Because of this, the entire dashboard, the windshield perimeter, and the rearview mirror were actually shrine areas, wonderfully ornate, and dedicated to a series of Santos, miraculous personages, and holy places. The more worn-out and dangerous the bus, the more elaborate the holy area.

In such places, ability, teamwork and faith override poverty with its consistent lack of resources and unpredictability. Success was not measured by outdoing your neighbor but by surviving the experience together. Riding a Grade B bus could be a spiritual experience, and only a fool or an atheist tourist would ride in one without a dashboard shrine.

Although I loved the Grade B buses, I was exhausted from the day's events and wanted to get moving, so I boarded the fancy bus and slept. A thousand forgotten corners of days I'd had were magically bred to days yet to come, and their children were the dreams I dreamt as I slid in and out of that world between done and destined, snug in my seat as the proud bus trundled down the mountain.

I lifted my lids a little after sunup as we squealed to a crawl and crept past an accident in a canyon off on the narrow highway. Everybody on our bus had jumped to my side, genuflecting and murmuring phrases of shock and pity. I craned my sleepy head out the window. The smell of burning metal and rubber sickened the air, and through the black smoke I saw to my right the inert, odd-postured bloody corpses of seven Indians, two of them women, I think. A bus was upside-down, burning furiously, with a sound like sucking wind down the side of the ravine. The brush was burning back up the slope in a wall of flame, toward us.

My heart speeded up as it sank, beating me out of my dreams with fright and dismay. I was sickened at the sight, and my heart tried to swim out of the pool of great shock and empathy for the wailing and disoriented crowd who could do nothing for the remainder of the passengers burning in the white-hot Grade B bus. Even the windows had melted.

In a disheveled, bloody short-sleeved white shirt and gray pants, third from the left, one arm under him, lay dead the *ayudante* who had kicked my friend the old road-sweeper in the ribs. Blood raced to my ears and eyes, and I had to suck in a deep breath of air to stay conscious as I came to realize the bus aflame in that canyon was the very bus I had tried to board earlier but didn't because of the old skull-faced road-sweeper. To my horror, the families I had sat with earlier had met their deaths here, and most were burning before my eyes.

One of our passengers, a copper-faced Mazatec woman with a handsome *gabacha* (apron), began to weep and wail, as she had recognized a relative amongst the dead. Though she flung herself at the bus door to leave, the bus driver refused to release her to the pandemonium and confusion of the crowd. Eventually several other women and a handsome old Ladino took her into their arms as she flailed and convulsed, weeping and slobbering onto the floor, infected with the weighty force of her heartfelt grief and helplessness. She tried to fight her way to the earth where her tears would feed life and the ground could eat her pain, as is only right, for real human beings must do this or be ill for not doing so.

I myself was sick, devastated, grateful, hurt, alive, and very proud of this grieving indigenous woman, but disgusted also with what part of me was like a North American who seemed to be such an amateur in these matters, considering grief and beauty to be sideshows in life when they are really the left and right hand of the goddess called Life, in whose arms we are all suckled. The driver started us on our way again, and after an hour of tearful, birdlike chatter, rehashing what we'd thought we'd seen, sleep invited me into her nest. We passengers all settled back into our journeys and into a sense of normalcy—not stoicism, fatalism, or denial, but life, which would go on, not despite such a misfortune, but directly on account of it. The tenuous nature of life in a place like this made the living of life a precious obligation. An awareness of the high stakes of mortality can re-sensitize a jaded person's sense of taste, and life becomes a delicious meal no matter how basic the recipe. So I wept, talked, and fell into a delicious slumber, actually more at home than I'd been in a long while.

3

THE COAST
OF TURTLES

It has always seemed hopeful that people passing the same spot of earth, on the same day, at the same time in their lives, could have utterly divergent experiences. Other people have gone where I have gone, and met some of the magic beings I knew, but it wasn't in their destinies to experience what I did. There are layers of realities before us, behind us, around us, and in us, and we stay in a layer no matter how far we travel until the spirit admires our courage and grace and allows us to sprout into another zone of experience.

Because of this, it would not have been enough for me simply to arrive in a Mayan village to learn shamanism. A village is composed of many layers, and at this point, I needed to be carved by life into a shape that fit the layer I was destined to enter by birth. I wasn't shaped right yet. Though by now I had a strong feeling of destiny, somewhere in the future my training had already begun, unbeknownst to me. Long before I'd meet any human teacher, life would put me through a kind of boot camp, college preparatory course. This was in order to change and strengthen me enough to receive a more subtle and strenuous shamanic instruction among the Maya. I was still too green and rickety.

From the day I left Oaxaca my life entered a zone of mystery. This wild, mysterious existence would become commonplace for me, but I never lost my sense of awe. The adventures that ensued forced me to have mental courage. I learned not to jump, melt, or become hysterical. Instead, I dug deep into my natural soul where my ancestral ingenuity was enthroned. This kind of courage and ancient originality were the very natural attributes that had allowed our ancestors to thrive and survive with grace.

For the next year and a half, knowing full well I'd been born for it, the spirits were to force me to find a way through a magically designed maze of unfamiliar situations. The spirits knew I had no real choice in the matter. I must learn to swim through the wonder and difficulties of the next years or be killed by my own natural soul, who would hate me for keeping it back from living out its life because of spiritual cowardice and laziness. Whether I knew this or not I can't remember, but my soul did, and for whatever reasons I had at the time, I went on with it all, never turning back.

Only slightly recovered from that narrowly missed bus wreck, I landed hot and hungry into the commotion of the matriarchal Zapotec town of Tehuantepec. Before I could even get off the bus, an elderly Guabe Indian man dressed in his people's traditional whites caught my dead mother's suitcase full of useless hardened oil paints. With this in hand, he proceeded to stride out of town, toward the northwest. It is common for men to hijack your luggage off an incoming bus to a hotel, forcing you to follow in hopes you'll check in where the luggage lands. This old fellow, however, never stopped, he just kept walking out of town.

I chased him, dragging my guitar case, yelling at him in the coastal heat for miles, unable to overtake the strong little man. Finally, I gave up, and when I turned to trudge back to Tehuantepec, he put down the suitcase in the sand and came nimbly running back to me to comfort and cajole me into continuing forward in my unfed, exhausted state.

We eventually entered his family's cool thatched hut set in the ocean breeze far from Tehuantepec, in the heart of the land of the little-understood Guabe Indians. Famous for their ceremonial masks made of armadillo shells, horsehair, tin, shark parts, and wood, the secretive Guabes had at that time eluded close study by anthropologists and outsiders. This made what followed even stranger.

The man I'd followed here showed me a book he kept inside a smoky old wooden chest. The text of the book was written backward in a self-styled phonetic Guabe, and the old man periodically entered into the book the thoughts and events of his people, as others had done before him. Contained in the book's pages was an ancient ritual chronological account of the Guabe. The text had to be read in a mirror held by an assistant, and apparently one outsider needed to witness the traditional out-loud public ritual reading of the book which took place every four years. This time it was me.

It took days to accomplish. A younger Guabe translated to me in Spanish as the older man read it out in the mirror. I was never to tell anyone the contents. I never have. Arriving on foot and on horseback, hundreds of adult Guabes attended the reading. We were all well-fed on iguana meat, armadillo backstrap, and shark, accompanied by large, beautiful corn tortillas made by the handsome, gold-toothed Guabe ladies.

The ritual ended as unexpectedly and oddly as it had all begun. After the book had been read and ritually replaced in its coffer, the same old man who coaxed me to his home then had me fed and packed up with traveling food. He walked me to a field blessing and sent me off to wander again.

I had begun to feel at home, but this was not my village yet. However, I had tasted the possibility of home, of indigenous village life, and it would linger forever, pulling me forward to the object of my longing. Trudging out on the strand, small, alone, and feeling somewhat humiliated, I finally collapsed, exhausted, into a deep sleep on the untrammeled black sand beach in a little cove on the Coast of Turtles.

Unaccustomed to the sea, I slept too near the tide line, and awoke eyeball to eyeball beside a big dead shark washed up by the surf, both of us half in the water. I jumped up, stunned. My guitar was floating out to sea, so I swam out and got it, unaware that I had paddled unscathed right through a group of marauding live sharks, who were teeming to hack up the still immersed back half of the deceased monster.

After several days of living above the tideline in some extraordinary cavelike holes of stone, I met a woman who began to visit every day around noon, bearing food neatly wrapped in handwoven tortilla cloths. Magali was thirty or so and maybe not so pretty, but well tuned to the ocean, and magnificent. The jilted wife of a fisherman-turned-sailor, she had three children who were little bushy-headed creatures with hair red-tinged from the salt breeze. They scoured the tidal pools for small shells, like quick mammalian crabs, scurrying, giggling, then squatting to ponder some wonder along the beach. The rest of the day they spent puncturing and stringing their morning finds on fishline to form necklaces for sale to tourists in the villages.

Magali would walk with me on the black sand beach after our lunches and stand peering past me with a faraway gaze. Her rough hair with a narrow white stripe, wild in the breeze, her face creatively sculpted by the winds of grief and her ability to negotiate her life's load with grace, reminded me of the long-standing wind- and water-tortured columns in the caves where I'd taken up residence. When she smiled, her teeth were like pearly tears in a cavelike depth of mystery.

She brought me food for weeks, and that meant a lot to me. The ocean was trying to loosen up my hide little by little, like a molting snake. The two of them, Magali and the sea, meant to polish me into a smoother, more solid thing. But I was still too unformed, too embryonic to carry the weight of Magali's hopes, and like some men do to many women, I disappointed her. Scared, I thought to move up to the mountains of Chiapas, to the Maya, to greater heights I suppose, away from her beach and ocean.

She was not a woman. When I think back, I know she must have been the ocean, the ocean turned human, as a woman bearing food, the sea as a lover come to visit. The Goddess sent again and again to save me from me, from what I thought I knew, and lead me to see out of the eyes of nature.

———

Just as I had resolved to resume my wanderings away from this beautiful woman, hordes of determined mother sea turtles began sliding out of the night, onto the sand, launching an invasion up and down the whole coastline in both directions, in their annual effort to make more of themselves. At first there had been only one trying to swim in the moonlit sand. Heavy out of the water, she dug in her fins, and with an enormous effort she advanced herself up the sparkling blackness of the beach past the tideline next to my little tower of rock.

The fine lady leatherback dug and dug, her sweet round eyes crying thick, sand-encrusted tears as she labored. Resting a while, she went at it again and some more until finally, backing out of the cavity she was creating, she turned about-face in a kind of slow, desperate way, then moved back into the nest in the lunar night. From her funny tail she squished out a plump pile of perfect little wet moons. She frantically paddled on top of them finloads of previously excavated sand to form a little hummock, in front of which, exhausted, she rested, her birdlike beak pointing toward the pounding surf, praying as only turtles can that her little ones might survive. By dawn her treadmarks showed how she'd again merged with the water.

With such natural magic going on all around me, I forgot about leaving. Magali and I walked through the turtle fields every night, hopping over turtles, strolling around them, entranced in the spell of miles of turtles in moonlight and the intensity of the mission in their big hearts. Finally one night we, too, succumbed to the ocean's organic tug, scooping and scraping out our own little sandy burrow and making love all night, paddling and trenching ourselves into the luscious beach and earth right alongside those lovely jade beasts, resting and resuming, pulled like the turtles by an irresistible obligation to be making life to the sound of the sea and a thousand turtles lurching and tossing in the moonlight.

Spent, we slept like two little eggs nestled in our wallow as the neighboring turtles sporadically sprayed us with sand, trying to bury us like their incubating eggs. We laughed and rode the ocean's rhythm to our dreams, asleep on the Coast of Turtles.

———

For days afterward I waited for Magali and for the baby turtles to hatch. Though I waited and waited, I never saw Magali again. But one day after the mounds and I had been cooking long enough, out they came, tiny little versions of their turtle mothers, cuter than a baby's nose. The tiny turtles dug their way out of the sand, rolling and flipping their way over the strand into the surf, where they took off like aquatic butterflies, flying into the water far out to sea. For days they made their exodus, many becoming food for foxes, opossum, pelicans, and gulls before reaching the safety of the open ocean. I picked some up and made a big prayer for them to take to the Goddess of the waters. Then I released them flat and squirming into the waters, my prayers spreading to the unseen with them. One day they, too, were all gone. The beach was just black and sparkly; no Magali, no turtles, no food.

Magali's sailor man had miraculously returned, and she, like a mother turtle, had gone back to her home. I, like the little turtles, went searching for mine, dragging my guitar and my dead mother's suitcase full of heavy, hardened paints. Pulling myself out of the sand, feeling heavy and sad, I headed for the cool mountains of San Cristobal.

The mist of San Cristobal de las Casas felt cold in the pre-dawn darkness and its dull teeth gnawed into my joints and bones, which had grown used to the torpid coastal heat. The major thoroughfares of this ancient mountain town were cobbled in river stones like the scales on a sea turtle's leg, and over these slick, dew-glazed scales, out of the smoke-spiced fog, waddled a well-dressed dwarf not a meter tall. He offered in a dignified fashion to carry that infernal suitcase of my mother's. As we walked together, an occasional soot-covered Mayan shouldering a round, heavy handmade fiber net full of angular oak charcoal, much larger than himself, strapped to his forehead on a tumpline, would trot past us out of the murky night, throwing out the mandatory salutation between breaths:

"Señores." (Lords, Sirs.)

To which the dwarf and I blessed him with the required:

"Que le vaya bien." (May thou go well.) You could hear the thuds and slaps of those tough, sandaled feet long before you'd see him, and hear them fade away after the foggy night and steep stony roads had swallowed him.

These streets were chilly and deserted, and this little dwarf knew where I might sleep a night for four pesos or fifty cents American. That being the only offer standing, we took up my loads and trod our way up a side street into a longish building on a long slope of stone walls and red-tiled houses with courtyards.

We entered a courtyard with a non-functioning fountain, then climbed a dark and narrow stairway up to the unlit courtyard balcony. We took a turn inside, and came upon a corridor painted in bright green enamel with a few uncovered light bulbs glowing.

A queue of ladies of the night stood catcalling me, blowing kisses and showing me their product as each waited her turn for the Sunday night medical checkup, as the law required. They were of all ages, and quite sweet. I reckoned I was getting lodging in some kind of bordello, as many such "houses" traditionally employ dwarfs and midgetmen to run the door and look after the girls. Many Latin American whorehouses function as hotels in their off hours. Too weary to care, I flopped on a wooden cot inside a tiny, windowless room, its ceiling, floor, and walls armored with a thick sediment of green enamel paint.

The following morning, as I lay facedown on the shrimpy-smelling whorehouse cot, I was awakened by the sound of two raucous ladies downstairs arguing long and hard about something.

Having gone to sleep in a green room, I was astounded to find myself in a solid red room. Totally red!

I began to rise up out of bed and open the door to check the hall to see if it was still green, or if maybe I was in a different room, but my cot began to rock by itself, and I felt something cold and wet pressed against my left arm. I rolled to the side and looked up, and there, looming over me, stood a snow-white deer. A white doe with solid blue eyes. She shook her head and ears, scratched her front leg with her hind leg, leapt over me to the red floor, and walked elegantly to the door with her beautiful black nose breathing mist on the glass doorknob.

Only half awake, reeling from my dreams and opening a door for a blazing white deer with blue eyes in a fire-engine-red room that had been green upon retiring, made me wonder if I was truly awake or in the land of some spirit. But when I unfastened the latch to release the white deer into the corridor, another white deer, a buck with tiny velvet antlers, awaited her just outside. The two ran skidding on the tiled floor up to the balcony and sniffed the morning air, looking about, perfectly at home. Two white deer.

And the corridor was totally red to boot! I walked up to the balcony and looked down into the courtyard, which now had a very long black Cadillac car parked on the mosaic tile floor next to the fountain, which had mysteriously come alive, shooting water about its star-shaped pool. The deer followed me about, frolicking like dignified goats. Not a human soul was to be seen; our dwarf had vanished, along with the ladies; the only sign of people was the ongoing disagreement downstairs.

I washed up, got my suitcase, my guitar, and my string bag, clunked my way down the narrow stairs and searched the compound and courtyard for a person to reimburse for my night's stay. Every room was empty and devoid of furniture or signs of life.

Trying politely to keep my distance from the arguing, I resorted to yelling but I received no response. All attempts to pay up having failed, I cautiously crept up on the room where the disagreement seemed to be happening. The room was a very small, unlit bathroom with the door open and a heated two-party verbal battle going on. I switched on the light as I spoke a morning greeting, and all sounds went dead. No one was in there. But then a tremendous squawk split my eardrums, I wheeled, and there in the corner behind the door were two beautiful, ornery green parrots, excellent students of whorehouse debates. I began to breathe again, laughing hysterically at myself and the mystery of the day.

Leaving my four pesos on the hood of the Cadillac in the courtyard, I approached, for the first time, the world of the post-colonial Maya outside, entering by leaving through the threshold of an enchanted color-shifting bordello held by two white deer and two angry green parrots, and managed by a disappearing dwarf.

———

W herever there are Highland Maya people, a delicious, melancholy smell permeates the air. Carried on the backs of hardwood smoke, the perfumes of flowers, fruit, and roasting tortillas are spiced with the fragrance of pine needles.

Such a smell drifted through San Cristobal, chased by another smell, that of an old oppression. It came out of certain non-Indian class-oriented parts of the old town, and wafted into corners where Indians *were* welcome. San Cristobal's marketplace was one of these corners, and there for the first time I saw at least fifteen different village dress styles of Mayans— from Chenalho, Zinacantan, Chamula, Oxchuc, etc.—all wearing intricate hand-woven tribal clothing of distinct village design, each reflecting a different Mayan dialect.

Unlike many foreign travelers, I wanted to change or fix nothing about these magnificent people. With so much beauty and their living connections with their own ancient lifestyles all in one place, something in me was feasting on their excellence.

Indians didn't come to San Cristobal for fun, only on business. Everyone, including myself, wanted to get out of town as soon as they had concluded their errands, and get back to their mountain village homes.

The village of Oxchuc was having her annual town fiesta, and I very much wanted to see the sumptuous Mayan processions and ceremonialism, reputedly still a strong and vital part of life amongst these Tzeltal Maya of highland Chiapas.

The ride to Oxchuc was a steep one, passing over the balding green pine-topped hump behind San Cristobal and running the skirtlike folds at the hem of her ride, up and down for miles, then dropping into an odd little valley, on something of a wide log skid to the edge of the rainforest. No buses seemed to go that way, so I had myself hammered into a space in the cargo bed of a lorrylike truck going up to Ocosingo the back way, hauling a load of Mayan people from Oxchuc returning from wage labor on the coast. I looked like a toothpick in a box of bullets.

Cheap bus riding in Latin America was a kind of yoga. I had probably mastered it by now, but stuck-in-the-truck yoga took my training to new depths of balance and gave me an appreciation for the adaptability of a human body to assume any shape in the name of not having to walk.

Mystified, intrigued, smelling of piglets and sweat, I had no resistance to Narciso's inspired offer of a hot shower!

Narciso was a solid young Tzeltal man whom I'd befriended on our notorious truck ride to Oxchuc, outside San Cristobal. He and his wife Rosaria generously invited me to sleep in their well-made hut off the eastern boundary of the village. Sharing meals with Narciso and Rosaria, I lazed around for a day before the town feast got going, feeling too tall, culturally poor, dirty, and homeless. I longed to *be* one of these proud, edgy Mayan men, with a short-sleeved, long, handwoven tunic, shot through with red, a sign of importance, and carrying a machete under my arm whose sheath was heavily adorned with multicolored Moroccan cutouts, with an overabundance of metal eyelets and rivets, and braided danglers. I wanted to have three-inch-thick Michelin tread soles on my sandals with leather straps to match my machete, and a hand-knotted string bag of the most intricate manufacture off my shoulder. I'd cruise through the village with my household in tow: the wife, sisters, aunts, daughters, their bright-colored satin hair ribbons tied in big butterfly bows at the back of their well-combed heads, and the tails of the ribbons plaited the entire length of their meter-long braids, swinging over their white, red-breasted *huipiles*, long shawls over their shoulders, and sash-belted wraparound skirts, and with our children, waddling alongside like beautiful little ducks, with their tribal colors, just as present as the adults.

Hundreds of groups like these filtered in from all over: from the mountains, plantations, and other villages, they all arrived here, every year, like spawning fish, coming from as far as they had wandered, to be together, to do what Mayans all over love to do: stand and look beautiful together, regathering and tuning up the village soul, every person a holy chunk of the collective heart.

Not entirely a traditionalist, Narciso was more cosmopolitan in attitude and judged himself a progressive. He could read a bit, speak Spanish, Tzotzil, and Tzeltal. He loved electricity, of which there was none to be had just yet in this neck of the woods. He and Rosaria were anomalies in the village, and I would have preferred to associate with one of his more traditional, clannish relatives, but I was slowly learning to let go of my preferences to the exigencies of the moment.

And now after our evening meal, I could hardly believe my ears when Narciso spoke of a shower. There was no piped water here for one thing: no tanks, no motors, only a stream where teenage girls and women brought what water they needed in clay jars and plastic *tinajas*. I had been bathing cold in streams, ponds, basins, buckets, hotels, and so forth, but the last hot shower I'd had was almost a year ago. I'd been bathing cold ever since. Then I learned that Narciso was speaking of a public shower, and that the workers there would need to be paid. This ran about eight pesos, I was told, a whole dollar. That was a lot of money to take a bath, but who cared? For a hot shower and to clear up the mystery, it was worth it. Workers? A public shower in the middle of an ancient Mayan village? It was too nutty to turn down.

In the morning I was roused by three young gentlemen ceremonially attired and carrying staffs. It had thundered and rained all night long and I'd slept like a fossil, so they had to keep at me to get me up.

At first I wondered what taboo I'd broken, or what line I had unwittingly crossed to warrant a visit from these solemn-faced village constables, who served the village theocracy. But Narciso calmed me, reminding me it was "time for the shower"! These boys had been sent on a mission by the village hierarchy to make sure I arrived safely, where I was awaited down at the showering place. Having no notion of where that might be, I put my trust in these proud fellows, dressed in their tribal best, come to officially escort me to my washing. I'd never been paraded to a shower before. It was great.

We slogged through the squishing mud, one official in front of me and one on either arm, but only after I'd wrapped a home-spun towellike cloth around my middle. Other than some amulets of my youth and the towel, I was naked. The bathing place was a pretty fair hike, especially walking barefoot and trying to hold up the towel in the cold mountain air. I guess we created a pretty big stir as crowds of little kids and adults came trotting up to get a glimpse and began to follow us. We gradually amassed a loud, noisy retinue, and I felt a bit like a popular prisoner, some kind of honored sacrificial victim, but I think I must have been secretly eating it all up.

About three-fourths of a kilometer downhill, in a clearing by a trickling stream, stood an impressive line of older men smoking cigars and intensely togged out with fancy hats, sashes, sleeved blankets, and canes, big, exaggerated sandals, and ornate string bags. As we approached, one of my escorts hailed each man in a row, going down the line, with me following, comically holding up my towel with one hand and shaking the leaders' hands with the other in turn. Narciso hung close behind me. It was all quite formal. A ceremonial toast with the local liquor was made, and we were served a couple of shots, according to rank, of course.

Taking good care to leave the area in front of these beautiful old men clear, a large, milling crowd was forming. And then I saw it! In front of us stood an old antique, rivet-studded, black locomotive boiler with a steam whistle on top. Smoke was billowing out of her big old stack, and from this congruous monster stretched a two-inch-thick pipe running into a three-sided wooden box of well-aged, rough-sawn boards reminiscent of an old outhouse with no front. Where the black boiler pipe came through the back wall sat a couple of cast-iron valve wheels; then from there the pipe went vertically two feet up the wall to a big sprinkler-can head, dynamically fastened to the pipe with time-blackened wire.

There were no train tracks for miles and no road down into this swale large enough to drag this old relic down here, plus it didn't have wheels anyway. I loved this! It was insane and extraordinary to see an entire village line up for one bumbling outsider to take a shower, holding a scanty cloth over his bottom and privates, as if it were all an inspired religious event, a sort of absurd miracle. The best part was the fact that it was powered by an obsolete locomotive boiler with a steam whistle, here where the jungle meets the mountain, among a group of Mayans who were culturally still happy with the sixteenth century and where there was no running-water system.

My natural timidity was really on trial that day, as more and more villagers swarmed to get a glimpse of the shower guy, but it was the young unmarried girls, with their flashing eyes, who really made me nervous as they craned their smooth necks to get a look at me. Any one of them could have stolen my heart. Excited, whispering, and worried, they gestured among themselves. Having myself grown up around an indigenous village, I was expecting to receive the unmerciful taunting and goading of people afraid of something new, which in a small community is usually either slowly digested into the village matrix or driven out altogether. But in either case, even if you did end up being accepted, you had to survive a gauntlet of abuse.

It surprised me, then, that few people mocked me and most had rather anxious looks on their faces. Tossing down more of the ritual shot glasses full of a strong homemade libation, and still in line with the proud hierarchy, we awaited the signal from the workers. These were a group of highly energetic young men, busy splitting firewood and stoking the firebox under the locomotive boiler to heat my shower. It was to them I was to pay my one dollar.

Todavia—"no, not yet"—or *Ya mero*—"pretty soon"—they would excitedly, loudly announce every so often. Obviously cronies of Narciso, these guys were definitely progressives who wouldn't wear the traditional outfits and who were delighted by this idea of bringing in "advances" of non-Indian culture such as this shower, bringing them to the brink of participation in the Modern Age by firing up this old machine. Their first client being from the States was too much for them. They were elated and enthusiastic. "We'll signal you when it's ready!" they yelled to us, as they sweated and labored.

And since they were experts and all, we waited.

The crowd thickened, and a tense atmosphere of expectation poured through the throng. Hungry for life, I succumbed to the spell of my life's fantasy; to become, if only for these few delicious moments, a part of a people's life, a people whom I deeply admired and feared, whose full-lipped young, industrious ladies I thought must contain thousands of years of dreamlike secrets. And they were watching *me* and only me, the big man of the day. On and on my nauseating, deluded mind seduced my common sense, when finally one of the old kings tapped my back ever so gently, calling my attention to the workers. Perspiring and ecstatic, their chests heaving from their labors, they proudly coaxed me into the box. The shower was deemed ready.

The fire under the boiler was really fierce and popping, while the boiler was gurgling like a low-pitched hookah. So I sauntered into the five-foot-wide box. Designed for local heights, the roof just cleared my cranium by half an inch, and the sprinkler can shower head was aimed right at my shoulder blades. The crowd was about twenty feet away, shoving and stretching to get a good look. I turned around, my back to the audience, and in front of me stood two enormous ornate iron valve wheels, which I figured corresponded to hot and cold respectively, like the life-loving imbecile I was.

Unable to see the boys at the boiler, Narciso relayed their message to me, to open one of the valves slowly. So I did. It was like opening a rusty vault wheel, creaking and groaning, until it was fully opened, but—no shower. So I closed it again, with great bottom-wiggling, which the crowd loved. Narciso shouted they'd have it fixed right away. One of his sidekicks shimmied up to the roof of my box and started banging on the pipe with a rock.

I waited a little longer.

Then the signal came: an ear-splitting blast of the steam whistle, announcing that my shower had officially begun!

Those boys kept blowing the whistle. Everybody in the crowd had their hands over their ears, but their eyes were glued on the little shower box. I opened the valves as directed, the whistle blasts echoing beautifully throughout the whole mountain valley, but still no water. Turning to face the crowd, grinning, I squinted like a cat taking a poop, shrugging my shoulders to the crowd, as if to say "No water."

But then it came with a hiss, gurgle, and whomp, with the force of a fire hose out of a two-story-tall cappuccino machine, blowing the shower head clear into orbit, and me right with it, out of the box a foot in the air, and kerplop, face down, into a mire of four-inch mud, ten feet from the box, at the feet of the village hierarchy!

The crowd roared, the whistle kept screaming, and hot, hissing water sprayed the air, dissipating over the crowd like a geyser.

Some of the old guys rolled me over and over in the mud for my scalded back, picked me up, and feasted me jubilantly around the village, house to house. I was congratulated for a full day and night, plied silly with *nicte*, or flower water, until I could neither laugh nor stand. The whole town meanwhile took turns pulling the steam whistle, till it ran out of steam.

The flower water and the mud took some of the sting out of my blistering back. Being feasted took the bite out of my loneliness. But staggering around Oxchuc, arm in arm with crowds of old men and "progressive" kids, gleefully impeded by fits of laughter about my shower, actually being congratulated for making possible a majestic and foolish event for the spirit, made being alive so precious that for that moment I would have willingly died to keep it from vanishing.

I had never been admired for being a beautiful idiot, or rewarded for my spirit. That was the best shower I ever had!

4

HIS BACK PAVED
WITH STARS:

Lost,
Looking for Home

Hordes of little iridescent blue-backed sparrows made a sound like "plish" in rapid succession as they shot in and out of the curtain of water falling into a green pool whose banks were solid limestone carpeted in moss. The cascade concealed a cave where these birds had their village in tight neighborhood groupings of round mud houses that covered the echoing walls.

I didn't get lost right away; I had simply jumped out of a truck, onto a trail they told me would lead to a curative waterfall whose rare liquid was drinkable. My shower-blistered back had festered, and this magical place was reputed to have what I needed to put me right again.

Fevered and woozy, I felt the water's luscious fingers sneak into my soul as I sank my inflamed, crusty back into this big hole of chalk filled with cool liquid jade, while swallows and dragonflies fanned my face, one kind flitting, the others hovering.

Fondling an opaline bead I'd found earlier in the day, I decided to give it back to the immensity from where it had come, in hopes that the healing powers of this delicious place might look upon me kindly. The bead was different than most pre-contact beads in that it had been drilled with holes at right angles to one another, meeting in the center of the opal. Rainbows played within it. Maybe it had been the corner bead on some ancient Mayan vestment. It had been formed without the use of metal. I didn't know the old Maya liked opals: only jade, amber, serpentine, and so on.

The iridescent jewel had been staring up at me out of the mud like the earth's eyeball, right near a big chunk of toppled limestone carved around the edges with badly worn hieroglyphics from long ago. Embedded in a little rise, the stone formed a table where I took the last meal I would for quite a while, with a family of traveling Chol Mayans who shared their lunch of hard-boiled eggs, stewed dahlia greens in crushed *miltomates* and *chipiltepin*, some beautiful tortillas, and thin, sweet coffee.

Where I grew up, unless you knew what you were doing, keeping things that belonged to the ancients might be bad luck. I swam across the watery hole, through and behind the falls. Still in the water, between the falls and the stone, I looked up to see where the water came over the ledge. I could see the swallows' lair was actually a cave inside a cave. The steep, slick wall behind the falls formed a coincidal cavern, its deepest point perforated by a more tunnel-like hole where the swallows were coming and going. Up to the swallows' cave was a treacherous climb, and I barely made it. Crystal-clear water was seeping out of her, too. Still naked, I stood up inside and placed the ancient milky bead into the entry hole of one of the swallows' earthen nests, feeling a great presence. The swallows were her messengers and her eyes!

Later on, climbing out onto the bank, I dressed and meandered down the river to warm a little in the sun, as it hung low in the afternoon sky. I ended up on a boulder that jutted benchlike out onto the rushing river where a lot of fine spray was lifted over the stone. The sun shot it full of multiple rainbows, so I purposely positioned myself there in order to feel as if I were inside the opal bead I'd just given away. As I sat bathing in rainbows, enveloped in their spell, an immature tapir poked his gentle, elephantlike beak out of the impenetrable foliage on the opposite shore. With an elegant waddle, he launched his sleek, ample self into the water right in front of me! Hidden by mist and rainbows, he must have felt I was part of the landscape. I was certainly feeling a part of something bigger myself. Just his horselike head and ears stayed visible as he waded around, blowing mist out of his short trunk, while his eyes, full of the wilds and nothing of men, smiled above the water like a five-year-old farmboy smelling fresh, hot bread.

Some baby stars must have gotten lost and gone walking the earth, climbing on backs of animals, to find their way back home to the skies— some ending up sparkling in rivers and in the hopeful eyes of birds who soared, some in the eyes of young humans and frogs. This little tapir was carrying at least fifty of them on his back, ribs, and rump, all gorgeously arrayed in some ancient order, a constellation absent from the sky. The tapir was one of the Rain God's animals, and the stars on his back merged into the sparkling river. Since rainbows, like the spots on a young tapir, were destined to fade as soon the sun disappeared into dusk, the rainbows were the first to go.

Part rhino, part horse, part peccary, part elephant, the young tapir got to staring at me, his roachlike bristled mane quivering in the rapids when he realized I was human. He turned, laid back his ears, strained and pulled his cute, powerful rump up the mud embankment as fast as his massive body could take him, crashing like a seal-colored boulder at light speed, diving, stars and all, into the dense underbrush, disappearing like a noisy dream. Leaves and twigs dropped leisurely behind him after he was long gone. Without thinking, I swam the river, floating my mother's suitcase over and down onto the little beast's road, following the tapir's wake of damaged vegetation, deep into the forest. But I never caught another glimpse of him. By now it was so dark I couldn't tell up from down, nor could I hear the river or the falls. The place was very dark and getting more so, not black, but shades of green so deep that black looked bright.

It was strange how easily that tapir had enchanted me, pulling me right out of what I knew, into the water, through the forest, to this deep place where I knew nothing. Immobilized by the dark and my inexperience, I was compelled to make camp as best I could; all I had was my dead mother's suitcase and a small prison-made hammock, which I ignorantly began to stretch between what turned out to be two needle palms, which filled me with a barrage of hairlike poisonous spikes, like mini–sea urchins. Adding to the pain I already felt in my back, these thorns would make me swell, with symptoms like the flu.

Sleep didn't even cross my mind. After all, I wasn't lost in the middle of nowhere, but buried deep in the beating heart of a dense somewhere, invisible to everything I'd ever known. Nobody in the whole world even knew I was here. Jaguars began coughing and rumbling all around me in that dark somewhere. I got to feeling that I might be eaten soon, so I kept myself fully awake, which is not to say I could have slept if I'd wanted to.

About a thousand jungle crickets, a type of high-pitched whistling cicada, raised a relentless, deafening screech for the entire duration of the night, like a dissonant smoke alarm. And all this was syncopated by the birdlike brattle and beeps of widely distributed tree frogs, not to mention the hissing beetles who flew at night and liked flying into my eyes and other parts. Luckily, the mosquitoes quit after a couple of hours, only to return at first light.

Utterly unprepared, I'd wandered in here with no food, no water, no receptacles, and no fire. The last liquid I'd tasted was at the swallow's waterfall many hours ago, and it was beginning to turn my guts into Death's Ballcourt! Between the cracked and oozing inflammation on my back and the feverish reaction to the poison needle-palm spikes, by morning I was feeling pretty dry and shaky. In the half light of dawn, I found myself lying awake in a vigorous grove of massive trees. Some reached to the leaf-hidden heavens, but down at my level the area was thickly draped in a crisscross tangle of hanging vines, some as thick as my legs, and some like my arms, but most of them the size of my fingers. I itched all over and was probably full of tropical chiggers and ticks. I was scratching all over when I heard another jaguar growl.

Turning slowly, my fear and my macho in place, I glared in the jaguar's direction, and in a goose-bumped, shaky, adrenaline-inspired attitude I reached for a clublike stick. Then I saw that what I'd lain awake all night waiting to be killed and consumed by was, in the daylight, a few little drab birds the size of fat swallows, with big old beaks that growled and whined all night! They looked like they were smiling, self-satisfied, but like the beasts they mimicked, they nodded off to sleep in the day. Dizzy and dry, I unstrung my hammock, laughing at my all-night fear of some harmless birds.

Now that the light had come, it would be simple to track myself back to the river and slake my thirst, then up a few miles behind the falls to the road and on to Zapata for food and a rest.

Still chagrined at my brave vigil, I kept knocking one of many vertical green vines out of my face. Then I realized that this vine was eating one of my jaguar birds. This vine, which had hung over my eyes all night, turned out to be a highly poisonous tree snake with fangs in the back of its leaf-colored jaws. Backing off slowly, I got my gear and headed into what I remembered was the verdant hole by which I'd arrived.

As I pushed along, the rainforest seemed like the floor of a strange ocean, an enormous body of water trapped in the form of plants. It was an awe-inspiring woman with a million faces, not all friendly, not all hostile, not all caring, but each of her faces was a distinct species, a living form, and the wild jungle shone in every one of them. All of them together made her shine as one intense living female being.

To wander in her, for me, an American desert-raised fool, was to journey through caves of chlorophyll, a tangible carnal sea in whose lusty waters I could actually breathe. The dense exuberance of her body dazzled me. You could truly hear and see her before your eyes, so present in so many beings, coming and going, living and dying, rotting and breeding, sprouting and spawning, spreading and flowering, creeping and killing, eating and birthing, singing and hiding, screaming and sleeping, digging and drilling, flying and waiting; where the ground itself was not even dirt or rock, but a thick nap of humus and plant litter on a felted blanket of tightly interlocking networks of competitive roots on top of more roots.

Even the sky was green, paved in tree leaves like blades of jade, with the branches that grew them densely populated with mosses, aerophytes, ideophytes, orchids, fruits, screaming birds, bugs, and monkeys. With plants behind me, plants in front, plants to all sides, and plants under my feet, it became plain that I was in a house. This woman's body was a house, a temple, our mother's womb, my lover's face. The force of her sensorial newness, along with my feverish state, dropped me into an array of savage emotions, both ecstatic and terrifying—new feelings, unknown feelings. The new aromas, the new sounds, things I'd never seen before, spun me into a trance, amplifying my already well-established erotic relationship with the landscape and my verdant quest to find a way to merge and mate with the spirit of the world, which I'd hoped was in women, and had seen inviting me in girls' eyes. I now knew that this spirit surrounded me everywhere, and I was lost in it: The jungle was that woman.

But this was the dry season. There could be no ground water for miles and miles, and any water you did find would be stagnant and probably kill you. You had to learn which vines to cut, how to slice them, squeeze out the cool, secreted liquid into your parched mouth, or how to carve the trunks of the giant jungle dahlias, not poisoning yourself drinking the magic water. I didn't know any of this yet. And a person lacking this knowledge could easily end up melted by the seasonal heat, dragged down into the humus, transformed into the food of coyotes, beetles, buzzards, and carnivorous mice.

The deserts of my upbringing had similar rules, where water was the obvious blessing in a landscape so visibly dry. But here in this lush, arboreal sponge, I was deceived into thinking there was water to drink.

Literally tons of water surrounded me, pushed and pumped through the cellulose arteries of trees, palms, canes, and vines, sealed in the bloodstreams of animals and subterranean roots. The air was so heavy with moisture, it was indeed like breathing underwater: a vegetal ocean, a jungle sea where the fish are birds, and crustaceans, insects; the sharks are jaguars, coyotes, and pumas; rays are eagles, whales are tapirs, and dolphin, deer; eels are snakes, the undercurrents are the trees in the sluggish jungle breeze. And as in the ocean, nothing moved in a straight line. Everything crept, fluttered, stalked, strolled, surged, crashed, or grew in spirals, swirls, or undulations, and anything else meant exhaustion.

She was so inviting, yet unknowable, addictive and poisonous, dreamlike but very touchable, beautiful and deadly, changeable and uncontainable, where the discoverer is discovered by himself, walking on the bottom of the ocean of his own soul, surrounded by leaf-locked water while dying of thirst, devoured in the belly of this verdant Mother of Abundance.

She did not pity me as I staggered and yelled into her orchid-studded heart with my own dead mother's suitcase weighing me down with the past, unready for the Now, looking to belong and to be longed for. Unarmored, I walked straight into the mouth of this hungry thing, right over her teeth, stringing my humble hammock over her tongue, and fed myself to life, like a magnificent nitwit just waiting to be eaten by the Mother Forest.

Alone, naive, and uninitiated, I assumed, since the jungle was a woman and all women were "mothers," and since all mothers would want to feed and look after me, that the Mother Forest would do the same and would eventually come through for me. But this was a new kind of woman for me, and I had no relationship with her.

This time I was the *food* she gave to what she tended: Nature.

Trying every hint of a trail, and using every bit of ingenuity I had, I poked and crashed around over logs and under vines. But I never found my way back to the river. In my dry and debilitated state, I began a journey straight into the jungle of my own nature. Panicking, I fled like the tapir away from my human mind, into an anxious and disturbingly familiar animal acceptance of dying, not an "if" any longer, but a "when," and the "how" I should live until then. So I wandered and wandered, deeper and deeper, and still found no river, no road, no trail, no water, until, exhausted, I slept propped against a copal tree. My teeth chattering and shaking, I awoke vomiting. I was so dry and emptied I almost choked to death like my mother had when she died. By now I had diarrhea, which took more and more precious liquid from my skinny frame. Like a drunk artist, I listened with delirious interest to the ringing in my ears and how it mixed symphonically with the twitters, coos, calls, and rustlings of leaves. Losing more and more of who I thought I was, I was learning to stretch deeper into something I could truly call "me." The bold essence of frangipani came and went on the air, countering my weakness a little. Ticks fattened themselves behind my knees, while dive-bombing colmoyote flies buried their sharp heads deep into my hide like darts. I stood up, and, wandering and rambling, I strained my ears for the distant roaring waves of the howler monkeys. Like the scent of the frangipani, their guttural rumblings faded and recurred as I navigated toward the beacon of their deep sound. The monkeys would know where to eat and what to drink.

Mesmerized by the beauty and impervious immensity of the ever-deepening forest, I discovered that my acceptance of my smallness in the face of it all made being lost into a kind of being at home. How lost could you be if you felt at home being lost? I was very hungry but unable to eat, dehydrated and reduced to stumbling and trudging with my mother's hard paints and brushes. Then I brushed against the gum-smeared bark of a tree slashed in a netlike pattern with a cup nailed at its base.

This was a sign of people, most likely chicleros. Chicleros were men who penetrated the rain forest, gathering chicle for chewing gum or *caucho* (latex) for rubber, making camp in small groups. Chicleros were most often outlaws who roamed the jungle hiding from the authorities, tapping trees in season, trapping and shooting animals the rest of the year. They were not known for their scruples or compassion, but were notorious for killing, robbing, and raping Indians, going unpunished as they knew the forest well. Of course not all of them were like this; many were Indians themselves, tapping tree resin seasonally to make up for failed crops.

Chicleros would have water for sure. Darkness was coming on and I couldn't move any farther, so I strung my hammock, collapsing unconscious inside it, delirious and dry, full of fever and diarrhea, crying for the jumping pains in my guts.

Something was smothering me, stopping up my nose and mouth as I awoke, my eyes refusing to see. Terrified, I flailed at my face and bolted into an upright position when the clouds lifted. Spitting and gagging, still sitting in my hammock, I woke up completely armored in blue butterflies. From my hair to my toes, no part of me was visible. Thousands of bright powder-blue butterflies formed a three-inch-thick jittering husk of shining, sky-colored insects who'd hover when I stirred, then settled again, refusing to flutter off.

I walked a little, shaking my arms, and the butterflies came along like little pets, clinging in places as I moved, giving me a new skin of light, shimmering indigo. There were no butterflies anywhere else, none on the trees, the vines, or the roots, not even the air. I had them all!

Delirious, and never having seen this many at once nor this color blue, I lost myself and began dancing and dancing around, feeling light, euphoric, and very ill. When I jumped, my live blue sheath jumped, refusing to be bucked off. They were all over my hands, my arms, belly and legs, feet, back, my neck, my face, my hair, everywhere; I must have looked like a man made of blue butterflies. Rolling up the hammock, I felt a sickly exhilaration; charmed and blessed by this miracle, I began speaking to them, my new companions. Oh how we shined in the vaporous emerald light of this jungle dawn.

My knees like noodles, I wandered, still hoping for water, looking like a big ambulatory blue flowering tree. In hopes of keeping the butterflies with me, I walked along trying not to disturb the teeming beasts, staring point blank through a knot of powdery wings and hairlike feelers, only occasionally brushing the creatures off my eyes to catch a brief glimpse of obstacles waiting to topple me, giving little or no attention to my heading, as I was lost anyway. Each time I brushed them back, they crowded in again, instantly making it impossible to see anything other than butterflies.

For most of the morning I struggled along like this, hypnotized by this magic herd of butterflies, but unable to shake the feeling that I was being dogged. I was accompanied by more than the blue fluttering bugs; someone was there. I felt it so strongly that, brushing aside the swarming insects from my face, I turned to look and saw only the forest and the butterflies when . . .

Down I went, crashing over a cliff, tearing off my sandals, ripping away my toenails on an arching root, head over heels, down and down, speeding down, the butterflies hanging in the air where I'd been, and I hit the . . .

Here there were no bird songs, no breezes, no air, none of the natural rushing in the ears, no sounds at all. Nothing. Totally silent here, under the honey. The smell was sweet, very sweet.

The world was such a luscious place as I looked out upon it. My entire being was a big old tongue floating in an ocean of honey. The creation was honey. Every sense became taste, and that sense was drowning in the very rich sweetness of the honey. My eyes and ears were taste buds on the tongue of my desire, made to taste to the fullest my immersion into that immense deliciousness.

Staring at me, the rat's expression never changed, but when she went to blink

her eye, it took months to accomplish. I lay watching the rat's eye wink for a cou-
ple of months. This took a lot of my focus, but here in the honey creation I could do
it easily.

Everything had revealed itself, all things wore their significance without mys-
tery, and all things had meaning. I could see everything inside everything else,
merging and diverging simultaneously, products of their ancient largesse, and yet
see how each unfolded its unique face by its own personal effort. Every minute
thing that had a purpose in the whole, even if heretofore unrevealed, was now eas-
ily understood. You could see how all the pieces fit together or destroyed each other
in the perfectness of the push and pull, resistance and receptivity that made life
pump and function.

Meaning was honey. You didn't have to comprehend meaning, you ate it,
drank it, swam in it, became it. You could understand it, but it mattered not at
all, and you didn't even want to.

The rat had meaning and fit in a million ways in the ecology of the big pic-
ture, before, later, now, and beyond. Each of her hairs was significant, her fleas
had meaning, the fleas' hair had meaning, the tiles on the walls where I lay had
meaning, the thumbprint of their long-dead makers had meaning. The clouds,
the past, the sun, the future, the rain beings, they all had meaning.

Everything was here. Nothing good, bad, ugly, or lovely was omitted, and
everything fit in many places in the large picture, which fit into a larger picture,
and so on. What had been and what would be were one river. My dead mother was
here, but she had become a stone in the belly of a fish who swam here somewhere,
and I couldn't find her eyes. Unborn Gods were here along with friends I hadn't
met yet, some already old and dead. I was in here somewhere, but I couldn't focus
on him well enough just now. But all this meaningfulness didn't belong to me, it
belonged to nature and in this honeyed place I could know it all. In this sweetness,
knowledge was a merged, spherical thing, inseparable from the fact that it
couldn't be used here; knowing was an irrelevant and useless impediment to the
deliciousness surrounding the knower.

There was no "I" anymore, only the "I" that was starting to centrifugally spin
down into the honey, plunging like a whale made of honey that merged with the
honey where he dove, disappearing as a whale, as "I" disappeared as "I" into an
ocean of sweet, soundless merging, the hungry life being dissolved by life's hungry
belly. It was a digesting soup of everythingness, a oneness of all things, times, and
natures melted into each other, homogenized into a single point, a single place and

taste with a primal pull like a mile-wide magnet on a pin, an implosive cyclone, funneling everything into oneness. I had always considered oneness a good thing, but this oneness was a zero. This oneness was not life, because there was no diversity. Oneness was a noneness, where nothing was separated enough to see the beauty of another. All things were so merged that nothing longed for anything else. There was no desire. This was death, a lonely zero of oneness, where all things were nothing in no place. One big zero in a non-place.

A weepy, whimpering sound started somewhere far off and away. Something very distant began to miss me. A deep bellowing anguish, made to appear small by its remoteness, began a search for me, caring for me, grieving for me, coming a long, long way to find me. When it did, its cool cheek pushed against mine, then another found my other cheek as I sank drowning in the honey, sinking into the infinite, bottomless honey.

These cool, fat little cheeks against mine were the cheeks of the faces of my unborn great-great-grandchildren who wept for me, missing me. Their "I" not dead, having never been born, not wishing to lose the opportunity to live some day, they had to dive into the sticky sweet mire of the death to rescue their own faces by retrieving mine.

Realizing I was dying, I wondered if I hadn't already done so. Oneness was always lurking everywhere. It was nothing. Knowing was nothing. To know all about everything was nothing, knowing secrets and truths was all part of the big merging zero of oneness. To be alive was to unfurl the mysterious blossom of life, maturing it with the heat of longing, discovering its own nature. Gradually, petal by petal, at its own pace, its own reverence for its lack of knowledge driving it on to flower more, to discover more; its ignorance and its longing the parents of its beauty and desire to live.

To know everything, and be everything, and be able to do everything was death, because you were unneeded, and needed nothing. Living was being a vital part of something bigger than oneself, alongside a garden of a billion other diverse beings doing the same. The flower of life had to blossom in diversity, the oneness coming back alive in the dancing, interdependent many. Human beings weren't even close to being the center of that flower. We were a beautiful, ornery stripe on one of the petals.

Still in the bowels of death, I naively accepted the sweet, cared-for feeling of being digested in the Old Mother's belly. My juices might become the milk in her breasts, where she suckled all life.

This was fine if it was my time, but . . .

I had more deep eyes to gaze into, more pretty girls to love, more desire to feel this deliciousness and the willful human illusion of free choice against the backdrop of life's precariousness with its boundary of pain. There were challenges yet to confront, discoveries to make, more food to taste, more friends to make, more men to fight. My grandchildren would miss being born, and I would miss the longing foment of living life, so I decided. I decided to live.

There was no way I could drag myself out of here on my own, I was far too heavy now, full of knowing. Something alive, very crafty, would have to get me out. I called and called, beginning to hate this thick, imprisoning sweet goo of death. I heard myself begin to whimper somewhere far away, and I wanted to go find it when a lizard came. In his eyes were reflected the faces of my grandchildren's fathers, my unborn sons. The lizard ate an ant crawling between my eyes, his marvelous long tongue coming toward me for years, like a comet on its way. I pleaded with him to pull me into life, and I would owe him.

Moving his lips in a mysterious fashion, the lizard sang, hooking my nature like a fish on his song, hauling me up and up on the cable of his beautiful song, baited with the faces of my unborn children. I felt as if I were being mined, shot up out of a tunnel, spinning around like a water screw. The part that was me was being drilled out of the matrix of the universe. Unassembled, in pieces, my insides were strung out behind me on a beautiful thread of some kind, like fresh wash on a clothesline. My insides all had faces and voices. My heart was there, my lungs, my liver and pancreas, my gall bladder shone like a sun, and my intestines were a net of stars. My organs formed a council of deities and they began to sing, each in his own strange way, but together forming a chorus.

The thread that bound them together was a strong, pale, clean cable of light taken from the eyebrows of the Grandmother Moon who spun my life on a spindle of the lizard's song. The thread led off far to some other place. My body became a hollow tube of cooked bone, like the cannonbone of a horse, filled with eyes, instead of marrow, that could see, taste, and hear itself being dragged into life by the continuous low mumbling chant of the lizard, who moved his jaws from side to side like a toothless old man with a restrained hilarity. His chin was yellow.

Slowly I was coming back to life. Someone stepped on my back, below my ribs, becoming overpoweringly heavy. A deep, sick, intensely itching pain oozed from where they stood, spreading throughout my body into places I hadn't known I owned. In that place a rhythm commenced to echo to the lizard's song. I think this was my heartbeat. The lizard sent a duck for my face, who dove down and found it and brought it back.

Far away I could hear a flash flood coming, or a cyclone, or something like an arrow zipping in from an enormous distance. It was the lizard song—at first a hiss, then a windy, blowing sound, until slowly the deluge began to thump and crash, grinding like rolling boulders in a torrential, flooding river. In it gushed the mighty roar and rush of the sounds of everyday life back again, the silence cured.

I couldn't see everywhere anymore, just that rat in my face whose blinking came quickly now, while a sharp pain in my ribs rippled out in crippling waves to meet a deeper ache from the depth of my viscera. The honey had separated into air and ground, in between which I lay gasping in short, painful breaths, my broken ribs twinging at every movement, the air in my lungs both searing and putrid. My body was heavy like several tons of dead meat, unable to move any part of me on command.

The floor had not yet separated from my body, and my head seemed firmly melted into the concrete floor, wading in an awful pool of my own juices, out of which I couldn't budge, my eyes gushing with infection. The rat seemed to have taken some interest in my presence.

All was pain. The honey gone, a smile waited somewhere behind my face, having been fished from the deadly sweetness by spirit and my own nature back to life and living air. I knew that this suffering, this nausea, this painful breathing, these broken ribs, this nausea, this fever-tortured body, this foul-smelling breath, and this desperate uncertainty were the unmistakable signs of the blessing of being alive. The "other world" had shown me that there was a spiritual payment for the privilege to suffer. Suffering was not the price of living, but a part of the gift of being alive. Not a big deal, but a part of the deal.

I could now see how the breath of life did not come from people, but came into people from another place far away from human knowledge, thus bestowing life as a gift, not as an inalienable prerogative. This deliciousness, this pain, the befuddlement, mystery, and wonder, are generously handed to us by a hungry Deity force who wants our full, uninsulated participation in life as a down payment, beginning a lifelong series of ritual feedings into its starved belly. Instinctively I knew I'd been recruited to serve what had served me today, and they would hold it over my head until I came through for them as a reciprocation from me for my improbable return to life.

I was breathing and my heart was beating. I felt so sick I must be dying, and since I knew death was sickly sweet and noiseless, this deadly feeling must have meant that I was alive again. Only just barely, but alive I was!

In the deadly midday heat of a tropical spring, I returned from the land of the dead, sprawled on the floor of an abandoned room, face down in my own effluvia. Unable to move at first, I set my mind to regain the feeling in my limbs. Having held the same stiff pose for days on end, my legs were not too cooperative.

My sense of feeling and the ability to stir were like an old dog come home, sniffing out all the familiar corners and corridors in the house that was my body, in a sort of poky old roundabout way, until gradually most of me was more or less functioning and seemed to be at home with itself. Water was everything now, and who knew how long since I'd eaten—probably a week at least. I could've started yelling for help, but I didn't have the force to do it, and my throat was so dry my voice had disappeared.

Watching the lizard on the wall, I saw him scamper to the threshold of a doorless doorway some ten feet off. Looking back at me, he darted right through it. "I'd better follow him that way, too," I thought, remembering well his life-saving song still surging in my head: "He's pulling me to life."

On account of my extreme weakness, I had to plan for a long time how to crawl and drag myself out of this empty chamber, avoiding all unnecessary movements and unwarranted breathing because of my cracked ribs.

Entirely unaware of where I was or how I had gotten there, I had no idea of what awaited beyond the door. An occasional hum of life, the smell of dust, and the incessant chittering whistles and raucous beeps of tzanate birds had me guessing that I was in a villagelike place, but the torpifying heat made it improbable I could survive a visit outside the room by day. I decided to remain inert until nightfall, then inch my way a couple of feet at a time to the threshold, then roll into the cool out-of-doors. If I made it outside, I would reassess the situation, but for now I waited right where I lay, conserving the last little sparks of life force left in my broken body.

5

BY THE BRUSH
OF HER HAND

Fourteen hours later, around three in the morning, I crawled out of the deserted compartment into the moonlight sifting through the shaggy crown of a coyol palm, beneath which I lay crumpled in a stone gutter, panting in pain. Lucky to have the Grandmother Moon's cooling glow, I stared down the banqueta that lined a deserted rock-cobbled roadway with houses on either side.

After a fashion it came to me that I might be lying in the streets of a mean little rail town that I had visited earlier in the month en route to Lacondonia. If so, then about 150 yards farther down this same rustic thoroughfare stood a *tiendita-comedor*, a store-restaurant where I'd performed some guitar songs at a well-attended, spontaneous get-together after a very good dinner of *hilachas*, *plátanos fritos*, and *mamey*.

Three pragmatic approaches for getting to friends and food percolated simultaneously through my brain. My mind was as sharp as an ant bite in contrast to my struggling body. I decided to crawl two feet at a push, then rest, then crawl two more feet, then rest, pulling myself that way through the remainder of the night until I came upon the door of the *comedor*. If I got there by sunup, the owners would, hopefully, recognize me and come up with a plan for my recovery, as I could not utter one intelligible human word, my voice having fled with the water from my flesh. Cutting deeply, my broken rib bones limited my raw, whistling breathing. I collapsed after attaining each minor goal on my route, crawling along walls, to stones, up to a tree, to a palm, until, exhausted, I blacked out on an ancient curb with carved writing on the rock.

Street dogs licked me awake in the dawn, who, like me, were starving, and even less cared for. I was so dizzy in the sunlight, but I'd made my goal in around five hours. When I tried to stand, I sank to the ground at the doorway of the *tiendita*. The door was painted a fuchsia color with little flowers as a border. The walls of the store were a sky-blue with a Sal Andrews anti-acid logo painted at eye level by the entrance.

When I'd regained a tiny bit of steadiness, I managed to scoot a large pebble into my fist, and pounded the bottom of the beautiful door with it, killing a few of the painted flowers. Coppery ankles and a skirt hem were all I could see of a small, irate woman who flashed from the quickly opened door and kicked me hard, knocking me windless back onto the rocky street. When she spoke, she railed at my ugliness and began a squawking tirade about what I'd done to her door. These were the first human utterances I'd heard in a long while.

Gasping for air and curling up from pain and weakness, my disappointment was beyond description. I wanted to weep but there was no water in me. In some way her behavior was understandable, because after a couple of weeks of bad illness and exposure, I was unbathed, covered in urine, vomit, diarrhea, and dried blood. My toenails were bloody and missing, I must have smelled like buzzard guts and looked derelict and maybe even crazy and dangerous. I don't know. Obviously I hadn't inspired pity. But I couldn't afford the luxury of any romantic notions, self-pity, or understanding, so back up I crawled and banged again the best I could. Shutting my oozing eyes, I waited for another beating.

But this time a sweet-smelling and gorgeous little eight-year-old girl floated out of the doorway in a butter-colored dress. She squatted down and looked me over good and hard just like a little heron trying to decide if I were really something she should fish out of the water. She crouched on the stony old street curb, the shores of life, while I lay battling for air in a river of sunlight on a bed of hot cobblestones, when it hit her. She recognized the well-made black obsidian arrowhead I'd worn around my neck since I was no older than she was. She remembered me from the time I sang some songs for her!

She bolted into the store, pestering her merchant father to come save me, which he did. They dragged me into the courtyard behind the store and sat me on a chair at a blue-painted table, but I kept melting to the floor in a smelly heap. After spreading my arms over my prone head on the table, I stayed put. I didn't move anything except my lips for two days, slowly sucking thin white *atole* cooked with sugar and milk through a straw, actually living at that blue table until I could speak again and pee. I've been doing both ever since. May the powers be blessed that blessed me with that child's vision and her father's belief in her. Bless them both.

I was so happy to be alive that I was unworried about what anyone said or thought of me, and I began to be a different being altogether. The shop owner turned me over to Marvicio Gonzales Iturbe, the local M.D., who graciously arranged to have me nursed back to health in the sumptuous confines of his old colonial house. Wounded and sore, I tried to regain my voice and reinflate my dried-out body with a blessing of abundant water. Water had never tasted so wonderful. It was pure God. An Indian girl, one of the doctor's family maids, was put in charge of feeding me and keeping me cleaned up. She came every couple of hours, spooned in some food, spoke to me, and we laughed. Though I know nurses always seem like angels to wounded boys, her visits really meant a lot to me.

After I'd recovered somewhat, I was invited to take meals at the family dinner table. Unaccustomed to the attentions of servants, maids, cooks, and gardeners, I treated them as equals and friends. It seemed to me that one should at least be thankful to these people who were struggling to make life easier for their benefactors. But the doctor and his family criti-

cized me for being too familiar with the help. I was told to stop fraterniz-
ing with them, as it was beneath my station. They didn't realize that the
ancestors of these servants, as well as the people Dr. Iturbe healed, had
been the rulers of this land long before the Europeans came ripping into
the Americas with their hard hearts and militarily enforced merchant
cultures.

After a while I came to see that the doctor's family perceived me as a
man of breeding and means who had simply gone astray on a rain forest
trail during a youthful adventure. They didn't recognize me for the big-
hearted half-breed nature boy I was, a heartbroken fugitive trying to find
a less domesticated environment where my vision of life might flower.
Fond of my guitar playing, the doctor made me a gift of a new instrument,
and installed me in his little kingdom like a well-treated court musician,
long after I was ready to be released to the world. Marvicio had been stationed here against his will as part of a national program to arrange health
care for local villagers and poor farmers. The doctor, along with his attractive wife, three sisters-in-law, and a teenaged daughter, welcomed me
as a break in what seemed to them the uncivilized life on the frontier. Feeling like captives themselves, and unable to mix with the peasants, they decided to keep me there to entertain them. I was to bring a breath of culture
into their perceived isolation.

Of all the many gifts I'd received from Marvicio, money was never one
of them. This was intended to make certain I couldn't escape. Some of the
ladies of the house took a shine to me, and I felt like one of those old-time
Meso-American warriors who, when captured by rival kingdoms, received
every courtesy possible for the duration of one yearly calendar cycle.
Showered with all the food, clothing, honor, music, jewelry, and young
women they could want, at the end of a year these warriors would be sacrificed in a ritual context.

One midnight about a month later, after I'd recovered sufficiently,
I wrote Marvicio's family a thank-you note and stole silently over the
doctor's ragged, razor-edged walls spiked with broken glass. Feeling pretty
restless and nervous about my freedom, I dropped like an iguana out of a
tree onto the ground, with a new guitar, a monkey skin, and a Lacandon
Mayan bow and arrows, Marvicio's gifts.

I plodded north in the night a couple of kilometers until I came upon an asphalt ribbon reaching off to the east. In the muggy, moon-hiding windless night, an irritating mosquitolike mechanical clatter came out of the humid stillness right down on me in the form of a sand-colored VW bus. Its headlights flickered with the unevenness of the freshly paved road. I flagged the bus down, was brought on board, and we flew off at a top speed of five miles an hour!

An American hippie calling himself Bluejay manned the wheel. Both he and his young girlfriend greeted me, cheerfully ordering me to sit on the floor in the rear since most of the van's interior was dedicated to stacks of flats containing moist cow dung sown with the spore of several varieties of local hallucinogenic fungi. Bluejay was collecting these spores to cultivate in his native land of Washington state. Unwilling to jeopardize the welfare of his delicate mushroom project by jostling them around too much or by changes in the air, he refused to drive over ten miles an hour at any given time, and I can vouch for the fact that he liked five miles an hour the most.

I related an abbreviated tale about why I was broke, with no documents, and how this had all come about, making myself sound like a victimized hero while leaving out the parts about what had been mostly my own undoing. When my saga ended, the two of them made me an offer that was hard to turn down. Bluejay and Brenda described how, at this very moment, they were en route to the Guatemalan border. They offered to take me along, vouch for me at the border, loan me the requisite one hundred dollars one needed to show the immigration officals you had enough to live on, and make up a good story about my documents. They'd bribe someone if necessary to get me in. This way I would get out of Mexico with them. I would reimburse them in New Mexico as we passed through on their way to the Pacific Northwest.

Catching the only car on an abandoned road at two A.M., it was hard to believe such luck! There were a few details that had me thinking, though: like how long it would actually take to go the four thousand miles between Guatemala and Washington state at five miles per hour. But I was grateful just the same. I went along with everything for a couple of days.

Finally, to keep from going crazy, I took to opening the side doors of the van, jumping out and sprinting alongside the van, sometimes outrunning the car for a mile or so. Then I'd sit down and wait for them to catch up, then jump in again. After a few days of outrunning the van, we were not much closer to the border, so I caught a ride on a limestone hauling dumptruck with a pile of happy workers in the back. I ended up back in San Cristobal again, having made a full circle. I'd lost the good deal to return to the States, but it couldn't be helped.

When I came up on the plaza in San Cristobal, a playful ceremony was in progress. Young men had formed a big circle around a circle of young women, both circles moving in opposite directions. The girls were smashing confetti-filled eggs on the heads of boys they admired, who retaliated then with their own. The whole plaza was filled with beauty, laughter, and the loud music generated by a large, white-suited Ladino marimba band with lots of horns.

Standing there with my guitar, monkey skin, and arrows, I watched these kids, feeling like an old exile, though some of these young people were only a year or two my junior. My experiences during the last couple of months were beginning to carve me into a different shape and had left their brand on my manner. Bit these egg-smashing kids were sure of their identities. However innocent they were, they knew whose children they were and what culture they must promote. Watching them, I sank into a mire of melancholy and despair. I realized how different I was becoming, how this way of thinking had kept me apart from most other people.

My deep loneliness and tendency toward homeless wandering were the direct result of my mission to be seen in the same way I saw. This was unreasonable, of course; after all, there were no girls who held my vision of life dear. Were there? I refused to appear as something I couldn't believe in or maintain to get a warm woman to love me. I had drunk so deeply of grief and innocently gambled so hard with fate and irony that a special kind of vision was gathering in my eyes, not entirely clear just yet. This was the same look people saw in your eyes when you have died for beauty and come to live accepting nature as life with no promise of paradise, and mad at people who couldn't see that.

For some people, that look in your eyes seems dangerous. Women instinctively knew that a greater woman, Nature herself, a Goddess, lurked somewhere in your past, and in no way could a man, having known that immensity, be trusted to strive for material well-being or be satisfied with the smallness of the everyday struggle for security. Women knew that this great mother would call on this kind of man again someday, and, powerless to resist, he would be pulled like a bird into migration.

Nonetheless, I, this man barely returned from the land of the dead, desired in the deepest way to belong to an actual place, a tribe, a people, possibly merging with the land by loving a woman from a tribal domain.

As I troubled my heart with these kinds of thoughts, a balding man in a tank top, wielding a pint of brandy, pulled himself out of a boisterous knot of older Ladino men and drunkenly pestered me into playing him a song on my guitar. The marimba was blaring so hard, he wouldn't have heard me anyway so I tried to beg him off, but his cronies surrounded me and held me firm. Venting my anger and sorrow into a fast and showy tune, I hoped they'd let me off with that.

But they wouldn't hear of it, and dragged me into a coffeehouse just off the main plaza, where the entire non-Indian intellectual male student elite of the town sat drinking beer and coffee, playing chess, as every table was a chessboard. Climbing on top of one of the chessboard tables, my new old friend announced my arrival and declared that all young men should listen to my music! Of course nobody paid the slightest attention to him as the jukebox blared over his lordship's proclamation.

Not to be deterred, my drunken patron pulled out the plug on the jukebox in the middle of a song and resumed commanding the now attentive crowd of boys to listen up. He then popped me on the head as a signal to strike up a tune. He wanted me to stand on a table while I performed, and this was very embarrassing. But I did it, and played a very fierce flamenco rhumba with plenty of passion and a complex series of golpes and riffs and sang my pain away to boot. I had nowhere to go and nothing to lose.

Unexpectedly when I stopped playing, the whole coffeehouse rose to its feet with cheers, applause, and whistles. They stuffed me with food and beer and prodded me hour after hour into playing, until everyone was singing and more guys brought guitars and we traded songs and poems till dawn. Just before light, the old man sent someone to fetch his guitar, which turned out to be a magnificent Ramires flamenco instrument. This was Mexico, what was this Spanish masterpiece doing here with us drunks? I'd never seen one before, only heard tell of them.

Well, the old drunken Elias decided to present his guitar to me as a gift. I roundly refused, knowing full well he'd regret it when the liquor and this fine evening had dissolved back into the plainness of daily life. I argued, and we finally struck a bargain where he would give me the instrument at lunch the next day at his place. Or he wouldn't, if I was right!

After searching the pine-scented town for hours through the torpor of a serious hangover and a cricked neck from sleeping in the woods, I ended up in the inner sanctum of a gray stone *cabildo* right on the plaza. Passing through a couple of guard stations, Elias met me dressed in a suit. He motioned me formally and unemotionally to a seat at a long table set with soups garnished in avocados, lemon-marinated roasted meat, good Chiapas tortillas, *rice horchata*, and coffee.

Elias turned out to be the appointed governor of the State of Chiapas, a very dangerous and powerful man of the right-wing style. All the men in the street with him last night were the political bosses of the region and their armed bodyguards. Gone was the passionate lover of life, the effervescent drunken songster. In his place sat a hard-nosed, heavy-fisted political ruler feared by all the Indians and, for the moment, by myself.

He ordered the flamenco guitar in its case brought and placed it in my hands. A visiting dignitary from Spain had given it to him. He insisted on giving it to me, and as I figured no man should be without a guitar, I left him with the one Marvicio had given me. Elias saw me out, and off I went with my prize, dropping from the governor's palatial fort down the steps into the bustle of the town.

My hangover began to lift as my full belly put me into a life-pondering trance. Hugging my incredible and unlikely gift, both happy and bitter, I meandered with no real direction. But as irony would have it, as I stalked off the plaza toward nowhere, Bluejay's noisy van came creeping by at its ever-present five miles an hour. Glad to see me, he reiterated that his initial offer of delivering me back to the States after making the rounds in Guatemala was still good, if I wanted it. I hopped in without a second thought. We crawled out of town sounding a lot like a big old sewing machine, blasting Deep Purple's "Smoke on the Water" out the windows, startling the dogs and heavily loaded Mayans trotting to their smoky homes in the pine-tree–filtered sunset.

When we arrived at the border crossing, La Democracia, the Mexican side, paid very little attention to us, I suppose because we were leaving the country. But once Bluejay and his sweetheart got stamped in by the Guatemalan immigration officers, had shown their money and had their tires sprayed, they hopped up into their microbus quick-like, and I watched them, for the first time, drive as fast as they could manage—far, far away from me. They left me and my guitar stranded between Mexico and Guatemala with no documents, no money, no one to vouch for me, and no explanation as to their change of heart. The worst part was, they left with my Lacondon bow and arrows and my monkey skin.

Scared and betrayed, trying not to let on, I was led by the Guatemalan police to a side room behind the Immigration office to await the *Jefe de Migración*, or Chief of Immigration for Guatemala on this particular border. He would decide my fate; I could be jailed here and held until an "authority" could vouch for me, or transported to the capital Ciudad Guatemala, for serious incarceration, a hearing, and eventual deportation. None of the choices sounded as good as my guitar, so I played it. The Jefe was not due anyway until around sundown, and it was now about ten A.M.

Since there were no vehicles waiting to leave or enter Guatemala, one young man, whose job it was to spray all the automobile tires with pesticide, came in and sat down behind the little counter and began to chat. Arturo listened patiently and compassionately as I described the extent of my wanderings and the reasons for my lack of money and papers. He was mystified as to why the Americans had abandoned me. His curly black hair bounced like springs when he strained to see my guitar.

"Can I play it?" he asked.

"No, maybe not," I said. "It's all I have left now, and if you take it, it'll be in Guatemala and I won't. Maybe it'll disappear and I won't be able to follow it!"

Arturo smiled and nodded, scratching his stubby chin understandingly. "Then play me a song, something I can sing to. You know I sing a little?"

So I grabbed my newly acquired instrument and sang "Probablamente

Ya," a tearjerker sung by Lucha Villa (a famous Mexican lady singer who was born a Guatemalan just south of where we were). I threw in all the moans and cries, while Arturo sang a fifth higher in perfect harmony. We really got into it, and pretty soon we attracted three "blue birds," as they call Guatemalan street cops, because they are dressed all in blue and have a whistle. These were stubby, well-fed Indian-looking fellows with their flat cop caps tilted to the side.

Once in the room, they got in on the next song, crooning fine three- and four-part harmonies. I was astounded at the sincerity and beauty of their voices. By the third song, they had their hats in their rough, chubby brown hands and their arms around each others' shoulders, including Arturo, who was now playing with me on his own very bad cheap guitar. Between songs, we congratulated each other, and the policemen laughed and poked fun at their great camaraderie, knowing they'd be in trouble if anyone caught them out of their tough-guy stances.

We were still going at it, singing "Luna de Xelajuh," when a man in an unbuttoned white shirt, gray pants, slightly balding, with an unholstered nine-millimeter semi-automatic pistol stuck in his waistband, tottered in, stood listening to us, weaving to the rhythm of the tune. Only I could see him as he positioned himself behind the singing cops.

As the song came to a high, melodramatic closure, this onlooker bugled out a military-sounding order of *"Atención!"* Arturo and company muttered apologies and began to scatter back to their posts.

This was our Jefe. He was unexpectedly early and a bit drunk. Calling back his sheepish employees, he announced that we should all go and eat lunch together at Mama Lola's, actually a tent with tables where home-made sausages were grilled over handmade oak charcoal, thick yellow tortillas called *pistones* were slapped out and toasted freshly on the spot, and many other wonderful viands were to be had. In Guatemala, such tent restaurants are facetiously called *humo en tus ojos* or "smoke in your eyes" restaurants. "And let's bring the American guitarist with us," added the Jefe.

Well, at this point, Arturo, the tire sprayer, explained how I couldn't go to lunch with them, as Mama Lola's was at least two hundred meters within the Guatemalan border, and as I had no papers or money, I wouldn't be allowed to enter. In his inebriated state, the Jefe took all of this to be a direct challenge to his authority over this border, not to mention the challenge to his personal desire to have a party with his co-workers and his very own imported guitarist. How dare the law defy his authority! In a full tantrum, he yelled out:

"*¿Cómo que no tiene papeles? Aquí hay papeles, pa' que tanto hay papeles. ¡Nosotros tenemos papeles!*" ("How's that he has no papers? Here there are papers, plenty of papers. We have papers!") "*Por la Grandísima Puta, a mi no me van a contar que no puede venir un artista a cantar y comer con nosotros por no tener papeles. ¡Ha!*" ("By the most Enormous Whore! They're not going to tell me that an artist can't sing and eat with us just because he doesn't have any papers. Ha!")

And with that, he reeled to his desk where an ancient black cast-iron typewriter was enthroned. Putting on his little glasses, he hauled out a stack of legal paper bearing the official orange-colored seal of the Republic of Guatemala and began typing in all the required prefatory bureaucratic nonsense, adding in my name, my age, country of origin, my mother's name, my father's name, dates of birth, and so on.

To this he typed and attached several more pages of beautifully crafted florid drivel about how I was known to him, the Jefe, to be the personal friend of the governor of such and such place, and the mayor of some other place, and the loyal servant of the colonel in charge of protecting whatever, and I was admired by some friend of the president, who himself was aware of my outstanding character and indispensable service to the people of Guatemala, who were all proud and secure in the knowledge that such a meritorious, heroic individual such as Martín Prechtel had been chosen to be in the bosom of the country and that by the month and day of the above year and below, as such and sundry, etc., I should be given safe passage by any person or agency petitioned and provided with transport to any destination required by me, recognized in full by some highly feared so and so who'd be answering the call if these aforementioned wishes were not carried out in full. On and on, until he had five pages full of unintelligible, imaginative, valid-sounding nonsense.

There was more! He took out a hole-puncher and placed six holes in a vertical pattern on the left-hand margin above the seal on all the papers. Then out came a riveting device with which he powerfully set six lovely brass eyelets into the holes, scrunching up his sweaty face as he did so.

Now he laced five satin ribbons, a blue one, yellow one, white, red, and green one, through the brass-lined holes connecting the pages, then braiding their silk tails creatively to their tips!

After that, he squished his official seal into each page, then stamped the hell out of all the papers arbitrarily with every rubber stamp he had: square ones, round ones, rectangular ones, and triangular ones, his well-practiced hand a blur as he went at it. Then we all signed: me, the cops, Arturo, and the Jefe, and put our inked fingerprints on every page for good measure.

Finally, the Jefe carefully folded his work of genius into three, forced its bulk into an official pink immigration envelope, stuck it in my shirt, then poked ten quetzales (ten dollars in those days) into my pocket and in a kind of triumphant, nonchalant way proclaimed:

"Now you've got papers, you've got money; bring your guitar. Let's eat *por la Gran Chingada!*" We followed him into Guatemala toward the lovely smell of food. I loved this place!

The forested mountains at the border held up a brilliant April sky and reverberated our singing and joking for more than three hours. The delicious smell of *ocote*, smoke, cooking coffee and corn perfumed our clothing, drifting off into the cool mountain air to feed these hills who'd seen so many ancient cultures live, breathe, and leave right through here.

Making the best of friends, we smoked and ate, while explaining our mothers, our brothers, our fathers, our sisters, our lives, our upbringings, singing so hard and talking so long that the duties of the border were neglected. But in the end, the collective frustrations of close to a hundred waiting buses, cars, and trucks, all honking, plus the yelling of their drivers, grew beyond our capacity to ignore. The officials I was with were sent for, and I returned with them to their posts. Since we were inebriated and the backup was beyond belief, I got deputized to help stamp transport tickets and take bribes from truckers, which I handed over to the Jefe. We were checking people through like crazy men so we could get finished early enough to sing some more. I was really glad Bluejay had deserted me.

They closed the border early after we got everyone processed. It was about five o'clock when the Jefe sent Arturo to buy some Gallo beer with the bribe money. Repairing to the newly built and still empty customs house, the *aduana* building, we prepared to sing again. The floor was slick and shiny, with a reverbation like an amphitheater. We sang, much impressed with ourselves. A new team of cops showed up to relieve my friends for the night watch, so they were off duty to party now. The Jefe asked me:

"*¿Pues*, where are you going from here, Don Martincito?"

I was still on the border and lucky to have gotten this far. Initially I'd meant to come to Guatemala as part of a plan to return to the U.S.A., but now I was falling in love with this country. My new friends had plenty of suggestions and wrote down lots of names of places and relatives where I could visit, eat, or stay. Some of these people are my friends to this day. The Jefe suggested I sleep there in the customs house and catch a bus early in the morning when the border opened again. The last bus going in tonight had already passed us by.

As we all babbled and chattered, a red car floated up to the barricade, its persistent car horn bugling out its master's impatience. The police took a look and decided that this was a piece of good fortune for me. It turned out to be a brand-new Bronco driven by what the Jefe assumed was one of my American countrymen, a *paisano*, who would obviously give me a ride if they opened the border for him to do so. They, however, didn't understand that I was much closer to all these Guatemalan cops and bureaucrats than I'd ever been to a privileged Californian with a new Bronco, who looked at me like he thought I was some freeloader who would smell up his car. This was made worse by the fact that I was unmistakably in cahoots with a very cheerful bunch of drunken armed Guatemalan officials. We looked pretty scary.

Be that as it may, my Guatemalan friends all insisted that I communicate my needs to this frustrated man, just positive he couldn't refuse me a ride to better lodging. So I reluctantly asked him for a lift, reiterating their offer that though the border was actually closed until morning, they would let him pass if he gave me a ride.

"I'm not taking any riders, and I'm in a hurry," he stated nervously.

When I translated this back to the Jefe, it incited a riotlike wave of protest from the inebriated crowd. Quieting everybody down, the Jefe urged me to translate as he calmly stated:

"In that case, please tell this self-centered, moronic, motherless ingrate of a gringo that if he doesn't give you a ride wherever you want to go for the next two weeks, we'll have to disassemble his car, bolt by bolt, and impound the parts as we search for whatever we find!"

I tried not to laugh, to have a proper feeling of shame for this poor guy, as I translated. He had everything anyone could possibly want except the flexibility that comes from experiencing life and irony. There I was, on the other hand, with nothing at all to my name, the child of irony; and all I really owned were my wits. The Californian must have been terrified as I translated the Jefe's creative ultimatum, but he gave in like an indignant boy who felt he was being robbed of his entitled autonomy. No doubt he now had me figured for some brand of undercover narcotics agent, or something equally official and threatening, since all my buddies on the border had uniforms.

Now that I'd found a ride, an hour seemed too short for my new friends to find an easy way to say farewell. The American wouldn't smoke or drink with us, so we had to let him sit and groan in his new car, thrashing around, stomping his feet, and punching his dashboard in his frustrated impatience. He was very entertaining, but finally the moment of departure arrived, and amidst hugs and handshakes, eternal promises, and the clumsy lighting of each other's cigarettes, I was lifted into the boot of the Bronco with my guitar, as the driver wouldn't have me in front.

Full of good food, friends, *aguardiente*, new songs, lots of documents, a carton of Rubios, and a week's worth of Guatemalan wages in my pocket, off I sailed with my personal chauffeur to discover a new land full of mystery and irony.

Content, I hung my head out of the back, as the red Bronco ground up and down hills, swinging around a million tight hairpin curves, through a bejeweled landscape dotted here and there with bright-colored birds and the occasional Mayan woman rhythmically surging up a hill with a full forty pounds of water in a spherical fired red clay jar balanced on her head.

Every village had a unique style of dress. Brightly wrapped mothers trudged alongside the road with their little daughters proudly bobbing behind with toy water jars on their determined heads, perfect miniatures of their parents. The evening glow was still on the oak- and pine-covered slopes, when out of a ravine appeared two Indian soldiers in olive drab with hats and carbines, who signaled for us to stop. My California driver, Stan, was scared, and refused to pull over. The soldiers fired their guns harmlessly over his hood, bringing him to a complete halt. Powerfully built, the little soldiers piled into the boot with me. I told Stan to hit it, and we did.

"How come he didn't stop at first?" the soldiers asked me.

"He doesn't know the local rules," I explained. In those days in those countries, all forms of transport were required by law to give rides to military personnel or National Police, as only officers had access to jeeps, radios, or money.

Many areas were patrolled by pairs of conscripted infantrymen carrying outdated carbines and few bullets, like these two characters who were actually Mam Indians, a truly ancient Mayan tribe from this very area. They were just trying to get back to Huehuetenango to report to their superior and get some time off. These two young men had been forced into the military in the normal illegal way: by crews of thugs who enter Mayan towns and villages, chasing underage teenage boys like schools of fish, beating the ones they catch with two-foot rubber hoses.

These boys are then loaded like cattle into lorrie-like trucks and ransomed. Often their freedom is achieved only after the sale of a family's only acreage to convenient buyers, who often come with the conscription officer, who then takes both the land and the money, paying his procurer a salary. Sometimes land deeds are handed directly to the officer. Sometimes land is put up against a loan, which is used to bribe the officers to release underage "draftees." Officers thus paid off can secure the freedom of the young man who is sometimes the sole support of aging parents. But since the family becomes land poor, many of these boys have to leave the village to work for wages, which breaks up the family anyway. They can't win.

Illegally shanghaied boys whose families have no means to ransom them end up in a hideous, demoralizing boot camp where only the staunchest men retain any vestige of their identity. The lucky ones, like these two guys squatting in the back of the truck with me, get sent to regional patrols, which carry a little more dignity and freedom.

Chatting away in the boot, we, too, became good friends. I gave each a pack of Rubios from my recently acquired carton. Pretty soon we were driving Stan crazy as we started singing songs again.

One man had a sister who ran a *comedor* in the area of Huehuetenango, so I directed my driver toward her establishment. "Mr. Stan, we are going to eat at his sister's tonight. Take a left up here and follow my directions!"

Stan's trek across Guatemala should have taken him less than two days, but I misled him into a two-month, questlike detour, during which we visited Mayan ruins, living villages, jungles and caves, markets, deserts, waterfalls, and hot springs.

We got into some funny situations.

Pointed toward Panama for some car deal, Stan was initially terrified of me, thinking that if he didn't do my bidding some horrible Latin American retribution would descend upon him. So we cruised the country at my command, using the itinerary my acquaintance on the border had provided us. That kind of ride is a terrible thing to waste. Some of the magnificent places and incredible people we encountered are now nonexistent or impossible to visit. Stan was almost getting to be more human toward the end, and when he did, I let him off. But not in the beginning.

A kind of sweet nostalgic melancholy came over me as we trucked and hairpinned our way through the Guatemalan highlands, a strong feeling of having been once taken away from a place to which I was now returning home. The smells and colors, so familiar, seeped into me. I began to remember these hills from that series of eleven intense dreams I'd had during a blizzard the previous winter in my native northern New Mexico.

By now, Stan let me sit up front with him, but one day I got away from him and he came looking for me! We had stopped in to test the boiling waters of a volcanic hot springs by the pueblo of Zunil outside Quetzaltenango in the ancient Quiche Maya tribal district. A procession of music and wailing rose up from the village streets. Walking fast, I caught up to a little marimba, hammered plaintively by a single able Mayan man, playing as he walked in the procession, his instrument borne along on each end by two men. Behind him was a chirimia player and a drummer. A somber crowd came along behind, but up in front several disheveled, very drunk, leaping, weeping, moaning, wailing, clapping, staggering men and women took turns dancing with a still drunker guy, held up by two more sober helpers. This fellow was magnificently attired in a totally traditional ancient Zunil ceremonial outfit of hat, head cloth, *rodillera*, pants and sash, sandals, and coat. The women wore ample, bright orange-red *huipiles*.

I reckoned by the look of it they were installing the very drunk, well-dressed man into some sacred office. This must be how they went about it, I surmised, by overplying him with *cuxa*, a local liquor provided by his grateful constituency, and dancing him down the village pathways. People ran out of their houses as the official went by. They put money into the pockets of his black handwoven jacket and held him as they danced along. They'd pass him to the next person, then drop into the crowd walking behind the little band.

Getting up my courage, wanting to belong in the worst naive way, I was allowed to take a turn. I danced away. Man, this guy was sure dragging his heels, I tell you; I had to do all the work of dancing. His head just kind of bobbed along and his hands were pretty cold. This fellow was the definition of drunk stiff. After handing him off to the next person, I dropped behind and followed the procession with the rest.

To my surprise and chagrin, we danced this man all the way to the cemetery, where he was put in a pine box with all his stuff and buried amidst howls, wails, and music. I'd been dancing with a well-dressed dead guy. This was a fantastic way to do things, to say good-bye to the whole village by mourning, singing, and dancing with every person in town. Dance your dead right into the other world!

Next, Stan and I descended out of the northern mountains, spiraling down toward Lago Atitlán like a couple of caracara scavenger birds pulling out of a thermal at the edge of the most exquisite lake in the world. Ten miles across, she was a water-filled volcanic crater, bound on her southern shores by three looming, heavily forested volcanos.

Jade, turquoise, and serpentine waters mixed and swirled on the bottomless lake. These were coaxed into sleepy waves by the fresh southern afternoon breeze, called the *Xocomiil*, causing the dugout canoes of Mayan fishermen dotting the shallows to lurch and bob about.

My eyes got wet; I knew this place, and it knew me.

Stan went on his way to Panama, while I, mesmerized by the beauty and the culture of the lake, stayed on in the village of Santiago Atitlán.

With two quetzales tucked in the sweatband of my hat, the pine smell of mountains, the sounds of lake birds, an earthenware cup of Mayan chocolate, and the touch of the smooth, well-sculpted, industrious hands of a solidly built Indian girl in her ever-present tribal clothing, the same hand that gave me the chocolate, I felt that home might be near. I could smell it on the air.

That Indian girl was like an archaic Mayan clay figurine coming alive before my eyes. She was dressed in traditional tribal clothing, her eyes both gentle and untamed, her long black hair carefully coiffured. Her appearance bespoke a ten-thousand-year-old pool of ancestral Mayan women.

Her luxurious red and purple *huipil*, made by her own hand on a back-strap loom, belied other secrets embodied within. Her hips were wrapped and bound by an indigo *murga*, a tubelike ankle-length skirt held fast by a wide red sash where she tucked her little things: her comb, money, weaving pick, and so on. Three large holes in her earlobes were laced with hanging shanks of red and violet yarns from which were suspended old Spanish *piastres* and *reals*, seventeenth-century silver money.

Five hundred years before, armored men, worried about money, metal, and maintenance of their position, had come from Europe to leach the soil and enslave the muscles of Guatemala. But this woman with the smooth copper hands, like her ancestors had, turned the Europeans' money into tribal status and allure. It was hard to tell who conquered whom. She certainly conquered me with her beauty. She was at home, an ancient home, the same home as when the conquerors came, conquerors who could never be at home. So her people were not conquered, exactly; they simply incorporated the invaders' money and metal into a kind of wearable trophy that seemed to broadcast a message to the ghosts of old conquerors and their modern counterparts. "You came, you killed, you didn't see; we are still here, where are you? We survive, we wear the scales of your monster culture in our ears, enhancing the spirit and grace you have never been able to take away from us!" Her people were not conquered. They never lost themselves, unlike those who came to take, whose faces melted right into their greed. Something ugly and terrible was conquered by her in the irrefutable truth that she and her people exist as they always have up to this very day. There was a victory in this very moment.

Then her baby cried, and she brought the hungry little package to her hips. Pouring out of the side of her *huipil* came a smooth, swollen breast, and from her mouth the birdlike baby chatter full of the milk of home.

I'd been here before, my eyes misting up like the white fog hugging these forested cliffs, unfettered for the first time, feeling like maybe the breast was finally coming to my own messy face, not just for milk, but as a subtle home for my desires, luring me like a trumpet flower, asking me to leave what I thought I knew and become the shiny bird I had to be. And all of this from the brush of a hand.

6

FLOWERING JADE WATER:

The Return of the Magnificent Orphan

Coming into the village of Santiago Atitlán as I did that day, after more than a year of roaming on my own, was not like reaching the promised land, but more like the homecoming of a spawning fish, or a migratory bird hatched elsewhere, following its nature, flying hard, not always sure of the way, but arriving at its true indigenous place of origin. I was coming back to a home I'd only glimpsed in my sleep.

Some say dreams come from people, from an individual's personal life, and maybe they do. To others like myself, a dream was simply a bud on the Tree of Life, a small leak from the other world's story, whose speech made life live. My life was a strange tale whose salient points had been broadcast to me in dreams long before I had to live them out.

Undeniably beautiful, Santiago Atitlán was a crazy, moody village of 22,000 Tzutujil Mayan Indians. Here the fifteenth century had crashed into the twentieth century and all the years in between. By retaining all the pieces of temporal wreckage and cultural displacement, Santiago became an indescribably mysterious and unpredictable place, dreamlike, some might say—where being truly Mayan meant accepting some non-Mayan things.

What for me seemed overpowering was not the obvious majesty of the geography, ancient lifestyle, or handsomeness of its people, but the quality of familiarity. Never once did I feel foreign or alien in this wild, enormous Tzutujil village. It was a new feeling: after being an outsider my whole life, here I felt like I belonged. Not that I fit in, because I didn't at first; not because I was welcomed by all, because I was not. But I felt good here, on account of I was actually *from* here in some way that I didn't comprehend.

It's true that when the skies were clear, they were bluer here, and the water of mixed greens and ceruleans was more dramatic here. It's true that the three tall volcanos describing the boundaries of Santiago's territory were covered from head to foot with a forest so thick and green as to make Ireland seem like a desert. Likewise, the young men were all princes, proudly erect and striding into the compounds of extended families with their hats cocked and oars over the shoulder after braving the choppy lake to return home to Santiago from those volcanos. The people were physically handsome, and still had a wild natural look in their faces. The girls waddled and their eyes flashed. It's true this was the most beautiful and alive place in the world. Like all Mayan villages, Atitlán was not always a kind place or an easy place, for it sometimes could be extremely dangerous. Often the simplest situation could become life-threatening in the blink of an eye. It was this special marriage of beauty and harshness that made Atitlán so perfect. That's why I stayed and continued to stay when it got near to impossible. Leaving here would become as unthinkable for me as it would be for any villager. After all, you didn't stay in Santiago because you liked the place, you stayed because it owned your heart, and people can't live without their hearts.

My love for this place didn't take time to develop, as one might expect, but was present very much from the onset, from the first instant I lay eyes on her. "How could this be?" I would think to myself, over and over, a bit scared and mystified as I gazed out over the Bay of Santiago. Below the cliff where I stood, hundreds of uniformly dressed Tzutujil women of all ages stood knee-deep in the boulder-strewn shallows, their red wraparound skirts rolled to mid-thigh. Energetically slapping and wringing their handwoven laundry on the rocks, they raised a high-pitched melodic roar reminiscent of a million nesting cranes, with their chirping and gossiping, happy to be the women they were here in the Center of the Universe. The Tzutujil called their lakeside village Rumuxux Ruchiliu, the Belly Button of the Earth.

I had dreamt of all this the previous year before setting out on my travels. I even recognized two *tienditas* (little stores) in the town, and realized I had dreamt correctly the name of one of the owners! The pier where the tourist boats docked had been in my dreams; the water, the hills and laughter, the smell. Oh, the smells of the village were alchemically made according to the season, combining rotting smells with cooking smells, stone smells, lake smells, fish smells, reed and duck smells, flower smells, market smells, smoke smells. It was all so overwhelming, but I recognized it all. It fed my heart like getting to eat what your heart desired after a prolonged hunger.

This was only the beginning; as each day deepened, the feeling of coming home became better and more bizarre. There was so much I would have to learn, but for now what I'd already taken in by nearly dying in the jungle, negotiating life, by traveling about finding my courage and a sense of humor, all had prepared me for village life and the years that followed. I began to trust the spirits more, seeing how their stories in dreams had already materialized into a living village full of people already familiar to me.

I didn't come to Atitlán to become a shaman or to study Mayan culture, or to learn how to be a better person, or to get enlightened. I came because I was called there, whether I knew it or not; because the spirits had carved a space for me in the matrix of my destiny and, fishing me out of the womb, had reeled me slowly but surely into this ancient citadel of

Southern Quichean Mayans in a time when their own destiny was imperiled. The spirits had a job for me, and I would do my best for them.

I knew this place. I had smelled and tasted it hundreds of times as a child, thinking it a place found only in dreams. So when I drifted into Santiago, I recognized my own arrival home, welcoming myself into my own heart, unaware that I would be welcomed into the village heart as well. For so long I'd been fighting and fleeing what in the United States was killing my heart, that feeling of being unwelcome driving me deeper and deeper into what I believed was a state of inextricable exile. Little did I know that this time, as I fled out and away, I was approaching the Center of the Earth, a place where I belonged.

For three whole days, I searched in vain for a hut to rent, thinking I could just walk into such a village and say that I lived there. In those days, this concept seemed bizarre to the regular Tzutujil villagers. First off, none of the women understood Spanish. If they did, they wouldn't speak it, and I didn't speak any Mayan yet. If the women didn't understand or want what you were asking for, it didn't happen. A few of the men spoke Spanish, but most didn't, and the few who were willing to listen to me seemed baffled by my request.

"Excuse me, but did you say you want to give me money to live in my house alone?"

"Yes, that's right!" I'd reply.

"Well, where are my people supposed to live?"

"In another house," I'd say.

"What other house?" they'd ask.

"One that's not being used," I'd answer.

"Well, why don't you live there instead?" they'd ask.

"Where is it then?" I'd ask.

"There is no such house!" they'd finish.

And so forth.

Or:

"You want to give me money to be alone in a hut with no womenfolk, children, elders, or dogs, and no village standing?"

"Yes," I'd say.

"Why?" they'd say.

Or:

"Why don't you build your own house, like us?" one guy might ask, and I'd say back to him:

"I don't know how."

"Let your father and mother or uncle help you. Where are they? Where is your village?"

"I don't have any land or people to help me."

"Then you are an orphan!" they would state.

Or:

"Why do you want to be here? Don't you pine away for your tribe?"

It was inconceivable that I should want to be alone or far away from my home, as no one here could ever want either. And a man couldn't actually have a house unless he knew how to build one, which rested solely on his standing in the village, since building a house meant you were related to people who wanted you to have a house and who knew how to build one. Land wasn't simply bought or sold but held in a complex way according to the historical relationships of long lines of ancestors; where you lived and how you lived was a matter between the unborn and the already dead, with you forming a vital link between them.

If no one knew your parents or your children, you had no home, no relationship, no link to the village dynamic. You were then an orphan. The whole modern culture was an orphan culture, a place with a lot of houses and no village. You couldn't simply buy your way into being at home here. You had to become a relative to belong, and oh how I longed to belong here and be at home. To get a house, you had to come from a house to begin with. I had neither.

The Tzutujil don't have a real word for "door," but they do have a good word for "doorway." This is *chijay*, meaning "mouth of the house." Mouths took in food and spoke out delicious words. Doorways were for letting things in or letting them out, not for keeping things in or keeping things out like doors did. For the Tzutujil, a house was a place to put a doorway in order to show the ancient Mayan etiquette of hospitality, by allowing people to come be at your place, and allow you to leave to come home to your place. A door impedes both.

Unwittingly, I was looking for a door and not a doorway, something to hide behind and think private thoughts, not a conduit to let the community into my heart. Loneliness was the worst punishment imaginable, and I was trying to rent it.

I ate only once a day then, and that was just after dawn in the open-air public market. Guatemala has been famous for her markets since pre-Conquest times, and Atitlán was one of the most noteworthy because it had a very large daily market and a beautiful nighttime one, too, where fish were sold by candlelight. For thirty-five cents, I could hurt myself pretty badly on market food. So by day three of my fruitless quest to rent a hut, I was getting prepared to enter the thick crowd in the *K'ibal* to buy a little leaf-covered package of *patin*, a native recipe of tiny toasted dry fish simmered in a paste of home-ground tomatoes, ground on *metates* with toasted squash seeds, mouse chilis, wild banana trunk hearts, wrapped in maxan leaves tied with *zibaqui* and steamed, as it had been done for thousands of years, in big old clay jars.

Well, that's what I was heading for anyway, and willing to brave a shoving, animated crowd of determined Tzutujil women to get it. But just shy of the market entrance I felt someone grab my collarbone muscles so hard I went to my knees. A voice behind my head chuckled and croaked right into my left ear:

"Porque veniste tarde, Colocho?"

("How come you came late, Curly?")

Late? What did this person mean?

I was released and jerked up to my feet by two powerful hands. I turned and saw the silhouette of a finely dressed old Tzutujil gentleman lighting his cigar-stuffed pipe in the blaze of a hot March sun. Covering me in blue tobacco smoke, he continued, in bad Spanish, where we stood in the crowded market entrance:

"For two years I've been calling you over here, and you're just finally getting here. Then when you do get here, you don't even come to see me. So now I have to come look for you after three days, as you can't be bothered to get to work. To make matters worse, you embarrass me by roaming aimlessly around the village, harassing people into letting you sleep in their huts when you've got a perfectly good place and people too. Quit being lazy. Let's get to work!"

Though at least eighty years old, he spun around away from me, leaning his long, magnificent frame into his heading, and with billows of smoke tumbling out behind his big old shaggy white head, he turned and beckoned me forward with his powerful hand whose long tobacco-dyed nails looked like a monkey's.

I ran up beside him, stunned, with nothing to lose, as he shot me a big yellow-toothed grin off his old Mayan face. His sandals creaked on the volcanic stones, and, laughing his famous laugh, he trudged with me up the steep path to his home.

I'd seen him before. This was the very man, wrinkles and all, albeit dressed differently, but the same old fellow who, in one of those eleven magical dreams I'd had the previous year, had been teaching me how to breathe underwater and how to lay great planks of jade to make a big sea-bottom mask as a gift to the Gods. He was the same man who'd appeared, dressed all in black, in that dream where I'd been a monk and he had gotten killed after showing me how to turn lead bullets into beautiful jewel-like corn by using a cast-iron cornbread pan. For sure, it was him. I didn't even know his name, but he was so beautiful and compelling that even if I hadn't remembered him I would have followed him up that volcano to his big old compound. But I did know him, and so much of the village, too. Something with a plan bigger than my imagination and better than my vision of spirit was pushing and pulling me around that day.

This man's wife, irritated a little by his seemingly spontaneous detour, remained in the marketplace to trade, merging into the throng of purple-striped, bird-embroidered, red-haloed, haggling women, while he and I panted and plodded up the volcanic trail of cinder and rock to what turned out to be his large sacred house adjoining his living hut. This fellow's compound was the largest in town; jammed full of huts and people, it was almost a village unto itself.

Encircling a giant coffee-drying patio were women kneeling as they wove on their backstrap looms. The looms were suspended high from the outer ends of the roof beams under the eaves of the huts opposite the compound's boundary walls, which were made of thick mounds of basaltic boulders.

Salutations were blurted out all around as we strode into their midst; the younger girls ran bugling a friendly alarm to their families' huts, announcing our arrival, while the weaving women scrambled to their feet, their looms still attached, staring, fascinated by us.

It turned out that he had three wives living there. The lady who'd remained in the market was the youngest. Ya Chep was her name. Childless and in her forties, she was the only actual active wife, and she took good care of that great old man, as I would come to learn. The other two wives were quite ancient women in their seventies and eighties, both voluntarily retired from active wife duty. Each had her own house, and they were well attended by their children already in their sixties and seventies and by fifty-odd grandchildren and forty great-grandchildren, many with children of their own.

The man they'd married and whom I followed up the volcano skirt that day was Nicolas Chiviliu Tacaxoy, maybe the most well-known shaman in Tzutujil history and famous throughout the entire indigenous southwestern Guatemala highland and lowland alike. Notorious for his creatively effective and atypical approach to just about everything, while maintaining a staunchly traditional Tzutujil Mayan vision, he had asked the spirits to bring him a new student from afar to carry what he carried, to ensure its living survival. There were other reasons, too, but in his characteristic matter-of-fact way, he simply went out and got me, having seen me also in various dreams. He dragged me to his compound, gave me a home with no qualms and questions, and began immediately to teach me without any breakfast!

At the time I knew nothing of this, but I was destined to pad along at his heels for years to come. Every time, just like this first time when we rounded those dusty stone mounds into his compound, we would be engulfed by hordes of delighted squealing kids. There would be little girls holding big-headed shiny babies for their moms while happy little tykes in well-worn handwovens grappled our thighs and sashes, standing on our feet to get a ride.

They all scrambled for the attention of old Chiv, who'd laugh his famous laugh, tease them all, and poke their crazy ticklish bellies. Invariably a couple of dusty five-year-olds would screech for us to look, and commence to wrestling in the funniest bandy-legged way, so earnestly that everybody would have to laugh as the kids tried so hard to show off for us adults. Slightly more timid, their mothers, tired and beautiful with their little ones on their hips, between peals of waterlike laughter, tried to be serious and admonish the little creatures for drowning us in their joyful flood. Chiv lifted as many as he could, holding a skinny little girl up to his monstrous chest, kissing her head and asking her if she had made him some wild dahlias for lunch with some new corn *joc* cakes. She of course said yes, and got handed to one of her uncles.

Eventually we dragged our legs loaded with kids into Chiv's uncharacteristically roomy sacred house. When my eyes had focused in the cool dimness of the nearly windowless hall, I noticed how a gigantic prehistoric fish stuffed with moss had been hung overhead so as to swing freely from the old smoke-encrusted cross-beams. It had fierce pointy scales, thick as a dragon's armor, each as big as a man's open hand, and enormous teeth.

Below this beast and back a bit stood a noble corps of images, the throne of all ancient deified forces. Although unknown to me yet, they formed in a deep living way a veritable standing history of Tzutujil spiritual life, from a time before the Nahuat overlords, before the Spaniards, during and after the Spaniards, and up to this present day.

Way back and on a higher platform sat a row of elegant clay images of pre-contact divinities, most of them crouching on their haunches, male and female, standing and waiting to be "fed." Beneath and forward a little stood a row of massive stone heads, with heavy brows, pursed lips, deep eyes, and ropes around their necks, draped in scarves and exquisite hand-woven headdress cloths, waiting in a deep, timeless hunger. On flanks of the altar and further forward rose three seventeenth-century Spanish saints. These were two males and one female, one male on a small horse with very big eyelashes, the other standing with two fingers up, with a staff and a gourd, a pink face and gold hair. The lady saints wore what all Tzutujil women wore, but in miniature, all covered up except their bright faces, and draped in necklaces of old silver money. In front of all these lay an orderly array of deified jade jewels, long obsidian blades and micro flakes, from the hoard of "One Wind," the last Tzutujil king before the European invasion of 1524.

Standing closer to us directly under the magnificent old fish was a simple divination table, covered in a *zac zut*, a white and purple cloth with symbols of the earth and time woven in. A plump little divination bundle sat square in the middle. On the ground and in flames stood a row of pumice offering bowls, black with soot. Carved with the faces of plants, animals, food deities, hands, feet, and flowers, these were the receptacles in which fat was originally burned. Now many candles stood arrayed consuming their beautiful handmade shafts as food for the hungry deities. Large rawhide boxes, black from smoke and slick from use, hung free, off the sides from the cross-beams, their contents a mystery to me then. Hundreds of white and yellow tallow candles flickered in groups of three covering at least a third of the packed earthen floor, their smoky orangish flames misted somewhat by the thick white curls of incense smoke wafting from three separate burners.

Twenty or so unused copal burners were piled in a corner, a sure sign that this hall had housed big village Deities and public feasts in the past. The benches on which the Gods sat were cut out from the bottoms of big old worn-out hand-carved flat-bottomed canoes, usually of wild avocado or tropical cedar wood, and well over a century old themselves. These in turn were carpeted with sweet-smelling layers of the very finest thin hand-woven reed mats called *tzapalu*. Many other secret beings and sacred tools lay concealed under and around these benches, and formed the real power behind the God images visible above them, but this was none of my business yet, and I knew nothing of them then.

Though thrilled, my mind and soul were imagining less than the truth about these images. As the months went by, I would be gradually admitted to the depths of the meanings and functions of those spirits who were Chiv's alone. When I would finally be introduced to more spirits and Gods belonging to the village itself, I could then begin to receive my own images of the same village Gods, and images of my own personal Gods, much, much later. At this point, though, I was altogether stunned. I knew I'd been admitted into a rare and almost off-limits sacred place that only a few had ever seen.

I had an instinctual feeling for the holy by birth and blood, and a sense of awe for the wonder and beauty of sacred things as a result of my early involvement in the Pueblo way of life back on the reservation in New Mexico. You couldn't say I didn't hunger for spirit ways. But I was too shy and respectful to search in an active way, and what I found in Santiago was beyond my expectations. I would have to be willing to go the full route, walk the maze, learn to be what I was made to be, get strong and humorous, humble and able before the gift could be handed over to me for safekeeping. For now I simply sniffed at this magnificence as a big-eyed fox kit sniffs at a hen house, hoping someday to have enough adult finesse, spiritual adroitness, strength, and innate ability to serve these spirits and win the prize. For now I would just have to sniff and smile and try to learn as taught.

Old Chiv handed me a couple of thick reed mats big enough for my knees and pushed me down into a kneeling position on the luxurious layer of pine needles that covered the floor. He addressed the exalted entourage of Gods and spirits, just as he would a row of human chiefs or queens. Although I spoke not a word of Tzutujil as yet, I could understand well the respect and the ease with which his prayers flowed out of Chiv's ancient belly through his precise, well-practiced old mouth like a torrent of perfectly polished liquid pebbles.

For fourteen hours I remained in that position while Chiv went hard at it, praying, pouring liquor into the Gods' mouths, shredding flowers by the armloads, giving tobacco, water, foods, burning seven varieties of "tree blood" resins, copal the least among them, until finally, with the help of two teenage great-grandsons, I was lifted to my numb noodle-kneed legs. We danced all his bundles and each God in turn to the tick-tock of the slit log drums played by Ya Chep until dawn. A long bench ran against one wall, and there we sat as other old men and women began filtering in and sat with us smoking cigars hard until midmorning, when a feast began appearing, carried in carefully by a retinue of some of Chiv's big-eyed orphans.

Well-off families and shamans in particular were expected to take in orphaned children and babies. Life is not easy in a Mayan village. Men and women die young from overwork and malnutrition, or drown in storms in overturned canoes returning from work in the mountains. Men are crushed by boulders or massive falling trees, killed by snakes or buried in landslides, snap under heavy loads and roll off big cliffs, lose limbs and sometimes their minds. Women die in childbirth or of tetanus later. The people's everyday life is earned by the strength of their backs and the determination in their hearts, their hands deftly and carefully struggling to feed their children, spouses, and extended families. But it was very easy to die. Nevertheless, parentless children were never seen; though many lose their parents, they are immediately absorbed into family groups of the village, so that at no time are there any groups of unincorporated or unwelcome people. At least that's how it was then.

Chiv had so many orphans that he couldn't distinguish them from his own great-great-grandchildren, not to mention the kids from his famous love affairs whom he also raised. To make it better, almost all of the little boys, with his blood or not, were named after old Chiv, and the girls after his mother, so that only the women could tell them all apart! They were all like a pile of happy pot-bellied puppies, giggling, shuffling, playing and waddling through the dust, thinking up crazy things to do, in the constant human coziness of the compound, welcome everywhere, making it near to impossible for any of them to worry who they really belonged to, since they belonged anywhere they went, safe in that at least.

Much of Chiv's family were inside eating with us now, bowls of cabbages cooked with rare meat in chilis and lime juice with large paper-thin *leh* tortillas, the best of the best, which Tzutujil women take extra pride in making. Sweet coffee and a great deal of commercial liquor arrived. Chiv rose and thanked publicly all those present, especially his handsome forty-year-old daughters who'd cooked it all. We all followed his lead and ended by weeping intensely, the whole room, for about ten minutes, which turned out to be a pretty normal part of a family feast. I wept like everyone else, for sad things, for happy things, for the hard truth of being human, and for being alive to be here with all of them.

Chiv started making another speech, and his young wife shushed him up after a while, which is only right, as he was praising my arrival, and a praiser should never have to stop praising of his own volition, but be looked out for by another. It occurred to Chiv then as he was introducing me to the crowd of friends and relatives that nobody knew my name. We all laughed so hard we started to cry again.

"*Cómo es su gracia vos?*" Chiv asked me in good sixteenth-century Spanish ("How is thy grace?" or "What's your name?").

"Martín Prechtel."

"*Naq?*" ("What?")

"Martín Prechtel," I said, pronouncing the *ch* as a *ch*.

"Martín Rech tel? Ah, Martín Tel Rech!" Chiv bugled.

The crowd went berserk, convulsing in laughter. Old Chiv was a victim, as I am today, of primitive tropical dentistry, missing as he was a great number of teeth. Certain consonants got spoken in creative ways or not at all.

Rech tel means "his buttocks are showing."

"That will never do," Chiv declared. "This man is called Rilaj Meba A Martín—Martín the Great Old Orphan."

7

THE VILLAGE

Chiv's laugh was so famous that I knew of people who practiced it privately. Novice spirit doctors (shamans) learned to listen for it, as it had come to signify the voice of Holy Boy, a deity much beloved of all the Tzutujil shamans, whom old Nicolas had served as priest for twelve years.

Audible for at least a mile over water, Chiv's laugh was his trademark, sending waves of anxiety through his enemies and a feeling of protection and friendship to the rest of us. It combined the qualities of an elephant trumpeting, an old man's cough, a teenage girl getting the punch line of a joke, and the deep sigh of our old Corn Mother goddess after her baby corn was harvested and she was left alone in the mountains. His laugh contained all of this and more. Joy, terror, and grief, they were all in there. Shamans can aim sounds to make things happen, and Chiv's sounds were a powerful possession, which he never misused. But when his laughter descended over a person, it took you over, destroying every useless thought in your grinding mind, removing unhappiness, forcing you to laugh right along, but calling you to focus on the issue at hand.

After Chiv brought me home, he would never push me away, no matter what might happen. He was sure I'd been born and bred to be here in the Canyon Village, which was the name shamans used for the people of Santiago. He was equally convinced I had returned to my rightful home at this exact point in time to get my soul "cooked," and train up my content (power), all in order to be an advocate of the Village Heart. The Village Heart was an actual bundle containing the life force of the village, but the term also meant all the ways and rituals that kept the power of the bundle viable and charged up. It was a magical Seed Heart, an ancient relic that could turn into a person or godlike ancestor called a *Nawal*, who would walk among the villagers, teaching them and getting fed. Its wives were the Holy Mothers of all sustenance, who would visit the village on occasion. In the end they would return back to the other world, leaving us holding their spirit power in a bundle called the Village Heart, from whence they could be summoned in emergencies.

Chiv had seen and heard from the old *Nawales* that the Village Heart would someday become a refugee, a fugitive in its own land. It would happen during a destructive time of change when the delicate and complex ways of its rituals would be trampled, or diluted to nothing. Chiv had heard the missionaries harping about some "Nuevo Mundo," a New World, and he figured that was what it would mean for us traditionalists. Whatever didn't get crushed, according to Chiv's communication, would be *sold* or performed for entertainment for an invasion of hording materialists and tourists unable to see the gossamer power of the old ways and the true Mayan world it had maintained in nature for thousands of years, becoming a sideshow on a tour of a land they didn't really know.

I myself thought I understood what Chiv meant, but it wasn't until I truly had to carry the Village Heart with my own Gift many years later that I actually came to know firsthand the extreme desperation of the age, and how rightly Chiv had envisioned it. He said the Village Heart would have to be disassembled and broken down to its original component parts and each of its separated powers would be put in the individual steward-ship of a group of specially prepared people, who would disperse over the earth in different directions to ritually feed and keep their piece safe, keep-ing it fresh and viable, like a seed, until the call came in from the *Nawales* to reunite all the original chunks back together after the dust had settled from the war, sickness, and ignorance. Chiv tried to tell me in the begin-ning that I'd been brought to Santiago to carry my part after getting initi-ated as a shaman, but I wouldn't really know what that meant until I was initiated. The Heart's other powers would have to be tucked back into the trees, rivers, lightning, and the canyons, back to their original homes where the old *Nawales* had found them when they made the Village Heart to begin with long ago.

Although elated and relieved that I'd come to be his assistant, Chiv was cautious not to give me too much power or visibility right off, because he knew I wasn't strong enough yet. That force which wanted to kill the beauty and delicate power of the Village Heart would try early on to stop me from learning all I needed to learn by offering me fame, notoriety, and assumed shamanic power. As I was still young, I might be easily seduced by all that and divert my attention from the Village Heart to myself.

I had so much to learn, and of course in a village it's all on the job train-ing. There are no courses on being Mayan, or on language, eating, walk-ing, dressing, farming, etiquette, or anything. All things were learned by osmosis in the oozelike current of village life. You didn't just learn the lan-guage; you learned everything at once.

After I was accepted by most villagers, by Chiv's endorsement, I simply blended into the village like an ingredient in a stew. I grew into a new form in the same way as those knowledgeable old village crones cook up a big clay pot full of *pulic*, a Tzutujil soup for which they are rightfully famous. They don't separate the meat from the squashes, or cook the manioc sep-arately, or take corn to cook elsewhere, or boil the water on its own, or postulate about adding chilis, or consider the avocados; they throw it all in together with just the amount of chaos, just the right amount of calcula-tion (you know how old ladies do!), and stew it all in its own good time, with just the right amount of hardwood fire under it, watched but ele-gantly ignored until they know it's ready. Thus in Santiago I was cooked like a root in a stew, in the village pot, gradually transformed and educated about every aspect of village life, speech, respect, and the making of things.

In less than a year I would be a fluent speaker of Tzutujil and could take a sweat without fainting. I would have learned a lot of the etiquette very quickly and could take and make intricate jokes. This all went to prove to the people that Chiv was right; I really was a child of the Canyon Village and was only now finding my home. It fit on me like my own skin. And little by little a smile crept into this exile's eyes, and I became an oddly shaped villager at the cooking fires or with my young friends on the plaza playing music or listening to the tales of old people. I was like a big strange bird hatched in a nest of little finches, whose small adopted parents went about accepting me as one of their own, in love with my strangeness and I with their friendship.

The main thing about the village was the laughter. At all times, working, playing, or resting, the people loved to laugh. They loved to be together joking and laughing about living.

But living in the village was not passive. No one except the aged sat around watching the village go by, but even those older people were always making something. Everyone old enough to carry a hoe or a water jar was involved with the struggle for life. All the fascinating little prongs, nets, cords, mats, jars, antlers, sticks, gourds, and handmade devices that were hanging around the huts were used in one way or another, at some specific time of year, to help keep the family groups alive. Everything had a use for making or collecting foodstuffs, making cloth, bringing water, making huts, and so on.

Almost all of the men farmed. Some were lucky enough to have ancestrally held garden plots in the limited rich flatland at the lake edges, but every family farmed somewhere along the skirts of one of the three volcanos. Some people's land was so steep that in order to hoe it they attached themselves by a rope around the waist to a tree, so as not to careen to their deaths!

Every altitude had its seasonal date for clearing, burning, turning, planting, hoeing, breaking, and harvesting. This was all done without any draft animals, plows, or machinery. Each altitude had its own anciently inherited open pollinated corn seed, specially adapted to the five different climates and altitudes around the southern end of the lake that the Tzutujil considered theirs. Multitudes of varieties of native squashes, pumpkins, tomatoes, and chilis of every shape and color were grown at specific places and times known to all the people. There were more than thirty varieties of native beans with beautiful names like "baby bird beans," "gift beans," "weasel beans," and so on. Avocados of incalculable varieties, the best in the world, grew all over. People cultivated more than fifty kinds of wild fruit trees, mostly by simply not cutting them down. These were jocotes (*kinoum*), Nantzes (*tajpal*), cuxin (*atzaal*), zapotes (*tuluul*), zunzas (*mixpi*), caimitos, bananas (*saqúul*), plantains (*nimaq saqúul*), to name just a few. The villagers harvested many kinds of wild mushrooms and fungi, and tons of wild edible plants, edible tree leaves, tubers, wild beans, three varieties of sweet potatoes, three varieties of manioc roots, and quiscil squashes of eight or so varieties.

When any harvest came in on the backs of the men and boys, the younger kids and women would run out with handwoven towels of bright colors to wipe the sweat off the men's tired faces and bodies. The little plazas in the family compounds would fill with the jewel-like presence of all these products of the Mountain Earth, from the volcanos that gave it to them. When preparing a field, the men would fell the trees earlier in the year, then split the wood into very exact neat little sizes and tie the pieces into traditional packs taught them by their fathers, weighing about seventy or one hundred pounds. Attaching these loads to their foreheads by means of a tumpline strap, they hauled them on their backs to their family compounds. Often they carried firewood fifteen or twenty miles, sometimes having to stop at the edge of the lake, load the wood in their dugout canoes, then row it all home across the bay, load it on their backs again, and haul it to their houses.

With at least fifty varieties of firewood—hardwoods, conifers, wild fruit trees, and medicine trees—at cooking times the village air would be filled with the incenselike perfumes of their distinct smells and smokes. The people all knew every kind of wood, crop, meat, and wild edible plant. They knew which part of which plant was edible, and which part was for rope or burning or weaving, or was poisonous, and what was good for what at what time of year. I had to learn all this, too, or I wasn't carrying my weight in the compound.

The women carried heavy loads, too. But Tzutujil women balanced their cargo on their heads, never on their backs. Mayan women from other tribes did use the tumpline, but the Tzutujil women wouldn't do that. They did, however, use the exact same tumpline strap for a woman's type of work: weaving on a backstrap loom. Men never did this. A backstrap loom was an ingenious device invented several thousand years ago to weave native cotton into the strong, ornate clothing of all Mayan peoples. It was nothing like a European floor loom, where heavy timbers, beams, poles, pins, treadles, shuttles, strings, metal, and pedals intimidated a row of poor little threads into becoming cloth. The Mayan backstrap loom consisted of a few specially shaped polished sticks held together by the cloth itself as it was being woven. When the cloth was finished, you were left with a tidy little bundle of sticks.

Tension is maintained in the loom by the weaver herself, who sits on the ground attached to the long tier of unwoven warp threads by this very tumpline strap over her kidney region. The opposite end of the loom way out in front is tied by a Y-shaped rope to a tree or the eaves of the hut. The weaver simply leans back as she works, and the tension is maintained. The loom is full of sacred connotations and has a lot of taboos and regulations.

When a lady wanted to visit a friend or another compound, she took the whole affair with her, with the kids in tow, rolling it up and reattaching it at a friend's tree, where invariably all the women there tied up with her, radiating out like a fan. There they worked at their weaving, chattering till it was time to get the fires going back at the compound.

This strap that goes over the forehead for men is the same strap that goes over the woman's kidneys, but it is named differently, according to gender use. A man calls it *Ruqa ejqan*, "the hand of my burden." The women call it *Ej cabal*, "tool of my pushing." Men carry life on their backs; women give birth, pushing it into life. Mayan women have their own words for things, and men have different words for the same things. This is because they are used in male or female ways, and though the objects may be the same, they function differently, just like men and women themselves. The Tzutujil understand this. It permeates the whole culture.

Though all men farmed or knew how to farm, there were also several hundred fishermen on the bay. They all fished out of small dugout log canoes, using long spears, nets, or hook and line, depending on the time of year, *what* they were fishing for, and *who* they were fishing for. Women wouldn't fish with spears, nets, or hooks. Things with points that cut and pierce, and knots, belonged to men. Women had their own methods: They fished with baited clay pots immersed in the shoreline waters, or with fish blinds among the reeds, beating the fish into the traps with sticks and stirring up the water. Men claimed they couldn't fish with pots or blinds, as the fish would laugh at them, and because pottery belonged to the women and the twilled reed walls of the fish traps were like weavings, female areas of expertise. But all the fish tasted good, both men and women eating them all, and everyone did well at what they did.

It wasn't that women couldn't do male things or that men couldn't do women's things; it was that those things remained male or female no matter who was doing them. They *belonged* to the women, or they *belonged* to the men. For example, Mayan women wove almost all the clothing of their people: ornate blouses, called *pot*, covered in embroidered birds and rainbows; men's shirts with little tabs over their belly buttons; women's shawls; courting shawls; short work shawls; towels; diapers; food cloths; head cloths; baby hats; long heavily decorated men's sashes to hold up the pants called *scav*. Heavily embroidered also with birds and other tribal symbols, this garment came only just below the knee, a style developed for life in a canoe.

Everything woven was worn and used, but conformed in every case to traditional dimensions and design format, which never varied. Because of this, every woman wore basically the same outfit, and every man wore the same man's clothing. This uniformity was a large part of knowing where a person was from.

But within those styles and forms, the women were free to use all their ingenuity and propensity for adornment, decorating every available space of cloth. Some women were legendary for their abilities; it took a lot of strength and know-how. But all girls knew how to weave pretty well. They began to learn at four or five years old, weaving little leaves and fibers alongside a sister or mom, graduating by stages to greater efforts over the years, until by the age of twelve or so, they could actually add appreciably to the family economy, carrying at least their own weight.

So too with the little boys, who, having graduated from their mothers' sides at the age of seven or eight, followed the fathers to the mountains, over the lake, to toil and proudly haul what they could, learning early on all the ways to cut, tie, dig, chop every fiber, wood, leaf, root, meat, and crop in its time and prime, until they, too, by the age of twelve or so, carried their own weight and more in the household. Both boys and girls were proud to be contributing to the welfare of their compounds, knowledgeable in so many things related to survival and communal living.

All the villagers lived in compounds, invariably ringed with a jumbled wall of basaltic stones, some approaching a fortresslike rock fence. You could always tell how neighboring compounds were getting along by how high the *koxtun* (compound walls) were piled. Within the compound, family huts lined a little plaza. Usually a grandfather and grandmother had a central hut, out of which the compound had sprouted. Around the inside circumference of the *koxtun*, their married children, sons-in-law, and daughters-in-law had their huts in order of when they married. The center of each compound is where life was lived, crops were dried and winnowed, reed mats were braided, and the chickens and turkeys ran around at will, dodging the little kids and fighting with the ever-present dogs. Often there was a central cooking hut or two, and a granary hut where all the compound's womenfolk communally cooked and where the whole compound clan took their meals together, out of communal clay trays and bowls.

People loved flowering trees, fruit trees, and flowers, and many compounds even sported crops growing in them as well. Mayans rarely decorated the insides of their huts, but they decorated themselves and each other.

Really old men liked hammocks for sleeping and expounding. Little babies had special hammocks with a vine hoop inserted so it couldn't capsize. It was common for an old grandpa to string his hammock alongside the baby's hammock, both of them dozing off as they gently rocked away. The very old had to rub together with the very young in the compounds. This was preferable in Tzutujil thinking.

Women, though, preferred to have nothing to do with elevations, refusing even to sit on stools or chairs. Some even disdained to go up into the mountains. Only an uninitiated girl would sit in a hammock.

Tzutujil women liked to sit with their legs pulled back to one side in their tight, ankle-length skirts, on a couple of small tule reed mats placed flat on the earth. They liked being down on the ground, as the women considered other ways of sitting to be dangerous to their wombs. Squatting, kneeling, side-sitting, these were their preferences. Some men were so stiff in the joints from decades of carrying heavy loads that they could not get to the ground without great pain. Men preferred to sit on little stools of balsa wood, which the men carved with animal heads or any way they felt.

Every morning before sunup, hordes of men, boys, and little kids poured out of their family compounds into the arterial village trails that led into the cool mountains or to the canoes. Thick coils of rope crisscrossed their chests and backs, and broadaxes and heavy hoes were shouldered, their machetes in one hand; a string bag hung off the opposite shoulder, containing hot tortillas wrapped in a handwoven cloth. They'd grown the corn and made the bag themselves, knotted from fibers of the maguey. It all came out of the ground. Everything. Usually the men foraged for wild greens to eat with the tortillas, once out in the bush. The little kids ran alongside, carrying the water jug and their miniature machetes. These men could really cover ground.

As soon as the men were off, the women grabbed their water jars and trotted to the lake, there swishing out into clear water, filling up and balancing the full jar of forty pounds on their head cushioned by a coiled-up cloth woven by them especially for that purpose. Then they'd sway and surge, their faces sweating, their coppery brows furrowed, back to the compound to pour their load into a big water pot or barrel that everyone used to get their water for washing and cooking. Some of these ladies had to go up to a mile each way to the lake, some much less. But most of them made eight trips every morning. During feasts and ceremonies, more water was needed, so a woman might go to the lake as many as fifteen times to get enough.

Some women might head off to the open market to sell something they grew or made, to buy or trade for something somebody else grew or made, returning with the food and tools they needed. Women didn't like to look scruffy in the markets, so they always got good and dressed up at least once a day. Young men and eligible maidens dressed up every afternoon after returning from the fields or their work. They wandered in gender groups of five, fifteen, or twenty to show off to prospective sweethearts. People liked to be together all the time.

Women cooked big clay tubs of corn in limestone water over a low fire at night. They washed it in the dawn over and over. This cooked corn was ground on a grinding stone called "the molar of the house." Mothers fed babies asking for solid food by pre-chewing what everybody else was eating, and then like a bird transferring it bit by bit to the baby's hungry mouth, right out of the mother's mouth. Children were very holy to everyone.

The grinding stone, the molar, did for the adults what a woman's molars did for the babies. The hut was seen as a big head, the door was called a mouth, and the grinding stone its teeth. The people lived inside, eating food grown and brought by men, cooked in water brought by women, over firewood brought by men, ground on stone by the women, to feed everybody. The compounds were called nests, the bringers and preparers of food the Parent Birds, and the little kids nestlings. Eating together at the end of the day was the main goal of one's existence: that all one's people should have returned healthily from danger and difficulty, to be all together in their nest where there was enough food to eat, enough wood to cook it with, and happy to eat without warfare between us as relatives and friends. This was what we all wanted: food and togetherness. Every person struggled to maintain this very thing.

8

PRIESTS AND SHAMANS:

Remembering the Umbilicus of the Earth

Unlike their neighboring Quiche and Cakchíquel cousins, the Tzutujil of Santiago Atitlán had no remembrance of ever migrating from somewhere else before landing here in this place. They were living in the *Rumuxux Ruchiliu*, Umbilicus of the Creation, the very origination point of all life! Since the world was born here, they never had a chance to go anywhere else. They never figured out how to leave home, not because they liked it here but because there was only one honest to goodness place in the world, and that was this village. Everywhere else was somewhere else. It was no use living somewhere else besides the middle.

Atitecos (Atitlán villagers) measured the remainder of the world in concentric rings of villages and mountains, rippling out from the village like pebbles thrown in a pond. This world around us had sprouted from our village plaza, somewhere under the old temple, and had spread like a squash plant, radiating out in all directions. But the whole creation was firmly rooted right here in Santiago.

Everything in the village came in layers. In a sense, there had been a migration, but the Tzutujil had stayed where they were, while the world changed around them, right on this spot. The place the village was at now didn't always look like it does today. There had been four other worlds, or creations, before ours. They had all materialized in four concentric layers right here where we lived.

The Tzutujil are a tree and bird people. Everybody is metaphorically a Bird or a Tree, depending on what you're trying to say. The tribe is a tree, rooted in the first placenta of creation, with its trunk coming through the other three layers of heartwood, xylem, and bark, into this fifth world of the fruit, as it is called, or *ruachuliu*, meaning Earth Fruit. The other four creations were still happening right now, just like the fifth one, and everything in this fifth one was rooted and created in one of the other four. All these creations were taking place right under your feet. I knew a guy who showed me a rock you could pull up to see them!

That's why *Atitecos* could never leave home, because the whole world was Santiago Atitlán, and any other place was another world. Tzutujil language has no word or phrase to say, "I am leaving home." Linguistically, you could only leave a place that wasn't home, to come home. You could leave Guatemala City to come home, but you couldn't ever leave Santiago to go to Guatemala City. It was built into the language that as soon as you took one step out of the village, you were already on the journey home, which of course was complete when you returned, but the "going" was part of the returning. No matter what, we were always pointed toward home, heading home. So when I arrived in Atitlán, I was coming home. That was not hard for the Tzutujil to understand.

Every child born into the village had already been born into and passed through the other four layers of creation, one layer at a time. In each of these consecutive creations, the child received an essential layer of his/her own physical and spiritual composition. After having received and lived these four layers of lives, the child was given form and born into this fifth layer of the Earth Fruit, the world of form, this world. In this way, all of us humans relived the history of the world and actually were diminutive earths walking around in the earth, with everything inside us in miniature that was visible to us on the outside.

The first creation was stone and fire; in this layer you received what was hard and hot. Here you got your bones, your heart, and your gall bladder. Grandfather Fire lived in your bones, and the Mother of Life lived in your heart. Your personal soul was housed in the gall bladder. Dreams originated from the gall bladder, and its tenant was called *Q'aq'al*, or Fire Soul.

In the second layer you were given your flesh because this creation had all the food plants, flowers, and trees. All Tzutujil people know that flesh comes from eating plants. In the third creation you acquired the layer of your blood and nerves and all the liquids of your body, because here was the land of water, rivers, rain, lakes, springs, clouds, mist, and lightning. In the fourth, a layer of breath, vision, and movement was tied into you, this being the layer of wind and animals. Then you were born into the fifth layer, here to have form, becoming fruit on the branches of the Old Life Tree of the Village.

Two Deities, an Old Man and an Old Woman, sat in each of these creation layers, and they were the ones who assembled you. In each creation, Deities did different things to put you together. The Old Man would be putting male things together to make a child, and the Old Woman in each creation would be doing female things to add to the child's makeup. Every child got both elements, regardless of gender.

As each pair of Old People did this in each creation, they uttered special magical words and phrases. These words became the very things they described. The Gods spoke the world into life by continuously repeating their names. When they reach the fifth creation, the Deities' names take on physical form and function.

These words were a kind of counting, sacred prayer counting. In one creation layer, the Old Man tied knots to make a child's muscles, while his consort wove a story into its life. As the Old Man and Old Woman did this, they counted out roll calls of sacred things your body needs. These counting prayers never ended, going from one layer to the next, being basically the Mayan calendar. We are made of words, and those words are places in our bodies and on the earth, too. The fifth world gave all those Old People's words a place to have form and run around, happy to be alive and eating together.

Each pair of Old Folks passed you to the next creation, where the next pair got busy putting you together, and on to the next, and so on until you were passed into this world, where hopefully the village and your mother's midwife were waiting for you to welcome you Home. A child was actually counted into life by the Gods.

I knew nothing of this when I came home to Atitlán, and I wouldn't for years even after I learned to speak Mayan well. The Tzutujil people didn't believe my lack of knowledge, and didn't care; they just figured I'd forgotten like everybody else in the village. They told me nobody else could remember having been in those other four worlds either, at least not right away. When you were born, a little of the spell of the magic of those Deities and their worlds stayed in your memory, sparkling around you for a while. But finally every human being succumbed to some degree of forgetfulness.

That's why it was so easy to become a part of the village, because every Tzutujil started out in life as a sincere amnesiac who spent the rest of his or her life putting back together his or her memory of the other worlds, enough so as to serve the greater good of the village and the World-Earth Fruit, and teach those new amnesiacs to remember. This meant I was in the same boat as everybody else, just twenty years behind. Just like the rest of the villagers, I worked hard to catch up.

Not only did we owe our births to the Deities of the other layers, but our tactile life of movement and eating, the Earth Fruit existence, was fueled and kept alive by other Deities and forces living in these same other worlds, spirit worlds. Just like the tree, our world was the fruit, and the Deities were the Roots, Trunk, Heartwood, and Bark; and through these the Gods of the other worlds pumped the sap of life into our world, where we enjoyed what they could not.

Though the old Gods and Deities of the layers made our lives possible, they still had to stay in their own worlds. Yet this fifth world is so delicious that they desire it. A spiritual contract between the people of the village and the Gods said that they would keep life coming to us if we promised to send them remembrance. The fruit of our remembrance was this earth and our lives, and we had to send them some of its deliciousness by means of ritual.

Just as each villager worked hard to carry his or her own weight in the economy of each family compound, the village as a whole had to maintain the spiritual expense of its existence by giving the food of remembrance to the spirits, Gods, and forces of the magnificent layers of the other worlds. Just like the old people in the village, the Gods were never left out or forgotten. We always sent to the elders gifts, food, and a percentage of whatever we had to remember them by keeping them well fed and healthy. By remembering our elders, we learned not to forget the Gods. The old reminded us today to feed what had fed us as people up till now.

The Gods gave us life so that we could remember them, to keep *them* alive. The Gods of all layers ate remembrance. The Gods gave us things they didn't have, so we could create beautiful rituals, speeches, objects, and ways of being that remembered, put the Gods together again, just like they did us in the womb. A forgotten God was an angry God, or a dead God. In either case, the life sap would stop flowing, and all this life would be as if it had never existed. We would cease. All of our rituals in the village, whether personal or public, were memory feasts for the spirits. Being remembered was their food. Our forgetfulness of where we came from killed life and the Gods, and was a major impediment to a happy life.

That is why the village needed and prized its elders, because true elders were those of us who'd lived long enough to learn how to remember. They knew how to *vek*, or reassemble what the trauma of birth and the trance of everyday survival had made us forget: the words and spirits that made us. They were initiated.

When you had to work planting corn, fishing, weaving, hauling water, running after children, getting fires going, you didn't worry much about all of this. After all, one of the ways to honor the spirits for having given you life was the Tzutujil feeling of an obligation to live it, together, well. The elders worried about remembrance for you, understanding the demands put upon you, but gently nudging you toward thinking about it.

The final feeding to the layers for our time here, eating and being alive together on the Earth Fruit, was our deaths. This was the lease agreement with the spirits. Death was the balloon payment for credit extended by the spirits, against all that we consumed out of nature. To make a good final payment, you had to become a good gift. To do this well, one wanted to be spiritually ripe, heavy and full, so that in old age one's death fed the spirits like a sacrifice. To achieve such a thing, one had to have passed through all the layers of remembrance while alive in this fifth, Earth Fruit world.

This process was the process of Mayan initiation. Each layer of creation one had passed through before birth would be passed through in this world again in a ritual way, only in reverse order.

These layers look just like the stages of one's life. The first layer in life is the last layer in birth. This is the fifth world of movement. The first layer of remembrance is childhood, the time of movement, where you become a visible, moving part of nature and the village.

The second layer is the crucial time of adolescence. This is the layer of visibility, vision, and breath, the layer of wind. This is the layer of emotions. The young men and women of the Tzutujil are like shining warriors and shimmering girls full of visibility. This time of life is a time when remembrance becomes a way of life through large public ceremonies of initiation. Next comes the sub-adult layer of creation: the creation of water is the layer where one began making life, the layer of baby-making and marrying, the making of blood and blood relations. This is the layer of abundance, crops, rains, middle life. Here one's initiation into the public hierarchy begins, and here initiation ceremonies differed a little from the adolescent, as they were done in small, more private settings.

Then comes the layer of trees and plants, the land of being an adult or elder. A person became a full adult only at the stage of becoming an elder. We called the adult-elders Big Trees, Big Vines. These elder-trees provided the shade for the other layers to grow and develop.

Finally one gained the layer of stone and fire, the world of original memory, the world of roots. These very ancient people were dried by the heat of memory, which is why they were so slim. At some point after entering this stage of initiation, they began to remember everything, and they actually turned into memories themselves, memories that would echo through the layers of creations. These people were called *Culba Vinaaq*, Echo Persons. You could tell who was an echo person by the fact that anybody who saw them wanted to live more than before. Their words and very excellence of being echoed long after they disappeared, inspiring the rest of the world to sing, harmonize, and try to echo, too.

Village life was wrapped in these layers of life, layers of creation, but the Tzutujil did not penetrate or pierce these layers of life and knowledge. Unlike scientists or information gatherers who want to peel away layers to discover the heart of the truth, the Tzutujil Maya actually *added* these layers of remembrance to the bulk of their souls. Though it felt like discovering new knowledge in all these initiations, you were actually remembering what went on before birth that we had forgotten, things we were made of. You didn't remove the bark of a tree, cut the xylem, grab the heart, and say you still had a tree. No, we remembered, we put back together. That's what ritual initiations were for, putting back together what we tore apart on this earth because we'd forgotten who we were. We put back the heart, covered it with watery wood, then finished it with bark. That's why Mayan elders are often called Bark.

You became what you remembered by remembering it, because it was very literally in your body before birth. As you relearned these things, you gained them and you wore them around. This was something very Mayan and very visible, because people on the ritual Road of Remembrance actually wore more clothing as they went deeper. Each layer of initiation had specific ritual clothes added to one's everyday attire. Anyone could read such a person's clothing, recognizing at a glance where they stood in relationship to knowing and remembering the layers they were carrying.

For the Tzutujil adult, layers of initiation were done with the husband and wife. Each had to be present for either to succeed, but each gender had separate routes. Just like the Old Man and Old Woman in the other worlds, the human man and woman did distinct things to make a common third thing happen. This was the layer of adulthood.

As layers of knowledge and remembrance were gained, one began to be a living embodiment of tribal and spiritual memory. The elders carried the village, the umbilicus that connects all life to the spirit world. They carried time, and they taught the rest of us how to replace them when they died. When such a person had been initiated in and out of all the layers, they were spiritually "ripe," like the Earth Fruit, and they died as a gift of gathered remembrances, the juice of their ripe fruit souls flooding back to the hungry Gods in their creations. And it could be felt in our everyday lives, as good weather, health, increased crop yields, and more happiness.

After someone passed away, the villagers dressed that person with the layers that he or she had remembered. When people of great ripeness were buried, you could hardly see them in the grave for all the layers of clothing they wore as they passed out of this layer into the sixth. To die, well-adorned in remembrance clothing, was seen as feeding the world for unborn generations.

In the Canyon Village, what we all wanted was life. Life didn't come from people, it came from spirit. All life flowed directly from an Ancestral Root where the spirits worked hard to send us that sap of life. Because those roots and Deities needed to be kept alive by our remembering them in rituals, the adult villagers relied on two main types of "memory experts," two types of ritualists.

One of these groups was the village hierarchy, a highly organized group of theocratic priests, both men and women, who were in charge of all rites of passage, through the layers, while feeding the Deities of Time and Creation layers with public rituals.

They were a magnificent sight, when they moved as a group through the village streets, to or from their ceremonial obligations. Walking slowly and majestically behind the music of a large tribal drum and a cane flute came more than 150 men and women, dressed sumptuously in the ancient clothes of their layers, looking like noble flowers in clouds of white copal smoke. The body of male and female chiefs walked side by side in the middle, the men in long tailored black blankets and fancy headcloths with their staffs of office covered in flowers and insignia, the women in ground-length gowns, red halo head ribbons, and undyed native brown cotton shawls. All this, the old dress forms, was the memory of ancestral beauty, remembrance walking. Everybody would come running to see them.

The other group of ritualists wasn't really a group, because they never got together. These were the shamans. Though both the hierarchy and the shamans were dedicated to the continuation of life through rituals of memory, they differed in function and how they went about it. Non-Mayan people, not having similar institutions in their own societies, often confused the two types, especially since shamans didn't parade in groups, had no special dress types, and did most of their rituals in private or in out-of-the-way mountain shrines. Outsiders generally assumed that the beautiful hierarchy must actually be made up of shamans.

But the village hierarchy is *not* a hierarchy of shamans, and being a shaman gives you no advantage for admission in the society. There are shamans in the hierarchy, men and women, but none are there because they are shamans. It can even be a disadvantage to be a shaman if you were eligible to become a chief, if the other chiefs think you can't keep the two pursuits separate.

The main difference between the hierarchy and the shamans is the fact that the hierarchy maintained the village's spiritual relationship with the Layers of the Gods. This was accomplished with complex stages of overlapping prescribed ceremonies involving large groups of people in a system of many sacred houses maintained by sub-chiefs. The initiations served in these sacred houses fed the Gods, but they had nothing at all to do with the initiations shamans had to go through. Basically, the hierarchy maintained the communal good and was a public institution.

Shamans, on the other hand, dealt mostly with corrective rituals to repair damage done to human interrelationships with the spirit worlds by inevitable human forgetfulness and carelessness. Shamans were fix-it people. They did a lot of their work with individual parties or with a compound, not generally with the village as a whole.

The hierarchy maintained the flow, the spirit dialogue, while the shamans fixed any breaks in the pipes. Hierarchy chiefs were called *Ajauá* or *Xuojá*, man lords or woman lords. Initiates were called *Toltá* or *Tixel*, mutual parents. But together the chiefs and initiates called themselves the *scat mulaj ajsmaj-ma*, "our complete group of farmers," or "wielders of the planting stick," or simply "workers."

The most spiritually layered chief was still called a farmer or a worker, an exalted thing to be among the Tzutujil. All the villagers toiled to make life live, and the priestly chiefs and their workers labored long and hard just like people in the fields and compounds.

There are many varieties and specializations among shamans, but generically they were called *Ajcuná*, signifying "he/she who tracks it," or "he/she who finds it," meaning hunters. Shamans worked alone with individual matters, the hierarchy together for the whole village—the lone hunter and the communal farmer. Both kinds were great praisers and lovers of the sacred.

My life in Santiago Atitlán was filled with continuous activity, because I got pulled into the hierarchy service after nine months in the village, at about the same time I'd learned to speak regular Tzutujil proficiently. Quite fast, they say, because the Spirits and Gods wanted it that way. Chiviliu had me simultaneously on a road of shamanic initiation that had nothing to do with the hierarchy initiation. So I was going through two distinct ways at the same time.

Shamans were usually born frightened and more frail and timid compared to the more confident Tzutujil children. What scared them so early on was the fact that since they were more allied with nature, they were not blessed one hundred percent with the normal human spiritual amnesia at birth. Therefore they could still see and remember the other worlds where they came from; sometimes toddlers who were destined to become shamans spoke to these spirits in other layers. But it wasn't the other worlds that terrified them; they were made afraid by this world, the one they were born into. They just couldn't understand the inability of other people to see the big picture of all the layers. This world seemed harsh, and people seemed self-centered. The people thought children like this were dazed and distant.

Eventually this world's severity "bit the heart," *n cuxuna*, of the young shaman, and he or she would fall powerfully sick, unable or unwilling to live. Sometimes they did die—this world was too sharp for their tender soul. The shamanic nature power, the spirit, who had called for the child's birth, would come in the delirium of the illness or in a powerful dream to bring the child back to life. But then the little shamanic candidate was sometimes almost melted away and killed by the curing power itself afterward, as it can be so strong. So another initiated adult shaman would be summoned, and that person would, recognizing the plight of the prospective novice, cure him by ritually containing the child's oversized power.

Recruited thus by the spirits, the little shaman was directed to a teacher, or sometimes the attending shaman might take him under his own wing. An apprenticeship was designed to cook you like a pottery jar, so that at initiation the jar of your body and soul could carry the power without getting killed by its strength.

A shaman's apprenticeship was not organized by any specific tribal tradition. Except in certain cases, no living person actually knew what your
shamanic nature power had in mind for you. Nonetheless, a lot of guide-
lines and procedures common to all Tzutujil shamans were learned slowly
by simply serving your teacher as an assistant. This could go on for a long
time until your teacher was sure you were ready for the initiatory ritual.
But it wasn't prescribed. This period lasted three years for me. But even
then you weren't yet a shaman.

Most women shamans became *Iyoma*, and they got called by finding
objects as children, which were sent by the Lake Mother, the Moon, the
Holy Womb Mother. *Iyoma* were female shamans dedicated to midwifery,
pediatrics, and gynecology, if you will. I was very fond of the midwives. An
Iyom usually recognized a shaman at birth, because shamans were often
born with other souls, giving their mothers a unique and sometimes hard
time of it. The midwife wouldn't tell the mother, and probably not the father, but would announce it privately to the old people in the compound.
No one wants to burden the parents with such a discovery right away, as
parents never desire their children to become shamans. It was considered
too difficult and too dangerous. Shamans spent their lives dealing with
problems so the rest of the village didn't have to. That's why they were
well paid and materially supported.

The Tzutujil didn't have dynasties of shamans, or shaman families,
they just showed up where the spirits decided, in all kinds of families. Tzutujil shamans were not Holy Men or Holy Women. They weren't virtuous
gurus; they weren't required to follow anybody else's ideas of how one
should be, other than what their own natural spirits indicated. In Tzutujil
culture, the best shamans were not those who urged people to be like
them. The villagers didn't care how holy the shaman was: they called on a
shaman to help them fight oblivion, evil, and the sickness ravaging the
land and their lives, to bring back the spirits' favor and grace into their
daily lives. Shamans didn't do this by being good examples; they did it by
their natures, which weren't altogether human, but natural. They had connections in the spirit world, connections regular people had lost because of
their overdomestication.

The celebrity of a great shaman came from his abilities, but that was
not touted as a role model to a child, as how to live your life. For role mod-

els, the Tzutujil looked to good farmers, great canoe carvers, or a man who could walk long distances with heavy loads. They esteemed good weavers; a woman who could grind a lot of corn, remain cheerful, and inspire people to live; hierarchy chiefs and *Xuojá* who were the ideal layered adults. Celebrity worship of an individual hero came from some Western culture, not the Tzutujil.

Though we were spirit hunters and allied with nature, we shamans still had to live and function in the noisy turmoil of the village womb like all the people, but in the people's eyes we *Ajcuná* lived on the boundary of the village mind, next to the other worlds. The people revered us and they feared us. We were simultaneously admired and distrusted by those very villagers we served because they lived in a comfortable, polarized existence in one world only. Deep inside, the people knew we shamans went to worlds they could not, doing what they would not, often alone, receiving the mysterious grace of our atypical knowledge and medicine from a way of life that cared first for the welfare of the "Big Picture" of all life. Shamans only served the individual villager when doing so served the Creations. Human success was not a priority—the welfare of the village, yes, but our so-called power didn't come from a vision of life with humans on top. Unlike the farmers, we shamans did not draw our power from nature: we *were* nature.

There were families in which every two to four generations a shaman would appear in the clan. Once initiated after being an assistant, he or she would often gain strength and then change somewhat, his or her personality becoming intense, flamboyant, and very courageous. After your shamanic initiation, you waited till somebody dreamt about you and came over to get starred, as they called getting cured. A shaman was essentially a doctor. A shaman who didn't doctor people couldn't be called a shaman; doctoring defined a shaman. Nobody would ever say he was a shaman if he wasn't, because you'd be tested by some spirit and knocked dead quicker than lightning, or worse. Shamans didn't even call themselves shamans; people called them shamans behind their backs. You had to use code language with shamans.

The only time shamans would teach or even talk about shamanism is when they were helping novices become initiated. And even then they didn't actually teach you. They taught you how to learn, how to remember, and then they would make suggestions as to how to use what you'd remembered, so as not to blow yourself up. Some shamans called themselves "my owner's little horse," because the spirits rode us shamans hard! A shaman had to carry them, the spirits didn't carry you.

The village hierarchy had none of these problems. Shamanism was not a career or a choice; it was in you from birth, and you couldn't quit, either. Chiv held forty years of hierarchical positions, three times head chief and twelve years priest of Holy Boy on top of that. And then he retired, but he was still shamanizing in his nineties.

9

WOMAN'S WORDS, MAN'S WORDS, BELLY WORDS:
I Learn to Speak

Speech is in all things. The people of Atitlán believe that the nature of anything is its speech. The nature of grass to grow is the speech of the spirit of grass. The flowering of trees is the speech of a tree's spirit, as is the time of year when they flower. So when the Deity of that season speaks one of its phrases, the trees flower.

In the Tzutujil language, if a mouse rustles in the leaves, or a tree creaks in the wind, or thunder rumbles in the cloud, or wind whistles in the rocks, the people say, *"Xbi rubi,"* meaning, "He speaks his name." Because the speech of all things is their nature, these natures speak themselves into life!

The symphony of all things on the Earth speaking their names all at once is what makes this world alive. That is the song of the fifth world, the Big Picture. The Gods and their nature in the other worlds of creation don't talk *about* things, like us humans; they talk life into solid moving forms by repeating the sacred names of life over and over. In the other worlds their words are sounds with rhythm, like our words, but when they are born into this world, they take on form; they disguise themselves in a mask of form.

Just like shamans praying, the spirits have long, endless roll calls of life, which they speak forth elegantly and well. These words, these natures rise up the trunk of the Old Tree of Life, through the creations, finally settling as fruit in our world, where all we see is the sweet substance of life on the branch. This reality we feel, see, taste, and live in is *ruachuliu*, Earth Fruit. The word *fruit* also means "form." To ask, "What does it look like?" a Tzutujil will say, *"Naqa ruach rgan,"* or "What fruit does it bear?" even if talking about a sandal. The Gods' words took form here as fruit. We humans eat words, grow words; we are made of holy speech. The Tzutujil love to rename things, especially each other, but they do so to describe their natures. Everyone has names, inherited names, family names, but the only names anyone really pays attention to are nicknames. This way your nature is remembered every time your name comes up.

But the true names for all things are very different. These are the secret names, the sacred names, the Holy Names. The Tzutujil don't think any of the things in the world were named by people. They believe these words and names for things existed like seeds for the Old Tree of Life, in the old memory layer of the creations. These names are the spiritual DNA, the spiritual schematic from which all reality continually springs, conforming to the nature and form inherent in their names when uttered by the Deity, or origination spirit. These words are where life remembered how to make itself again. They are the memory of life.

Sacred words like those used by shamans and hierarchy priests are *our* memories of the other layers. People don't just use words like that out of ritual context. For a Tzutujil to speak in Tzutujil was the nature of a human being. By speaking well, one's speech magically developed one into a person, layer by layer. A completed human being is called *vinaaq*, or twenty. Because all the digits on your hands and feet come to twenty, each limb represents a different layer. So if someone says to you, *"Netzijon Vinaaq,"* "you speak like a Twenty," he or she means you speak well, like a completely created human.

Initiated people speak a language called Speech of Enlarged People ("Big Twenty"), referring to the bulkier character of one's soul as one adds layers. Chiefs speak *Xinkititkmama,* Grandma Grandpa speech, or Moon and Fire speech. But all layers have their opportunities to add to the whole village system of oral literacy. At every stage one could be an asset to the village by speaking well in your layer. This was called *kilajtsij,* or Delicious Words, referring, of course, to the sweet taste of being alive in the reality of the Earth Fruit.

All initiations were heavily charged with learning more and more magnificent ways of addressing the sacred and the people. It was here we learned all the stories of who we were and learned how to recount them. Learning to speak each layer of talk was perceived by traditionalists as the most worthy pursuit for an adult to follow.

The Tzutujil hid as much of their sophistication and worldview from outside people as they could, in order to survive the greed and ignorance of conquistadores, missionaries, and twentieth-century cultural pressures. These invaders weren't of a mind or ability to savor the depth, beauty, and spiritual richness permeating the Mayan vision of what it means to be a human. The Tzutujil didn't hide their culture in scrolls, caves, or museums. They kept it alive by hiding it in a living language, a language that protected its secrets by having layers. This way a deep, living well of memory was maintained in a live way where I found myself swimming to learn.

Even the Tzutujil had to wait their turns to learn how to remember, to speak and make life live. But once they came into adulthood, whatever was learned made them know that the language shouldn't be frivolously tossed about, given away, sold, or forgotten. Because it contained the spiritual map of their creation, it was guarded like a newborn child, and I would come to be one of those jealous guards. But first I had to learn to speak just regular Tzutujil everyday language or I wouldn't be a part of the village. By learning to speak, I, too, would become a real person. Only then could I move to the layers of hierarchy and into the complex, powerful speech of shamans.

To be useful, one had to speak well, and it was an obligatory part of every villager's early training. Of course I was getting this early start twenty years late, but I swallowed my pride and jumped into it with great application. The old ladies of the village, to help me out, fed me parrot stew, like they do with little kids, to make them speak a lot and bravely. It seemed to work.

As a musician, I learned the sounds first, practicing them over and over, muttering them to myself everywhere I went like the village idiot. I was in love with the rhythm of Tzutujil speech, and especially the sounds. Just like toddlers everywhere who savor the deliciousness of making sounds with their little mouths, I paid no attention to the meanings, entranced with the musicality of the explosives and clicks, and hisses, pops, slurs, gutturals, and slushy sounds, until they were all second nature. Then I headed toward the meanings.

The sounds tasted so good, speaking Tzutujil filled me like a dinner. Something in me was fed by speaking. I learned really fast, faster than a Tzutujil, faster than anybody ever had. Not because I am a genius, but because I was in love.

I wanted to marry one of these smooth-necked, suede-skinned, copper-faced maidens with flashy eyes and teeth of white shell, but we couldn't understand each others' words. I was driven to learn the language of what I loved, and by that desire to merge with her. By doing so I could merge with the village and the magnificent landscape of her people. I was driven by a mad longing and romantic love to understand this fresh frontier of Tzutujil thinking from the fine lips of a young Mayan woman. Learning the Mayan language was the first step in courting what I longed for, but without knowing, I courted my own soul and my destiny as well.

The older married women of the compound thought I was like a cute overgrown baby chick, and they kidded me and doted over me. They wanted me to wear *Atiteco* men's clothing, fascinated by the challenge of weaving something that big. Though I stood a small 5'6" in the United States, among the Maya, whose average height was 4'10", I was a monster. As much as I longed to wear the local outfit, I stated—with great self-denial, hoping a certain young woman would admire me for it—that I would adopt the clothing of an *Acha* (grown man) only when I could speak like one.

For that reason I could be seen, week after week, in the compound of the woman I was charmed with, trying to learn from her and her female relatives how to speak like a Mayan, so that I could talk to this girl and wear the tribal clothing. I'd speak and speak, through the women's eternal bubbling and joking as they worked, reckoning after a couple of months that I was doing quite well.

One afternoon as I met up with some young Tzutujil friends my own age, I tried addressing them with what I'd learned. They split their sides laughing so hard that it was a half an hour later before one, Maleep, could keep his face calm enough to explain to me that I was speaking, very eloquently, the Tzutujil of a forty-year-old married woman! The reason I wasn't ready for my man clothing just yet was that Tzutujil Mayan women and men have sub-languages with totally different words for a great number of the same things, and especially salutations and kinship terms.

There were a million differences. For instance, a mother did not call her son by the same kinship term as the father called him. Though it was the same boy child, the relationship of a mother to her son is different from that of a father to a son. We all know that, but the Tzutujil can't forget it, because it's in the everyday language. By the same token, that same boy doesn't call his father by the same term that his full sister calls him. Although there is no third-person pronoun distinction among *he*, *she*, or *it*, the word usages themselves are male or female.

Six months later I was certified to wear men's clothing, having finally learned to speak as a male. I'd already learned pretty much how to understand the speech of women, and talk as a boy, and now I could speak as a *qahol*, a young man. And this is exactly how every man proceeds: first at the side of the woman who births and suckles him, he speaks as a woman for the first four or five years of his life. Then he starts talking like a little boy with his wild little friends; then at his father's side he begins to learn how to speak like a young man.

Simple example of everyday speech's poetry:

"*Poq chic rubi nbij rajawal ral rilajj vinaaq, pinaaq, conoy ruchi ctie, rumac poq rie cdta.*"

"A great amount of its name it spoke, that one, a woman's child of the Old Complete Being [Twenty] searching for the mouth of Our Mother, because of the sharpness of Our Father's Teeth."

This translates more or less as follows:

"A great amount of its name it spoke," means: He made a lot of noise according to his kind.

"That one, a woman's child of the Old Complete Being," means: A Jaguar (a Child of Woman Hill, Woman Valley = the Moon).

"Searching for the mouth of Our Mother" translates as: Looking for the lake, water.

"Because of the sharpness of Our Father's Teeth" is how one says: In this great heat of the sun.

Or all together the meaning is assembled:

"The jaguar made a lot of noise, searching for water in his thirst!"

Cultures who lose this kind of complex poetic respect for what surrounds them are then cursed to try to keep their spirits alive in a bland hollow world full of unconnected things. Initiation and living well among the Tzutujil and most original tribal peoples depend on a willingness to learn that ancient eloquence. Though this appears time-consuming and inefficient to people from business-oriented societies, it is the true currency of our indigenous soul, whose stock is measured in the ornate beauty of our conversations with the worlds around us, spiritual and otherwise.

OLD CHIV
LIKE A MOTHER DEER

It takes years and years to know things, to learn things in a tribe. Education is a graceful, gradual thing among the adherents to traditional Mayan ways. Learning too fast or conceiving large knowledge too quickly at too early an age is considered dangerous to the soul and nonproductive to the community.

To contain shamanic knowledge one has to have a tough container because this knowledge is not located in the brain. Through initiation it is cooked into a substance that becomes one's actual bones, muscles, organs, blood, and breath of one's being. You become your knowledge.

My mentor, old Chiviliu, nudged me like a mother deer with her fawn toward this unique way of being, but not by teaching me heavy formulas or prayers. One didn't copy another shaman's prayers as a formula. This belonged to priests who learned set liturgies.

A shaman received his prayers and procedures from the power that "owned" him. Although the prayers fit closely into a basic format of shamanic rituals, they were always unique unto the individual shaman. This was not a balance between personal expression and tradition, but between tradition and the shamanic nature spirit's personality.

What I was being taught in my shamanic apprenticeship was how to court and approach the Gods. How to become visible to them, and hopefully welcomed. One shouldn't seduce the Gods, like a thief of ungiven knowledge, but court them as in a prearranged marriage between the shaman and his spirit power. To lust after knowledge is dangerous; to court knowledge with a go-between makes it more likely the student will survive initiation. My go-between, my advocate, was Nicolas Chiviliu.

The Old Man enjoyed scaring me at one or two in the morning by bellowing his trademark "Ah ha hai!" and rolling me out of my reed mats and *Momos tenango* blanket, pulling my sleeping head up by a fistful of hair, laughing at my comfort but deadly earnest about a ritual waiting for us somewhere. I was his assistant, and he needed me. By serving old Chiv, I was being slowly groomed and toughened for my eventual initiation.

I had to expect anything at any time and be ready to serve the needs of any given ritual without lending a thought to sleep, preference, or routine. As part of Chiv's crazy "jump up" style of training, I might be forced to jump to arms from the deepest sleep. I learned that some part of me was always awake, and, without chasing off the glow of my dream soul, I'd push myself to assess the requirements of the moment. Like a safari gun-bearer, I had to live day and night with my big handspun maguey string bag, full of offerings and ritual paraphernalia. I was required to have in hand, at all times, any of these items old Chiv demanded, passing them to him like scalpels to a surgeon. At the same time, a good assistant must have the ability to produce the ritual music appropriate to each stage of a particular ceremony, while still maintaining a flow of candles, copal, liquor, and flowers as needed by the officiating shaman.

Occasionally some ancient comrade of Chiv's would come along to help as sponsor for a group of Indian clients. His friend might be an excellent shaman in his own right, and I would be severely tested. Chiv would show me off like a new canoe or an exotic animal. Even worse were the times when a well-versed musician would mysteriously appear in a ceremony. These old-time people would breathe down my neck, scrutinizing my every effort with old glassy eyes, yellow from years of ritual smoke and sleepless nights. But these men and women were legends who otherwise would have been inaccessible to me. We would inevitably become close friends after passing an uncomfortable period of my winning them over with cigars, drinks, well-spoken words, and an honest regard for their spiritual rank.

When a ceremony had been successfully carried through, my teacher, like many shamans, would begin his "one-legged dance," in which he would spin on one leg. All of us guys, old men and young, would strike up the required Song Trilogy of Holy Boy. A friendly competition pushed us to heights of mutual excellence, which, in turn, pushed all participants to a level of togetherness I had never known before. We never wanted it to end. Our ancient, driving sound mixed with the smell and beauty of the offerings and was intended to be so intoxicating as to make the Gods drunk. It seemed the Deities couldn't resist the well-ordered frenzy and deep hearts of the people they created when drunk on dance and delirious prayers.

One night, after I had already assisted in at least a hundred rituals, old Chiv dragged me from my dreams. Grabbing my bag, he hurtled us into the darkness saturated in the lusty, narcotic stench of luscious pitaya flowers and belladonna. The old-time shaman pumped his long copper shinbones like piston shafts through the velvet sap of our high mountain paths, with me struggling along behind. He reviewed his proposed ritual strategy and the client's situation as we surged along those dark trails toward a ritual cave above Nishti'. This meant Place of Cactus, the place name for the Tzutujil burial grounds.

Our people (*kvinaaq*), as clients were always called, were being led to the cave by Ya Chep, Thorn Woman, Chiv's youngest wife. They would arrive at the shrine by a longer, less treacherous route that skirted the lake a thousand feet below us, with no cliffs or steep inclines like the path we were taking, but one that would safely take them to the cave shrine later than us. We, on the other hand, as we usually did, straddled the side of a tall, steep volcano called Pral, meaning "her children." This volcano was named for the three hero boys of the neighboring volcano called Ctit, or Grandmother Moon.

On this moonless night, the old man had to navigate from memory over the rock-embedded paths, surmounting large, unwieldy, sandslicked boulders, sometimes on all fours in the windy blackness, among heavy sighing trees and rich forest smells. I had to follow the smell of his cigar, struggling along behind this strong old man. Sweating hard but not too banged up, we arrived at the ritual entrance to the cave at least an hour before the rest. With nighttime ceremonies, timing is of the utmost importance, and a certain clandestine flavor had to be maintained. Prying eyes might add a distracting element in the form of the intruder's own history and spirit debt. This might complicate our work and confuse the issues with the Gods.

This cave shrine housed the Speaking Place for the Gods of Death and the Lords and Ladies of our Ancestral Dead. It was a strange and handsome little cave with rock masks all over the surface. The rock hole was used by shamans in their constant efforts to determine the whereabouts of deadly ghosts and realign any detours taken by the spirits of the recently deceased on their long journey to the land of spirit.

In this case, a renegade ancestral ghost had been stealing the *rukux* (heart) from the plants and cornfields of our client's tribe. The people we waited for were Cakchíquel Mayans from a village called Wall of Skulls some sixty miles from us. Nothing would grow properly for them, and all kinds of feuding and omens had ensued. The village had polarized into a couple of angry camps. Scapegoats had developed, and families were divided. These were all signs that some spirit of the dead had not been buried properly with all his rightful possessions. Having returned to get them, he was unable to find his road back to the land of spirit. Either that, or he had not been mourned properly and could not leave this earth. Spirits always looked for loved ones to warm them. The touch and presence of this spirit, made of death, inadvertently reversed all life processes in his attempt to reach his people. A typical case of "ghost sickness" had set in, not only in this spirit's family, but throughout his village.

At the cave, I busied myself setting up a fire and the incense pot and arranging our spirit-capturing devices. The presence and gaze of the Lords of Death, through no fault of their own, can be very toxic to humans. To make sure these deities were made less dangerous, we, the *Ajcuná*, or shamans, had to arrive first and ritually rouse the guardian dogs of the Death Lords and Ladies. We presented our case to these dogs, who relayed our message to their masters instead of bringing the deities into direct contact with us. When all was set, the Dogs of the Dead would take the essence of the ritual offering we made to their masters, the Gods, who consumed our ritual feast and would begin the reception of our words and shamanic parlay. Only in the case of dangerous deities were we required to deal through go-betweens; few are those who could survive the direct presence of the gaze of the Death Lords.

The Dogs of the Dead, mostly owls, crickets, June bugs, and shooting stars, arrived, riding on our songs and procedures. These spirits sat politely to our left. The Lord and Lady Deities of the Dead were charmed and contacted with certain colors, magic gestures, delicious terminologies, and smells, and were summarily informed through their messengers about the possible imminent arrival at the threshold of their world of the alienated soul we were to capture, who had mysteriously not found his way of his own accord.

The glowing little mountain cave was filling the night air with the sweet breath of *pom*, smouldering breadlike cakes of tree resin. Then Thorn Girl, Chiv's wife, arrived with a dozen respectful, beautifully adorned, open-faced Cakchíquel emissaries. They bore armloads of lilies, orchids, candles, long cigars, Cakchíquel ritual liquor, roosters, sugar, chocolate: all that Chiv had asked for the Gods, bundled in the long, handwoven yellow-striped cloths of their village.

When it was time to introduce, capture, and present the alienated soul, Chiv did so while I assisted him like a gunbearer. We jumped to it in a fulfilling and enthusiastic way with no mishaps or signs of spirit refusal. At other times a clay incense burner might explode, spraying grenadelike shrapnel through the crowd. I knew one lady who was killed that way. Sometimes bottles would crack or explode, or a person would faint, or the whole shrine might catch on fire. These were all signs of deity refusal and a failed ceremony. There were many versions of this and many reasons for it happening.

But on this lucky occasion, all went elegantly. The cave smiled brightly in the dark, as the Gods were richly fed by the hundreds of candles, ever-greens, flowers, narcotic perfumes, and tufa bowls filling the cave en-trance. The rock faces were fed fat, full of glowing cigars being smoked by the rock. Then we said our ritual good-bye to the spirits. We all returned to Chiv's house by the same routes we arrived on, as is the ritual custom. As he and I ambled up the hill from the cave, we saw below the glow of a smiling face, which was the shrine cave.

Our loads were a lot lighter now, so Chiv and I, his honored attendant, returned at a more relaxed pace in the darkness. At one steep, treacherous, rocky incline, Old Chiv stopped dead and stood stiff like a startled ocelot. He'd seen something dangerous in the dark, maybe a forest cat or snake, but he gestured with his lips as all us Indians do, toward an enormous fig-ure right on the path above us on the edge of the cliff trail.

He whispered to me like a hunter, *"Culel"*: "enemy." The figure's huge arms and outspread fingers waved in a strange, eerie way, as if in a rage and ready to crash down the hill and dispatch us at any second. We could barely see his primitive face, round eyes, and the phosphorescent glow at the top of his head. A strange moan came from the monster, who we thought might be *Mama' acha*, or the Ancient Big Man, a forest spirit who hated humans and got them lost by twisting trails or forcing them over cliffs.

Undaunted, the old man called for his arms, meaning his sacred equip-ment, shaman tools, which I nervously supplied. Old Chiv was yelling a tremendous, flowery speech to the monster in the wind, making promises of future offerings but with a little scolding thrown in, which I didn't think was a good procedure. In spite of this, the enormous dark enemy didn't budge, and didn't attack, but held his ground, making it impossible for us to pass on our way since he was blocking the only passage along the edge of a precipice, a narrow ledge whose borders went straight up on one side and dropped at least five hundred feet on the other.

We waited and waited, and still the giant wouldn't yield or attack. Fi-nally, with our machetes drawn, we rushed him—to find he was only a giant, poisonous arropa tree that had blown over the upper cliff in the wind and lodged itself on the path between the time we'd come through earlier and our return trip. Only two opposing branches had survived the fall. Each had one big, old, leathery, handlike leaf with five points waving in the breeze with a peculiarly humanlike motion, while the broken center trunk with its knots looked for all the world like a massive face. The purple glow came from the break in the trunk where a night-glowing fungus had invaded.

We almost died laughing, and Old Chiv almost rolled off the cliff anyway as we squirmed on the ground in total hysterics. I was laughing so hard my worms almost burst my belly, and I could hardly catch my breath before I had to squeal and hoot again. We were delighted with our stupidity, and how seriously we'd set our mouths, so threatened, and together bravely charging an old tree, the Old Man and me. Old Chiv taught me the magnificence of human folly, and the value of doing something beautifully, no matter how absurd.

When he could stop laughing to speak, the Old Man said, "Don't you dare tell anyone about this till I'm dead!" And I never did, till now.

The lake was our mother. We called her C'Tie, our mother. Other tribes called her Chi choy ya', a place of flowing water, or Chi ya, edge of water, or Chi Nam Ya, place of huge water. But the Tzutujil called her mother. She is a deep, beautiful Mother. Surrounded on all sides by thickly forested volcanoes, Her voice was the water birds in the reeds, ritually re-enacted in our village's sacred houses with musical instruments. Her colors were woven into the women's clothing; her reeds, crabs, and fish were her children.

Our canoes glided over her belly. Tzutujil canoes were logs hollowed way out in the jungle by certain Mayan families who knew the secrets of canoe carving. They were simply called *che*, or trees, or sometimes *Huku'*, meaning to pull one across.

Everyone had canoes, like city people had cars. When the canoes wore out, they were recycled into the benches used in the sacred houses. Dogs, kids, and men in canoes would choke the bay every morning at dawn. Everyone would be chattering, rowing, preparing to disappear into the mountains and fields on the opposite shore. Everyone's canoe had its little dog. That was our car horn. The dogs would sit in the prow of our canoes and bark when we came up behind somebody. "*Rup, rip, rup, yip, ayap, yow,*" and the slower boat would pull over and let us by.

My apprenticeship to Chiv was essentially a test of mental and physical endurance, a kind of flowery slavery to my teacher. Sometimes I even had to carry the Old Man home on my back when he was exhausted or couldn't get out of the bite of the ceremony. A lot of these journeys were accomplished in canoes.

One stormy morning, as five-foot-high waves crashed on the shores where our client's canoe was beached, we planned to cross the bay. It was a trip three miles one way, and then a four-mile climb up the opposing volcano to some newly acquired fields of Chiv's customer.

The fact that all the fishermen and canoe men had dragged their canoes to safety on higher ground, and that today absolutely no one was venturing out into the angry water, wind, and thick fog, made me confident that the Old Man would call it off. You see, in ancient times, the Tzutujil would sacrifice a captive to the angry waves once a year at this time. They did this to feed and honor the hungry spirit of the God of the underwater drowned. Drowned people in their afterlife are said to live upside down, eternally sustained by the spoils of raids wreaked on humanity by the dreaded Lord of the Underwater Dead.

Ever since the Spaniards banned human sacrifice four centuries ago, no deliberate ritual human sacrifices had been made to this underwater God. Yet the village knew that this underwater warrior God and his upside-down water army went on a foray every spring equinox, on a hunt that inevitably drowned at least one or two people, and some years more than that. The Spirits of these Drowned would be added to the ranks of the water warriors.

Modern cultures can ban gods, but they don't die or disappear; they simply go underground and get angry. Instead of being fed deliberately and ritually, they arbitrarily come and take their due. Old, alienated deities become enemies when you forget to invite them into your life. When you hold out an offering to an ancient, starving, forgotten god, he will take your hand off with the offering like a starved bear, confusing the giver for the gift.

So there Chiv and I stood, two small men, one an old, heavy-boned, smoky shaman, the other a skinny-boned novice, looking tiny on the boiling, steamy, foggy gray-green shore. We had a mission to cross the water against all odds in this very time that was long-appointed for a drowning to feed the underwater God. I think Chiv would have gone home, but he was training me and so had to risk his life many times for me. Of course he was risking mine, too. Humor gave courage to our hearts at times like this, so we joked a lot as Mayans do when confronted with death.

Then Chiv stooped squinting for a while through the clouds somehow at our destination on the opposing shore, smoking away, while the lake drenched us with spray. After a while, a woodpecker screamed on the right and Chiv conversed with him. This was the communication we had been waiting for. "Did you hear what he said, boy?" I nodded, having heard the bird say *"kixyiktaja, kixyiktaja,"* meaning, "Both of you rise to meet it!"

Chiv said, *"Utz ar ja majun xkin nbirubi camic,"* "Well be it, not one earred one says his name today," meaning "This looks good, no owls sing," meaning "No one is supposed to die today." Woodpeckers are shaman birds, highly favored by us diviners.

We went down to our client's little canoe, which was, unfortunately, a leaky, tiny fisherman's tree of less than six feet. This size canoe flips over on a good day with an expert inside, if one even slightly imbalances himself. Chiv called for several offering items from my string bag, and in his very clear voice, whistling through his three remaining horselike front teeth, he began a prayer to the north wind God, then to the sunrise wind God.

He set up a provisional shrine with pleasant offerings, of minimal quantity, as we needed the rest for our client's ceremony in the mountains. This shrine was a sort of spiritual promissory note to the Winds and Underwater Lords, the Lake Mother, and the Spirit of the Canoe to the effect that these meager offerings were only an aromatic whiff of a major feast we would provide if we could possibly survive the coming journey. He was giving these spirits incentive to keep us alive. The little offerings were a sort of spirit hors d'oeuvre, indicating a big feast in the future.

Then Chiv sang the songs of sparrowhawk and the butterfly, who are the dogs of the north wind and east wind, respectively. He kept singing, and within five to ten minutes the angry south wind subsided, and the lake went relatively calm. Jumping in the canoe, Chiv said, *"Ho'qá!"* "Let's get going before they change their minds!"

I pushed the canoe into the water and hopped into the log at the back end. My teacher was singing away in the prow where one's dog or honored guest or workload normally sits. From the prow no effective rowing can be done anyway, not to mention that there was only one extremely worn-out hand-carved, waterlogged oar. I couldn't stand in the normal position due to the rough waves and my inexperience, so I had very little leverage. Today I'm a fair canoe man, but on that day I was as yet unskilled.

Brave, foolish, and in love with life, we poled through the storm in an overloaded, dangerous, undersized dugout log, with an inexperienced skinny kid for a rower, into a deadly storm. All of this on the very day the storm Gods wanted to be fed a human life, and the experts decided to stay home and sleep. "If we die, we die," Chiv said with his usual good timing and laughing. "*Ho'!* Let's get going!"

I began rowing furiously, and we began going in circles, circles and spirals, going absolutely nowhere. When Chiv started chuckling, I noticed a gallery of about ten little seven-year-old kids, just bellies with legs and arms and big, round laughing faces, holding hands on the shore. Any Tzutujil kid knew how to row expertly, and the little ones were highly entertained by the comedy of my inexperience.

Finally I rowed away from their laughter, the little boat waddling out of the cove looking like some branch adrift with a couple of stranded weasels aboard. I rowed, while Chiv sang and bailed water with a little piece of gourd and on and on we went through the steam, the visibility about six feet in the middle of the lake.

Bit by bit, Chiv praising the winds, I got the old tree chugging along, rowing to the rhythm of Chiv's tapping hand on the log, his pipe puffing away, sparks flying in the breeze burning little holes in his handsome black handwoven wool jacket.

A sweaty hour later we arrived miraculously on the black pebble shores of Ptilpin at the base of the Elbow of the Earth, as this volcano was called. Of course, Ptilpin was where the higher percentage of unfortunates drowned, being the precise spot where the underwater army enters and leaves its kingdom.

We pulled the soggy log ashore, and loaded up our backs with the ritual offerings provided by the owner of the field we were to make a shrine and blessing for. The clients were not present, as this ceremony was to heal a very sick member of their family, the illness being derived from an imbalance with the spirit of newly acquired land. The family stayed in the village to nurse and monitor the sick person. We were like ritual surveyors sent to replumb the landscape of the ancestral soul of this family group on the land that fed its children.

A steep old canyon wall with a dense display of orchids stood between us and a very steep four-mile hike up the feet of the volcano. We strained and grunted up the sides and valley walls till we gained the shrine spot. Then it took us probably four hours to build and dedicate the shrine and offering feast. Traditionally in this kind of doing, we spilt liquor provided by the client in a special way on stones and wood, air and fire, and others, then drank the remainder as a communion with the deities. Liquor used in this capacity was called *Maqbar Ruachuliu*, Intoxicating Earth Face Warmer, which referred to the Father Sun, as the liquor was the Sun's Blood in this ritual.

On this occasion, however, our clients had supplied little clay jars of a liquor foreign to our experience. When poured into the fire it blew our eyebrows off to their roots. It was a powerful kind, and Chiv liked it.

We drank along with the Gods, getting real brave and happy, higher than an eagle's daydream. In the end we were as drunk as rabbits. There was nothing we couldn't tackle! We gave our ritual good-byes to the shrine and spirit of the place and headed down the cliffs, our loads and heads a great deal lighter. But when we arrived at our little boat, the waves had resumed their original angry style.

We had no intention of shrinking from the challenge, as the liquor, the excellent ceremony, our togetherness with Gods, and our pledge to carry out this ceremony nudged our common sense completely out of the picture. We entered the canoe with pure faith and a love for living.

As Chiv jumped into the prow and rolled over backward, laughing, I jumped in the stern after pushing the canoe into the deadly slosh from behind. While Chiv playfully rocked side to side as he sang the wind songs again, almost dumping us, I began to furiously row in circles again, going around and around. All of a sudden our little canoe somehow caught a trough in the waves and we started hauling effortlessly, the Old Man leaning over the edge, arms outstretched, giddy with his song prayers.

With our eyes like slits from the cold, delicious wind, our big drunk hearts praying hard, we busted through the fog like a couple of hungry herons heading home. We gained sight of our village shores in less than ten blazing minutes.

The sun broke loose on the lake, sparkling everything in sight. As we sped to the shore, a sizable crowd of villagers was mounting. Women and girls in their village outfits, many with babies on their hips, came running, whooping, and waving, while high-spirited teenagers and friends and men yelled and laughed, everyone delighted with our miraculous return.

I headed the canoe straight to the nearest shore as the crowd ran and trotted to the place I was going to park; they were all yelling advice and laughing, sounding like a hundred waterbirds. I couldn't understand any-one, as the commotion was too intense. Beautiful barefoot girls, old men, and uncountable big-bellied kids were joining the crowd at every moment. When I hit the shore, a loud cheer went up and the villagers closest to us desperately tried to get something through to us. Heedless, Chiv and I got out and immediately sank up to our chins in smelly, rotten mud.

The crowd went wild, in shrieks of laughter, many falling to their knees hysterical, some hugging their convulsing neighbors for support. More than two thousand people were dying of laughter with more and more trotting up every second, craning for a view of our two stupid little heads sitting on top of the mud, laughing right along.

I knew this place never had any canoes parked at its shores, which I thought was out of respect for a holy spire of rock that was here, called God Rock. This place was also called Bal bush ya', meaning Unstable Waterland, which was the real reason nobody put their canoes there.

A couple of farming men and young boys ran for their heavy firewood ropes and threw them to us. With some difficulty, we tied them under our armpits. The whole crowd pulled and cheered and pulled till we came popping and tumbling out like a couple of soggy corks, dragged across the bog to solid ground.

A surge of squeals and laughter resumed when it was seen that the great suction of the underground mud had completely snatched our In-dian pants off, leaving them in the bog. Chiv and I were standing there pretty much naked, covered in stinking mud with our funny little birds hanging out. Over and over we all died laughing till a group of high-spirited Mayan teenagers with their hats tilted lifted we two exhausted, happy, gooey shamans up onto their brave shoulders. Then, shouting and whistling for room, they ran us the mile and a half straight through the village to Chiv's sacred house, followed by the whole population, who were now in a great discussion about the power of the event and our passage over rough waters.

A crowd of at least forty-five very dignified and meticulously dressed foreign Indians from various tribes were waiting for an orderly reception with Chiv when we arrived muddy and bare, still on the backs of the youth. This, in turn, became a cause for great hilarity among Chiv's three wives, forty children, and sixty-six grandchildren, as we met these pious dignitaries who tried to maintain their decorum.

We were washed and graciously readorned with newly woven bird-embroidered pants, new sashes, and handwoven shirts. Our muddy pants, still stuck underground, stayed as offerings to the storm who had allowed us to survive that wild crossing. The whole world was happy; we were happy; the lake got happy; the children were happy; all life lived; and we feasted like heroes while our poor foreign Mayan visitors had to wade through the retelling of the day's adventures several thousand times, pretending they liked it in affirmation of what Chiv and I thought was a life well lived.

In the late nineteenth century, old Chiv had been a famous *Biyom Acha*, or trader. Before the entrance of wagons, trucks, and buses in the mid-twentieth century, Chiv had been a young man who trucked on his own sweating back as many as eighty to a hundred pounds of raw white sea salt from the traditional Indian salt works on the Pacific coast by Ocos. After walking over the old trade routes to Atitlán, over a hundred miles, he traded half the salt in the village. Then adding fifty pounds of dried silver-dollar-sized fish to the other half of his salt load, he marched up north to Nahualá and different points in a circle, trading and selling in all the main Mayan market villages. He made the return trip back home to Santiago loaded down with rare and wondrous items like needles, metallic thread, bottles, commercial dyes, sugar, and necklaces. He traded these for crops, livestock, and land use.

He became rich, but it did him no good. His birth had been requested of the other world by a famous Tzutujil Prophet, a *Nawal acha* called Francisco Sojuel. Before Chiviliu was born, his parents had five daughters in a row and no sons. Farming without their help, Chiv's father was hard put to feed them all. Chiv's mother was not a Tzutujil Maya but a Cakchíquel Maya refugee from the government massacres in her native Patzun farther up in the highlands. Her people are called the Red Blouse People.

One day Chiv's father got drunk and beat his wife. Disgusted with this behavior, the old *Nawal*, Francisco, went to help the woman and to discover why this man would do such things. Chiv's father explained to the Prophet that because his wife had no relatives in the village, and since his own relations had almost all been killed by diphtheria, he alone was left to grow enough food for six women. He got drunk and vented his rage.

The old *Nawal* cured the wife and said he'd ask the other world for boy childen to help Chiv's father farm the land so the family would prosper. There was one stipulation, however. The first child must be directed to pursue the path of a shaman serving what was called Food and Water Roads.

Chiv's father conceded, and, sure enough, five boy children appeared in a row, Nicolas Chiviliu the first of them. He was bigger, handsomer, stronger, and more egocentric than anybody else in the village, but he wasn't going to do any of that boring, hard shamanic stuff. He would become a merchant traveler, get rich, know lots of women, and be powerful.

No matter what the father tried to do to convince him, Chiv knew better than these unambitious old-timers, like many of us at that age in our early twenties. Well, he did get rich, by the Tzutujil standards of the day, acquiring many farms of avocados, corn, coffee, cacao, and oranges. He made his father and mother well off, but still he refused to apply himself to his obligation.

And so it went until one night while the village slept, one of Chiv's granary huts mysteriously caught fire, and over one half of the entire village of Santiago Atitlán was leveled to ashes in the wind-driven blaze. Chiv's wife and new baby were killed, and he went mad, driven from the village, barely escaping with his own life. The village knew full well that the spirits had sent the flames, and that Chiviliu had made the whole village suffer a great deal for his uninitiated unwillingness to suffer a little bit to become a shaman.

Chiv roamed the hills naked, slobbering, muttering to owls, saturated in grief and rage. Just before he would have died, a group of now legendary shamans and hierarchy chiefs went and hunted him down. They brought young Chiv back home trussed up in ropes like a wild pig, struggling and howling on the back of a shaman named Matec Reanda, who I had the privilege of knowing before he died.

It took weeks and all the shamans' abilities to bring Chiv back to humanness. Now his apprenticeship began in earnest. Due in part to the ill feeling against him in the village, he was sent on a pilgrimage of thirteen different Mayan towns, ending in Atitlán. Chiv spent seven years going from village to village, this time not as a merchant but learning other Mayan languages and dialects, gathering up his bundle objects, as I had now begun to do myself.

When he came home again to Atitlán, around 1910, he was still a scorned, ostracized man. Finally after a year of waiting, a woman having a terrible breech birth told her midwife she'd dreamt about this man Chiviliu, and that they should go bring him, as only he could alleviate her agony with his newly initiated power. Nobody believed her, but as the woman was going to die, they called Chiv in a last-ditch attempt. Both the child and the mother survived. From then on, Chiv gained stature, not as a rich man but as a shaman, eventually rising to become the most sought-after spirit doctor in the whole region.

His name became an adjective, synonymous with famous and shaman. Somebody might say to a person speaking authoritatively, "Oh, do you feel like a Chiviliu?" The Christian converts deridingly called Mayan traditionalists *"Nina' ix Chiviliu xix galaj."* ("You people are all Chiviliu, I see.")

Chiv never charged me for my training, though most shamans did. While training as a shaman, I had to maintain myself, and in order to carry my own weight economically, I had to earn a living. Though shamans are highly compensated, students, until initiated, receive nothing but training, as they aren't shamans yet.

To make my living while following my obligation as a student, I sold corn–grinding stones in Guatemala City every month. I commissioned them down at the edge of Our Mother the lake, where itinerant Quiche Mayan stonecutters from Nahualá plied their expertise on the local basaltic stone. They carved whatever style or size stone you might want right there on the lake shore, beautifully, with two chisels and a hammer. Instead of carrying the incredibly heavy finished product over the mountains, the carvers traveled to the village, pecking out the grinders from stones in the area.

Unlike these men, I did haul the delicate, weighty stones on my back to where a Grade B bus could take me to Guatemala City. In the richer districts of the capital, I'd find buyers among lonely acculturated Mayan girls of different tribes, who made their living as cooks and domestics in wealthy Ladino households. A grinding stone was the prime instrument for cooking any indigenous recipe, so these girls always nagged their mistresses to purchase one of my very excellent stones, as they were practically impossible to obtain in the city.

I took my earnings, which never exceeded sixty quetzales a month, and added twenty quetzales' profit by purchasing several beautiful handmade guitars for seven quetzales each in the capital, easily selling or trading them back home to the young men of the village at one quetzal profit per guitar, giving me a monthly income of at least eighty quetzales, double what most grown men with mouths to feed earned by working extremely hard.

There were a lot of expenses in a shamanic apprenticeship, and for this a student usually sought out sponsors among one's relatives. For me, it was different, as I was sort of an orphan. On top of that, I rationalized that I couldn't take from people who struggled so hard every day for every bite of food.

My meager earnings selling the grinders allowed me to continue with him. By the end of every month, when my savings dwindled to less than ten quetzales, I'd use that money to pay the stone carvers, if I could find them. I'd start the cycle all over again.

WHITE METAL, YELLOW METAL:

I Empty Out for Holy Boy

Chiv couldn't buy anything in his own village; everywhere he went the store owners and people in the market gave him whatever he desired free of charge. This was true Mayan retirement and village admiration for his past years of suffering and struggle to bring life to the village through ritual and doctoring. So when he had to buy offerings, he always sent me, to make sure they were purchased. If he went, they wouldn't let him pay. In Tzutujil spiritual economy, you don't get blessing from a ceremony if it wasn't a direct sacrifice or emptying of oneself or family.

One balmy afternoon, Chiv came tumbling into my hut, breaking my reverie. "How much money do you have?" he blurted, half out of breath, plopping his strong old being next to me on my balsa slat bed.

"About seven-fifty quetzales total," I replied, wondering what he was up to. Seven-fifty was five days' hard-earned wages for a grown man. Chiv pulled out a little white stone pipe with a short cane stem, pushed a half-spent half-cent cigar into the bowl, took the stem into the side of his mouth, turned the bowl upside down, and lit the whole affair, letting his words drift out on the blue smoke as he spoke:

"Holy Boy is being ritually assembled tonight, and I want you to use up all your metal [money]!"

I just stared at the smoke, my lips pursed, realizing how hard I struggled to keep in the game with this crazy old white-headed spirit doctor. All the prayers and ceremonies took every cent I had to buy offerings. I never had even a few cents left over to get anything I desired.

Granted, I was definitely no worse off than the majority of villagers, for whom the tobacco Chiv now smoked was a luxury. Actually I was better off than most. But the market for selling grinding stones was seasonal, and Chiv had me at so many tasks that I hardly had any time to make a living anyhow. So when asked to liquidate all my assets in one blow, I had to think. I had no bank to send to, no relatives to call on for money, no secret stash of silver dollars, just myself, my wits, and this old teacher who wanted me to get rid of all my money. I thought.

"Fine," I said. "What do I do?"

"You will see what Holy Boy contains and who he really is, but first you have to show your dedication by spending all you have left on him. Spend it on them that give you your life! Does this stay lit in your head? [Do you understand?]"

It was near to impossible to get to see the assembling of the Holy Boy, as every villager would be there crouching around a sacred house already packed to fainting capacity, standing outside the house, concentrically for hundreds of yards. All were grown men and women—little kids weren't really allowed. This Deity was considered too hot for their tender souls.

"Our Gods won't fill what's already full; they chase emptiness. You have to make a hole for them to fill, so spend all you have on offerings tonight. You'll see what happens!"

The Holy Boy would be put together this day, as every year, by a priest called the *Teleniel*, the Shoulderer, so named because of the fact that when the God is finally assembled, this man carries and dances him while the heavy God straddles his shoulder. He is also known as the Holy Boy's Horse for the same reason. On this night in utter darkness, the *Teleniel* had to fully assemble the God out of myriad component parts, each stage accompanied by the appropriate secret Tzutujil liturgy. The God would be dressed in the layers of creation with the rich Tzutujil clothing that went with each distinct layer. Then the candles would be lit and the heavy God lifted by a crowd of initiatory chiefs onto the shoulders of the *Teleniel*, who after dancing him to his three songs would place the God at his appointed spot between two guards sitting on large wooden stumps. The God had to stand on his own two legs; if he fell, the *Teleniel* would die before the year was out.

You see, the work of assembling done in the hot, close, utterly dark sacred house was tested by Holy Boy's standing up well. The *Teleniel* got no second chances, and there was no telling whether the God would stand or not. It was especially exciting if a totally inexperienced shaman was appointed to be *Teleniel* and to see if he could do the ritual properly, risking his life to prove his worth. For such a thing, everyone would come from miles around to see.

Chiv continued his instructive banter: "Go buy flowers, cigars, matches, *aguardiente*, white esteras, sacpom, and we'll use what money's left as alms to the God."

In the nineteen-forties and early fifties, Chiviliu had monopolized the Holy Boy priesthood, having commandeered the *Teleniel* position for twelve consecutive years until he was forcibly removed by the hierarchy. This had caused a political split in the village that was still at the heart of a lot of trouble in the village to that day, but Chiv knew this Deity better than any person that had ever lived. Anyone could tell you that.

Off I went to purchase the offerings, returning an hour or so later. I still had one quetzal left, which Chiv bound up in a silk scarf and tucked in my sash.

"Now we'll see if you have enough faith. Make sure you ask for some more money to help you live. The Holy Boy is rich; he's a great merchant, the great bringer of things, the negotiator, the ingenious Lord of Roads,

Knots, and Destinies. He'll test you, but you'll see his face." Then Chiv began the beginning prayer that precedes any ceremonial venture, making the leaving of the house the beginning of the ritual and the safe return to the same spot the ending.

Excited, Chiv smiled like a rabbit, and out we strolled, walking the village streets, yelling and mumbling salutations over the stone walls to kids, old ladies, men, and little girls, all my money converted into flowers, candles, and liquor heavy on my back. Chiv was still trying to light his crazy pipe. We headed for the house of the Holy Boy in the purple darkness.

Cushioned by the six-inch carpet of long, fragrant pine needles that was the floor in any sacred house, I awoke facedown not six feet from the guards of the Holy Boy, who fought to keep from falling asleep as I fought to get out of it. After losing consciousness in the middle of the ecstatic hubbub of the Holy Boy debut, I awoke more dead than alive, still poisoned by the requisite "canyon water" we'd ritually received the night before. Like everyone else in the village, I had a bad ceremonial hangover.

The Holy Boy effigy had truly come alive, standing well and steady after teetering for almost a minute, making him more alive. The *Teleniel*, his checkered handwoven shirt soaked in sweat, his headcloth over his brow, had thunked the God down hard with confidence. The tribal crowd of thousands all exhaled silently until the God stood well. Then the music broke in at the bidding of the sacred house chief, and the Holy Boy was lifted by his sash onto the shoulders of his Horse and danced to the thirteen directions, carried while the *Teleniel* knelt to each direction, rising to a standing position and then kneeling again effortlessly. The rest of us were amazed at the strength the Deity had bestowed on the *Teleniel*, giving him the ability to dance and shoulder two hundred sacred pounds like a ten-pound stone.

The Holy Boy had been returned to his throne on a reed mat called *pōp*, the ancient throne of all Mayans, between the guards seated on their stumps. The tribe had lined up especially to watch the most famous shamans do their *chit ri*, introducing themselves and their unique magical relationship with this Old Being, using the wild, magical array of cryptic eloquence so beloved of Holy Boy.

The Holy Boy had more than sixty public names, and then other secret ones according to how he chose to present himself to the shamans in visions. He was not always a male, but sometimes a woman, and not always human, either. Though mostly a controller of temperatures, he was the parent of heat. As the originator of human culture, he lived in fire. A patron of imagination, human folly, and chance, Holy Boy moves at the speed of thought, arriving instantly when called. He is always hungry, and only a few know exactly how to feed him. Thus the need for specialists or shamans when dealing with this God.

Ingenuity and desire were linked in him, as were trickery and addiction. He was the ritual manifestation of being alive. The Tzutujil, having no real word for time, had in Holy Boy a deified demonstration of living time. Since time was a story told, all the stories told at once were Holy Boy. In this way he became destiny as a feedable thing, manifesting mostly as fire. Though often touted as a God of well-being, it was being, period, that he manifested. He was the messenger between the Layers of Creation.

It was to this Ancestral Holy Boy that we went ritually to feed our nature as humans. There we immersed ourselves and danced with all the pain and joy, doubt and luck, loss and gain, certainty and unpredictability, all rolled into one polyvalent Lord around whom we gathered carefully filled with Burning Water and burning tobacco of vision, collapsing at his/their/her feet, happy to be alive another day. Being poisoned by the aftereffects of the ritual was a part of the ritual called the bite, a reminder of the very reality we had been feeding with the pains of our lives, all manifested in the annual re-creating of Holy Boy.

This God did not make our ancestors. Rather, this God, unlike foreign gods, had been made by our original ancestors. These ancestors, or Nawales, were the core natures of natural phenomena made manifest in human form. The magical interplay between those ancestral natures, poured into one being made from the wood of the Fire Tree, became the Holy Boy: our Nature. This God became a simple place to go feed our own complex natures as one being: The Grandchild of the Gods.

The people had fed the Holy Boy all night; they'd danced for him, given him big gifts, candles, fire, cigars. Liquor was poured liberally into his mouth, blown as a hazy mist over his head; shamans brought to him sick clients and kneeling men and women as the marimbas raged on. Emotions rose, and Old Chiv, bellowing prayers for me and for him, succumbed, weeping and breaking down as most all of us did. He passed unconscious onto the floor of pine needles beneath the low ceiling packed full of corozo palm flowers, whose smell alone could take you to other worlds.

I had made my supplications, and not long after I must have succumbed and passed out. Or, as the Mayans say, I became wounded in the soul's battle, and was therefore accepted by the power of the Holy Boy and under his protection.

When I awoke on a floor full of the wounded, I didn't care about anything except survival. I wanted only to get the nausea out of my burning stomach, the pain out of my head, and the shivers out of my bones. As I was lumbering to my knees, I felt a small bulge in my shirt pocket. Upon investigating I found a wad of crumpled quetzales amounting to twelve quetzales. A miracle! The Holy Boy had returned seventy cents on the dollar. At first I surmised that the old sacred house chiefs or that crazy old rich shaman, Mxcach, must have been ecstatically inspired. Maybe after having heard how I was made penniless by my faith, they had wanted to make sure I was provided for. This was a village, after all, and people cared about each other. Maybe that was all there was to Holy Boy after all, just an excuse to celebrate being human by getting together in a ceremonial way.

Anyway, I said my formal good-byes to Holy Boy and the half-awake guards and to the dozing chiefs and tottered up to my hut, determined to rest and revive in time to fulfill some hierarchy obligations later in the day.

Sleep had almost burst its sweet warmth through my exhausted body when I was retrieved from its depths by the yodeling of a Ladina lady in big-city Spanish.

"*Hola, buenos días, está aquí un Don Martín? Hola, hola, está aquí alguien?*"

I rolled and staggered to the doorway. The delicious morning lake air fled in front of an onslaught of heavy perfume. Not knowing who to expect, what I saw inspired me to fake a sober air. Here before me, in my isolated Mayan doorway, stood two immaculately dressed white ladies, one mature, one young, both with fancy hairdos, makeup, perfume, nylon stockings, high-heeled shoes, purses, gloves, and corsages.

Half-drunk, blinking in the sun, I must have looked like a newly hatched buzzard chick, gawking and unsteady. Undaunted and on a mission, these two incongruous ladies proceeded to interrogate me.

"Are you Sir Martín, the painter?"

"Yes, I paint a little," I replied, knowing that I had not touched a brush in over a year due to all my shamanic training and my lack of income to buy supplies with. Nonetheless I did have a stack of finished canvases piled and forgotten at the other end of the village in a hard-to-get-to hut.

"Well," the older woman continued, "we have just finished making our summer house down on the coast between here and Tziquinala, and we need your paintings to ornament the walls. We were told you might have some to our liking."

"Aha. Who may I ask told you such a thing?"

"Oh, a friend of my husband's. May we see your work, please?"

"The truth is, my paintings are all quite far away, on the other side of this village, and I'm not entirely positive you ladies could arrive there in very good condition in that footwear. You see, it's very rustic, and quite a climb."

"No matter to us! Just lead and we'll follow. We have to get some art."

This was strange, and I was in no condition to lead anybody anywhere. I'd never sold a painting before, and who were these irritatingly cheerful women?

Grabbing my string bag and hat, slipping on my heavy tread sandals, I eased my way up and over boulders, uphill through black sand, almost fainting for the dead liquor in my head, the heat of the rising sun.

Without one complaint or evil word, these ladies maintained a very steady, respectful banter as they chuckled their way up the hill in their fancy suits, laughing at themselves as much as I was about this whole scene. High-society Guatemalan women were swooning belles who usually hated Indians, villages, and rusticity, so I was very surprised. I actually grew fond of the pair, as much as my headache would let me show.

After thirty minutes or so, we arrived at the hut. The ladies were puffing a bit, but they had kept right up with me, holding their high heels in one hand and steadying themselves on all the big rocks with the other. I opened up the dusty, abandoned hut, shook out my old paintings, and started laying them out along the outer wall under the thatched eaves. After only thirty seconds of consideration, the older woman pointed to a painting of a Tzutujil girl grinding corn, and asked me, "How much?"

I was still astounded that anyone might want to buy paintings from me, since I'd practically forgotten I knew how to paint. I also had no idea what a painting like mine could be sold for, but since I was broke, I thought maybe I could get twenty quetzales for it. While I pondered these thoughts, in the middle of my long ruminations, the older lady piped up with an astounding offer:

"Okay, I'll give you five hundred quetzales."

I was so stunned that my mouth must have dropped. When I didn't reply right away, she blurted: "Okay, you drive a hard bargain. I'll give you seven hundred quetzales and no more, and I'll take that other one there for the same and this little one for two hundred."

That all came to about sixteen hundred quetzales, which in the early seventies I'd never even seen in one place before. I was still staring, not knowing what to say.

"We'd like to take you to breakfast. Just take these wonderful paintings to the entrance of the village and have our driver load them in the trunk."

Driver?! Breakfast? Where? There weren't any breakfast places out here!

Sure enough, there was the driver and a big old black Cadillac-type car right at the bottom of Chinimyá, surrounded by herds of little Tzutujil kids. We loaded the canvases, and I got in the car. All the little kids' faces pressed on the windows, yelling:

"*A Martín, a Martín, ba tzra n ket naka wa?*"

("Martín, Martín, where are they taking you?")

Well, I didn't actually know, to be honest.

We drove very slowly on the washed-out dirt road to San Lucas, over boulders and in the ruts, past all the noble Tzutujil men, young and old, shouldering their axes, hoes, produce, and armloads of firewood, their little sons at their heels. They looked sideways at me in this monster of steel, being taken God knows where. We cruised down the coast toward Tziquinala, and up a canyon back toward Chicacao. I didn't know there even was a road to that part of the piedmont jungle, let alone one so recently paved.

After a climb, we arrived at a house built into a high cliff. It was made of solid stone and had big plate glass windows that opened out on a breath-taking view of a great span of green stretching out forever, from the majestic cloud-wreathed volcanoes behind us, right into the Pacific Ocean.

The two ladies sat me down in the new cool dining hall, and brought me scrambled eggs, tortillas, black beans, sour cream, deep-fried plantains, coffee, and oranges, which I ate while everybody watched. It was all I could do to keep that good stuff in my liquor-poisoned belly, but I did so with great resolve so as not to dishonor my buyers, and not to ruin my unexpected sale of paintings.

After I'd finished eating and thanked everyone, including the pinafored Indian cook, the women hung my paintings on the wall. After bargaining me down a hundred dollars, they counted out a wad of Guatemalan money and handed me fifteen hundred quetzales, to which I could not argue. This was three years' wages in our village.

As the driver herded me back into the big car and I was saying good-bye, the older woman said, "Our husband will be very happy about your having come."

It was all so mysterious. I had many questions, but I had to return to the village so as not to miss the initiates coming out for the first time in a year today. As it was, I was sure I'd missed it all and was angry at myself. We'd left the village about nine A.M., and this house was an hour away. I figured I'd get back to Santiago around noon, two hours too late.

When we arrived in the village, however, it was still midmorning. I didn't know how this could be. I got out of the car at the edge of Santiago, thanked the uniformed driver, and walked into the village. I realized then that I didn't know the names of either of the women, the driver, "their" husband, or who these strange people were.

Chiv met me coming up the hill and asked me what I was going to do now, as if he knew all about what had happened and was testing my motives. I said I would give a donation to the initiating chief for his expenditures, and then I would go to the Holy Boy and with Chiv's help make a presentation of thanks.

Chiv said, "This is how it is with us, and this is how shamans function. You'd better get some sleep."

COOKING THE SHAMAN'S SOUL:
My Training

At first I was like a well-treated slave whom Chiv took everywhere, in every weather, to every shrine, in every mountain, forest, canyon, valley, shore, island, and village, introducing me to the keepers of these shrines and holy places, both spirits and people. Slowly but impeccably, he monitored the pressure and weight I could handle, navigating my patience, my physical stamina, and my tolerance of change and of unpredictability with a smile, working me up to a fine temper. He forgave my failures and laughed, assuming them as his own shortcomings.

My assistant days taught me how to serve and made my body durable to most of the hard conditions found in a village male's existence. Then

Chiv proceeded to push me toward greater challenges through formal exercises that addressed shamanism directly. First I had to learn the usual everyday techniques that were common to all village shamans, like how to spray water or liquor from the mouth. By spreading a fine, atomized spray over a client in the sun in four or five directions, you could bring in the deep-colored light of multiple rainbows. Shamans learned how to hang the droplets in the air for a long time. That way, a sick client would be bathed in rainbows, which was indicated in certain ceremonies and ailments, especially when dealing with fright. This came from gophers and tapirs who spray dust and water in just this way.

Ashes of different ritually burnt materials were blown over a suspected ghost's lair and then designs were drawn into the suspended ash particles. Messages were written with different objects to speak with the poor dejected spirits. If you had the shaman's instinct and strength, you could blow a conch shell, mist your water out all over the place, then instantly shoot a heavy load of sacred ashes through a bone. Lo and behold, you could see the shadowed silhouette of the ghost or sometimes a God, standing there in the room projected like negative light inside the water-ash mist.

When a shaman got really good at it, he or she could bring down a client's fever using this technique. I'd kneel under Chiv's big fish in his hut, take incense smoke into my lungs, forcibly puff it out over the hot head of our patient, and watch the hot smoke turn to a fine cloud of cooling water droplets. By the same token, the shaman could take a person in shock or with no heat in their body and make the heat rise in their shivering, clammy body, starting from the feet up through their legs, to the shoulders, over the hands, up the neck, to the chin, finally returning the warm red to their cheeks. This could be done in many ways, but it was really fun to turn water into smoke by blowing a fine mist of prayed-over liquid cut by a glass blade behind the patient's head and watch it turn to blue, fragrant smoke. I was really good at that and loved doing it, especially when people came back to life on account of it.

But these things were pretty common among the fifty or so professional shamans in the village. There were a lot more of these types of procedures, but they were not to be exhibited on demand or used to show off, or one could lose the ability.

Before you were allowed to try any of this, it was best if your teacher made you observe life. Most of my active training with Chiv before my initiation was involved with becoming totally aware wherever I stood. That meant becoming knowledgeable of the nature of all things around you at any given time, while also being aware of what surrounded you as one organism with you in it. This was accomplished by a series of disciplines. Gradually one's own natural soul began to define itself in the body in a sort of moving way, the same way the body defined its shape in relation to the nature surrounding it.

To us shamans, this was not really so esoteric; we considered it as natural as eating and walking. In the beginning, Chiv sent me so many paces in any direction, out in the bush, where I'd have to plop down and draw a circle around me in the dirt, sand, or leaf litter as far out as my index finger could reach. Having agreed not to look outside that circle for the remainder of the day, I watched the shifting shadows and activity that went on in that circle, and remembered them all. Just to stay sitting in such a tight spot was a challenge to anybody, but it always amazed me, all the lives and destinies played out in that little circle.

The first time I did this, I remember staring at what appeared to be a bare patch of ground, when a little amber-colored spider popped out of a tiny, unnoticed hole. His front legs bristling for a fight, he wheeled around like a gun turret, his little eyes checking out the turf, when another spider in the same grumpy mood appeared out of a hole on the other side of the ring. The first guy really got angry when he saw this challenge to his territory and started spinning around like crazy, saying all kinds of bad things about his mother and insulting the other spider who came in closer for the showdown. And there they stood, front legs waving in the air, teeth bared, all eight eyeballs rolling, face to face, revolving around in a tight little circle, raising what for them and their neighborhood was dust. It was like miniature sumo wrestling.

Finally one of them saw an opening, and hopped on the other. They rolled all over the place, pushing and grabbing, kicking and bristling, grunting and biting for the longest time, then they'd break, each panting in his corner. Then they'd go at it again until they finally agreed on taking a lunch break. Both spiders ran down their holes, turning a couple of times to make sure they weren't being followed.

After a spell, almost simultaneously they both popped up, still chewing the last of their lunch. They couldn't wait to battle some more, which they did, only now they were serious. The amber-colored spider finally killed the other one and, exhausted, dragged his enemy, armor clanking, down into his hole. After sucking the juice out of his rival, he reappeared out on the porch of his hole, cracking his knuckles and yawning, very proud of himself. Then out of the unseen sky came a very long, thin-waisted wasp. The wasp stung the spider good, dragged him down his own hole, and probably laid her babies in him.

Above the hole, a nervous speckled lizard had dropped out of a tree, and was doing quite a few push-ups. He kept looking at me like one of those frenetic guys you meet on Guatemalan buses selling vitamins or pencils; the guys whom you buy from just to get them off your back. This lizard sucked in that wasp the minute he stuck his shiny head out of the ground, and then jumped back into his tree. This patch of ground was worn bare, as it was the lizard's accustomed landing and launching place.

A crew of ever-present ants came and hauled out one of the spider bodies, and the sun went down.

This whole event was a form of divination. Anybody who wasn't able to read the dramatic stories taking place in all nature would never be able to read that nature in a human life. This type of looking taught us the shamanic understanding that all beings had to eat and live out their nature. That was a blessing, and that's how we saw it.

At other times, I was quizzed on how many toes certain animals had, or how many feathers were in a flicker's tail, or how many times lightning and thunder would flash and crash on what volcanos and in what order, before and after a storm, to figure how long it would rain. I was asked how many rows of kernels certain ancient varieties of corn had, or how many turns a certain beetle made before she went under her leaf, or how a jaguar whistled to mesmerize her prey. There was no end to this kind of learning. If you didn't know the answers, Chiv always sent you out to find out. This forced you to pay attention to everything surrounding you at all times.

The barks of certain trees told us how the coming year would be, weather-wise. The sounds of birds and bugs had different powers over weather and destinies. The belief was that the seasons didn't bring the birds, but rather that birds' language of magic sounds brought about seasonal changes in temperature and moisture—birds especially, since each bird was the voice in earthly form of some God. Ground animals were, too, but birds were always telling us things.

We could be going somewhere, talking, and Chiv would always turn and ask in a serious tone, "Listen! How many birds are singing? What kinds? On what side of your body?" One began to have at all times an intense awareness of nature's voice and presence in every aspect of life.

All these exercises, riddles, and questions were a kind of spiritual weight lifting where the goal was to discover your own nature and become what you hunted. However, instead of killing it you would become what you were hunting. When you finally understood that nature was the imagination of the Gods, you realized that your nature hunted your own soul inside this enormous imagination. Your own soul was the imagination of the ancestors living inside the imagination of the Gods. The discovered nature of your soul caused the shaman's soul to survive.

Chiv's exercises were designed for this discovery. Sometimes he took me observing water in canyons, in the ground, or in a cave. Eventually when I became aware enough, I casually graduated to the next stage of exercises, known as *Ntzikij*, or He calls it. Calling consisted of bringing animals to you, or birds to your hand, or changing weather by using the unspoken voice of your nature. A shaman used his heart instead of human words in this exercise. Words as we know them now hadn't happened yet in the Original Earth before people. In the Original Flowering Mountain Earth Navel, all nature was a story told, where plants, animals, winds, stones, trees, and growth were the words. The speech of the Gods was nature.

Finding that place within you that called specific natural beings to you, where they were trusting and unafraid, forced one's stubborn human mind to serve the storytellers of life: the Gods. If you could do this, you discovered your own nature little by little without the mind's always claiming that it had done something. You had to learn to distinguish between learned knowledge and remembrance of other layers.

Since all Tzutujil shamans, myself included, understand that the human body contains the whole world, in order to cure disease or pain a shaman had to become a charmer of all that world. A shaman had to become nature, not just an observer of nature. The wild mountain jungle, uninhabited by people, was the living manifestation of the other worlds inside this one. It was both our living imagination and the Land of Dreams in a very tangible, unsentimental, natural way. Humans weren't necessarily welcome there, but the true natural spirit of a shaman was at home in this, the verdant Belly of the Gods.

Chiv would take me out into a jungle area devoid of humans and put me into a shrine area in front of crossed-armed stone Gods, or big-eyed wood Gods, or holy trees, cliffs, clefts, or waterfalls, depending on what I was to call. Then Chiv "shot" me into nature's mind, blurting out the Respect Name of the animal or force he wanted me to call. Calling with your heart, your nature, means you cannot use speech or your native language. Noises were technically okay, but they had to come from your own natural soul, not be a creative contrivance of your mind.

Each shaman had to remember what worked best for him. The main point of calling was that it was not *chasing*. You could not order life to come to you, nor did you actively *go after* it. The secret was to get behind the eyes of what you wanted to call, become that being's vision, likes, and dislikes; understand by being what your subject wanted to go toward. Then you became the object of that animal's desire. One had to become fascinating to nature so nature would come! Becoming irresistible to what one called meant making yourself *visible* and delicious instead of becoming the power called.

The human mind, I found, has a low grinding sound that scares most nature away. So for me, I had to engross my grinding mind in doing something beautiful and quietly repetitive to keep it humming a more natural tune in its concentration. Mostly one failed at this, but even when you had a victory, you always scared it away by your elation, and then you had to laugh at yourself. But eventually you'd become a specialist at calling certain beings who would become indispensible in your initiations. Whatever you could call with some consistency would have to be ritually fed and given altar space in your bundle house, when that day came.

Chiv could call weasels, sparrowhawks, rain, butterflies, and fish. I became good at trees, hummingbirds, lizards, and winds. We had butterflies in common. This calling was considered a kind of precursor to tracking, to tracking a sick client's soul lost in the wilderness landscape of his or her body. Just like hunters, who track animals in mountain forests, the novice shaman had to be fluent in the Respect Names of all natural things, especially poisonous or large animals.

A Respect Name was thought of as the kinship term used among the Gods themselves for the different beings in nature behind which the Gods disguised themselves in nature. But it also served as a kind of hunters' ritual code, which they used whenever they were in the chase, in order not to scare away the soul of the animal they hunted. But all the animals and trees had to be addressed or spoken to in this way so that they didn't interpret the human as an intruder into the Gods' land of nature, but rather as one of them, something natural. Shamans were exactly the same, only each one sought out names told to them especially by the forces of life, which only that shaman used. This created a singular relationship between the shaman and the God of the animal, plant, or weather, or whatever. Whereas the hunters' language of Respect was pretty much a hunters' language common to all of them.

All adults knew most of the encoded Respect Names, because this rule of using special words for deified natural forces when in their presence extended to the general village to some extent. The Sun, for instance, was called *Qij*, but this term was used only at night or when the Sun was absent. When the Sun shone, however, all the people called him *Cdtá*, "Our Father," because of course he is. The same for the Moon, who was only called *Ić*, Moon, when she was hiding, but when she shone on us, we men removed our hats upon her appearance and addressed her as *Ctit*, Our Grandmother. The same was true for fire, lake, mountains, and many other natural forces. All these things were alive and had to be addressed as kin when in their presence, otherwise they would be insulted. The same etiquette used for humans extended to the world. Thus the things of the world were addressed instead of discussed.

Respect Names came from the hunters' tongues, and this was observed by all "layered" men out in the wilds, regardless of whether or not they were hunters. You had to use the Respect Names for all these animals and powers even if you hadn't seen one, because all their natural world was listening. This kept the relationship formal and good. For instance, the regular word for a deer was *quej*, or the borrowed Nahua Indian word *mazat*. But in the mountain they used the Respect Name "sister-in-law." A jaguar was called *Bajlam*, but his Respect Name was *Ral Bom*, "child of a woman valley." A snake, normally called *cumatz*, was *Tzibwa, Tzibawach*, "Painted Head, Painted Face." And so on for every beast.

But anyone untutored in all this could simply call any animal, especially the poisonous ones, by the word *Rilaj Vinaq*, Venerable Deity. This was the code word for "The Old Lady." The Old Lady was the mother of all undomesticated life. Old women in the village were also referred to as *Rilaj Vinaq*. This was a term of great respect, meaning literally "a well-layered Twenty (complete being)," or "a venerated being."

Any wild animals that stung, bit, poisoned, or attacked humans were referred to in their presence as *Rilaj Vinaq* by regular villagers. If a person was stung or bit, a shaman would have to be called to remove the *kii*, or poison. It was said, "The Old Woman bit you." Her poison caused pain because she hated humans for having torn up the natural world of plants and animals.

She was the mother-in-law of the villagers, because we humans had married her daughers, the "Corn Mothers," and she had never really sanctioned the marriage. So all her anger and venom was in snakes, spiders, scorpions, centipedes, and so on. Only shamans could "talk her down" and successfully remove her poison from the body. She liked shamans because they understood her, being rooted in nature and not humanness. She had taught each spider bite shaman or snakebite shaman her own language pertaining to their corresponding animal. They are very powerful and beautiful, these prayers.

Tzutujil shamans as a whole were defined by their use of ornate, polyvalent language skills. Instead of everyday words, they used ancient words no longer prevalent, whose meanings were revealed by their awareness of certain origination stories and how their own initiatory experience incorporated those stories into the shamans' everyday lives. For instance, a June bug was commonly called a *ver ver*, for their buzzy sound, when they got mad. The Respect Name for a June bug is *r xicanab chicopil*, which is an archaic plural word for "Little Winged Animal." On the other hand, the shamanic term for a June bug is a polyvalent word called *Ruqaruach knimaq kí*. This meant "the yolk of the fruited faces of our many now made great," which also means "the eyes of our ancestral dead." Those little charming creatures were considered to be the iridescent eyes of our old-timers come back to see us and report our progress back to the spirits. That's why we never killed them.

Hunting was still carried on by certain families in the village, but for most it was a thing of the past, since the coastal land had been ravaged under the metallic ring of American-supported cotton growers, foreign sugarcane planters, and fruit and cattle operations. All of these enterprises had cleared the coastal forests of the original Flowering Mountain Earth and offered only very low cash wages to a shanghaied Indian labor force who slaved and sweated in fields that in the intolerable coastal humidity actually intensified the heat now that the verdant trees' breath could no longer cool them.

The old hunters were my friends. Their ways were not at all macho, but quite noble. They had an intelligence about the wildness of the land and a kind of mythological rulebook by which they moved, hunted, and treated the souls of the animals they killed.

Ma Acabul invited me to my first feast of a hunter. Acabul was an enormous Indian, a fine, big-hearted man who was married to a beautiful coastal Tzutujil woman who understood him and was highly respected in the village. They lived in Chiv's compound due to the fact that Acabul's old grandfather and Chiv had made some deal long ago. Acabul knew that whatever he killed was the son or daughter of a God. He would be in charge of that animal's upbringing in the other world.

Highland Tzutujil hunters went mostly for deer, peccaries, armadillos, tepisquintles, coatis, rabbits, currasows, quail, doves, and so on, whose meat they often sold or traded for corn, firewood, or services. They killed mountain lions, occasionally jaguars and ocelots and cocomistles, but they never sold the meat of these beasts, as they were predators, representations of the keeper of all the other animals, the heart of the universe, and the hunter himself. Thus all the feline predators were "feasted" themselves by the hunter and his family. The beasts were cooked ceremonially just as the domesticated animal sacrifices were, in squash seed paste, wild chilis, and mints, consumed in formal feasts with honored guests, a little of the meat of each body part being distributed to the fire, the doorway, and the middle of the house (its umbilicus). The bones had a ritual destination depending on the beast and were never put in the fire.

I ate my first jaguar and my first ocelot in one of Ma Acabul's hunter feasts, and I must say that, expecting a tough, dry meat, I was utterly in error, for never a better meat was there on this earth, exceeded only by tapir, which we all hate to kill. The backstrap, or tenderloin, was given to me. It was wonderful and filled me with a sweet, durable, smiley kind of patience like the cats themselves.

Highland Tzutujil never eat primates, dogs, or any kind of reptile: lizards, iguanas, or snakes. I, of course, in the space of my wanderings, had to eat all of the above while attending reciprocal feasts of shamans in neighboring coastal tribes, who do eat them. All were quite delicious except the monkeys, which were like eating your little brother.

Everyone ate fish, but only cold, after cooking; otherwise you would explode. The belief was that anything with scales was cold, and if you ate it hot, it would cause you to swell with steam! The relationship between fishlike animals and snakes and lizards was well recognized, but because fish were wet and cold from living in water and not dry and cold like reptiles, they would cause you no harm. First, however, they must be cooked and cooled. None of their bones could be thrown in the fire, either.

Before the arrival of Europeans, the Tzutujil had a whole section of their population whose lives were dependent on deer. A shrine of at least a thousand deer heads lay at the entrance to one of the Mountain Gods' homes until it was destroyed by an American building a hotel there. Today, as in those days, puppies are raised and run in little herds to the coast, where they are sold or traded to the coastal Tzutujil, who raise them to eat as feast food. They also eat lizards, snakes, iguana, monkeys, grubs, locusts, and ants, causing the people of the two regions to regard each other with suspicion. But the shamans and old people know that the highland people are the Males, and the coastal the Females; and that the Male people eat Male food and Females eat Female things, and together they meet at fish, which both tribes eat. Thus the two types of life are necessary to make the tribes function.

But with modern ways, corporations and Christians moving in and clearing the land and the imagination (the two things being one and the same to us shamans), there are fewer and fewer animals. Now there are no hunters. Ma Acabul and his people have all passed on. I'm happy to have known him; he was one of Chiv's best friends.

Shamans are essentially hunters, and all the principles of hunting had to become second nature to the novice shaman. From early on, Chiv had me hunting, too. Going out every couple of days, it took me all of an intense two years to get any good at "calling" with my heart. Chiv would have me practice oratory praying, too, using common forms, not the deep stuff. I was just to get used to getting my throat and tongue around the words, so the delicious sounds could hammer their meaning deep into the bones of the listener, which at this point was either Chiv or the spirits.

When I'd become proficient enough at both calling and praying, Chiv made me begin to practice becoming what I called. I failed utterly, which was normal, since the exercise was not designed for one to succeed but, rather, was meant to tune your abilities to be in nature instead of around or drawing on nature—to *be* nature. Nature was made of a complex interrelationship of an infinite number of constantly changing "little natures," and mine was one of them.

Out we'd go to the bush, where no human would be likely to poke his or her curious nose. Chiv would set me up with no water, food, fire, or blanket, and instruct me to stay in one place an hour or so before dawn to wait until the next day's arrival of our Father the sun. I was to hear, see, taste on the wind, feel on my skin everything, every sound, every change of heat, humidity, coolness, footsteps, and breezes that went on around me until the next sunrise, without sleeping, drinking, eating, or talking. Learning how to listen like this was called "being in a place well."

You couldn't think about your life, or the life of others. There would be plenty of time for that, because to have time and place to just think about this and that is heaven to us. This exercise, however, was to make sure you didn't think. It was not like some Asian meditation where you empty yourself exactly, but was rather where you filled yourself with all the senses, with every cricket chirp and birdsong, every creak, crack, pop, and twitter. You were not to focus on what happened as an observer, but rather to hear, see, and allow it all to sink into the bottom of your body and bones like silt and seeds dropping into your river of liquid bone from the overhanging trees, while you gazed from the bottom of the water, very still, hardly moving, like an alligator.

If I did the exercise right, my soul would begin to merge with my entire diverse surroundings, and the edges of who I was would get increasingly blurred until my mind would jump and snap me back like a dog on a leash, scared of how far I might wander, and maybe never come back. Then I'd calm my mind, send it off and slowly begin to listen and see, until I started to merge again with nature and be snapped back again by my mind. Each time, however, I'd get a little farther into nature and a little better at staying there.

A current began to pulse between the mind of self-preservation and the mind of the natural instinct to become part of the life around me. After a year of practice, that pulse became so fast and habitual that it took on the character of a unique "third thing." That third thing that appeared was what I would need to have in order to survive my initiation as a shaman. While immersed in nature, not analyzing, not understanding exactly but becoming nature, one really did begin seeing how vast the human soul can be. It was this middle place, this third thing, Chiv and I were after, the place of shamans in the middle of the world.

After the first few tries, Chiv suggested I go out by myself without his tutelage and do the exercise. At one point he casually said, "Now you had better start hunting by calling. Bring back the whisker and feather of what you pull toward you." The whisker or feather, tooth or breath of a live animal was very powerful, as pieces of people are, too, quite possessed of the DNA of our souls. If you cut your nails or your hair, you always burnt them, because you could be hurt or controlled or used as an energy source by any unscrupulous sorcerer who got ahold of a chunk of you while you were still alive.

By the same theory, if you hunted an animal unarmed and succeeded in taking the fur from the tip of its tail or a whisker from its face, these being the two most powerful repositories of the animal's power, you could call upon the nature of that beast to help you when you were in trouble. By that time you would also have become very adroit at becoming that animal or part of nature itself.

The animals I ran into mostly frowned on the practice; none of them ran up to me and said, "Please pull this whisker out of my cheek!" One did not get that close to a beast by having power over the animal, but by becoming part of that animal's power, which the acquired whisker or whatever actually represented.

Modern people have no idea how difficult this is.

You first had to touch the animal with your index finger without its running away. Your mind and spirit had to be just so, as it was in the exercise of being in a place well, without getting excited, and then you touched the beast without being scared or preparing to do anything. When the opportunity presented itself, you simply reached up and quickly and tightly pulled at the whisker or feather in an elegant, whole-body way, knowing full well you might get bitten or killed. This was the only way you could succeed. If you had the method down, you had the whisker; if your human mind thought it was superior to the beast, you failed or got killed or worse. If you understood the magnificence of nature and the beast and the fact that both were allowing you into this deep place where no contrivance could help you, then you had to just be that and not think about it, or you would fail again.

The whisker showed you had graduated in this, but you were never allowed to show anybody. You kept it between you and the spirits.

I mostly failed, of course, but little by little my soul found the groove of the "middle place" and more and more often I returned with what I needed. I wear at this moment, among other things, the whisker of a jaguar coiled in a skin case, taken in just this way; the top crest of a roadrunner; and a side tail of a quetzal bird.

The village boys, during their formal public initiation into adolescence, were collectively given traditional tasks to perform, tasks upon which the sacred system of the village totally depended. Similarly, Chiv and other teachers gave their shaman students tasks designed to renew certain shrines or find lost sacred things. One time Chiv sent me to find the throne of the Gods who sat inside a special mountain, in the center of the Tzutujil universe, called Qelbal Juyu Taqaj (Mountain Throne, Valley Throne).

A foreign mining company had repeatedly tried to sink an exploratory hole into this strange little plug of a hill lying between our village and the coastal plains. Like the surrounding area, it was heavily covered by a thick growth of jungle and immense trees. The miners had desecrated a shrine of the greatest importance to the old believers. They had sawed down a monstrous tree that had been for centuries the "throne of clouds" with which Coastal Rain Cloud Gods had rested and could be coaxed into our zone with the right ceremonies. The base of the tree had grown oddly out of a crack in what was a solid plank of fine-grained granite on top of the mid-jungle hillock. Granite was very rare in this quaking volcanic country. After several centuries, the tree's branches had been carefully and systemically bent and curved to form a throne. As part of the end of every ceremony performed at the base of this tree, the twigs and branches would be bent, thus leaving a living reminder of every supplicant forever in time.

This hill was reputed to house Earthquake, a little brother of the Rain Gods, and it was said by men who had visited the hard-to-find place that the ground there shook and trembled on a regular basis. On top of that, it was easy to get lost or disoriented on the hill, which was most certainly covered by a thick carpet of clouds at all times, day and night, making it impossible to get your bearings.

Rowing three miles over the lake, we arrived at the base of Tuq an hour before sunup. Taking our string bags and machetes, we and the man who would end up becoming my father-in-law pumped our kneecaps straight up the water-soaked, orchid-covered ravines of the thousand-foot ridge. As we walked that ridge, our eyes were feasted with a breathtaking dual vista made of the pre-dawn volcanic highlands reflected in the turquoise mirror of our lake and mist-covered lowlands that stretched for miles out to the sea. Then we descended on the opposite side into a soup of rising clouds, off a cliff where a river burst out of a solid rock wall below the ravine. The pressure was so great that when I put my hat in the water, it shot out two hundred yards in a split second as if it were propelled by a firehose! The water tasted as if it had sugar in it, and we drank a lot of it.

Though it remained dark as early dawn, the sun must have been high. We saw no trail, only a faint, overgrown hint of a path used by larger four-footed animals of the rain forest. This led down to our right deeper and deeper, looking to me like the cloud-darkened underworld. After a spell of dense fog and foliage, we rose up again until we climbed out over a granite sheet carpeted three feet thick in leaf litter. Ahead of us, we heard a low rumble that became increasingly more audible as we reached our goal.

Then there it was. My guide had successfully brought us to the legendary mountain home of all the Gods and initiation chambers where certain ancestral humans learned to become Gods. This was Qelbal Juyu Taqaj.

The hill was indistinguishable from the sky, and I wondered how those miners could even have known about it, let alone found it from the air. It was so hidden in clouds and trees that we could hardly see it from the ground. Though we were only twenty miles from the lake and three more than that from the village, it felt more like a hundred miles for all the ridges, ripples, inclines, and canyons we'd covered to get here.

The top of the hill was delightfully flat, maybe the only truly flat land I'd seen in this hilly country outside some parts of the coast. Unlike the surrounding jungle, the trees grew every twenty feet or so with no vines or thicket beneath. The floor was solid humus, and the leaf litter went down as far as my machete went. Indeed it did tremble every twenty minutes or so!

Rumor had it that the miners had tried to drop heavy equipment on the hill from helicopters, which is why they felled so many trees, including our sacred tree, to clear space for landings and camps. Unable to find enough Mayans to work on top of the sacred hill, they hired only Christian converts, who were pretty few in those days in the late sixties. The miners were going to set up camps and start digging a big hole, but their cables kept snapping. Their helicopter crashed into the ravine, killing many workers, so the project was finally abandoned.

My task was to find the old shrine and, if possible, the stump of the old shrine tree. Chiv told me to probe around with my machete until I found the granite slab, then begin clearing using my heart to call the shrine after making supplications, which I did. It took us about an hour to find the slab and the shrine. The stump was there, too, and was growing back as good supple branches, which I bent into the shape I figured must be right from what I had heard described.

I set up a ceremonial layout and offerings according to Chiviliu's specifications, and then proceeded to complete a ritual to reinaugurate this almost-forgotten shrine. All this seriousness and proficiency on my part much surprised my future father-in-law, since he was a Christian convert: what in these parts passed for a non-believing rationalist.

We ate, and as we cleaned up our meal wrappers of wild banana, which had contained a delicious old-time *patin* recipe sent by the womenfolk, a shaft of brilliant afternoon sunlight cut through the fog and hit right where we lunched, bathing the stump and the shrine with a very appreciated bit of news about where we were and how much daylight we had left. I stood up with my string bag, admiring the light, euphoric about what seemed to me an acceptance of our presence on the hill, when I felt a warm liquid running down my bare calves below my sash. An acrid stench stung the air like smelling salts. I turned to look. There next to me, knocking me with his powerful, spotted leg, was a big old male jaguar spraying my leg as if I were a tree.

Gracefully, I found that middle place in my being between human and animal, a pure grinning awareness, neither fear nor courage, because for the most part human courage is just educated fear, and animals can sense that, too. Quickly I reached down, grabbed a long white whisker on the right cheek of this fine spotted Child of a Woman Valley, and deftly popped it out of his face with great belly force, no breath, and a minimum of movement.

He coughed and grumbled, tossing his deadly playful head to one side, showing a little tusk, then leisurely trotted off into the misty thicket. My companion returned from relieving himself as well. He'd missed the whole thing! Solidified and tested by the old cat, my natural soul, like the jaguar, was moving back into the fastness of its wilderness home in my Earth Body. The jaguar's eyes were on us, and like a twin with my nature, they both watched from out of sight, both within and without the small fascinations of the human mind. I could feel the jaguar staring at us while my companion became fearful of my eyes on him.

The air lost its light again to the Gods' Eyebrows, the Respect Name for fog. But the pan pipe trills, clucks, and chirps of thrushes, trogons, and a *pajuil* found their way through the thick, spicy air where I stood shaking. The Head Owner or God of this hill usually appeared as a jaguar when he walked out of the God World into ours. And I had his whisker!

Shaking, I kept trying to roll it into a hoop. It refused to stay round until Chiv later showed me how. It still sits over my heart, guarding my nature.

There were myriad tests, tasks, trials, teachings, drills, exercises, services, and riddles thrown at me through the course of my time with old Chiv before my true initiation. Initiation wasn't done to celebrate any acquired abilities or learning, but was done at a time when your supervisors thought you were strong enough to begin actually learning the details of the craft. I didn't get a course on shamanic procedure that I studied like a college student. I wouldn't get exams at the termination of any so-called training. One received ratification of one's abilities by the people at the same moment one was perceived as having successfully cured somebody. The power had to be in place; knowledge, although useful, was experientially gathered by on-the-job training, once the business of arranging your content by all these extreme measures was complete.

When you got good at being in the mountains, you began practicing the same down at the edge of the water, which was intensely difficult. Then you did it on the water in a canoe, drifting with life's breezes in lightning storms and so on; then *in* the water for long hypothermic hours with just your head sticking out. To focus without focusing, to stay attuned to the surroundings was really difficult there.

The highest shamanic ability was to keep your nature intact while surrounded by the goings-on of a human village. The mountain work brought you into the sap of the village of plants and animals, and water into the liquid living village of life. The human village, however, was the most difficult to be in, as you couldn't use your quality of being human to merge. Since it was already effortless to be a human, one could easily function as oneself. The trick was to not be human, but to be a part of nature while among the humans.

Chiv had done this for himself back around World War I, going to thirteen villages. I only did it in a couple.

Chiv deemed it practically impossible to have your nature's spirit ways intact in your own village where everybody knew everybody. So instead your supervisors dressed you down like a beggar or bum and put you on the plaza of some other tribe's village, where you couldn't really get the language. There you were expected to sit in the middle of the hustle and bustle of the people in utter awareness of your surroundings, precisely as you would in nature. In this way you would become as much a part of the unseen nature of a village as the dung beetle pushing a chunk of manure to a cornerstone, on the urine-soaked stones where you lay.

When I did this no one ever really *saw* me. Like nature, I was taken for granted, my heart beating just as well and hard as if I were well-dressed and clean, speaking and eating in a hut with a passel of relatives and friends. Due to my own nature's immersion into the holy, the sacred sap-like matrix of nature, I became covered in an everydayness that armored me as effectively as a one-inch steel plate. My apparent invisibility to humans became a talent I would use the rest of my life to harvest the whining demons that plagued the naturalness of my clients, in my struggle to make life live or fight ghosts and sickness. It also occasionally saved my life in this world, too.

My amazement at this discovery made all the other exercises I'd done come to a point of relevance. I began to realize how we humans pass through each stage of creation, coming in as blind amnesiacs, then becoming mesmerized by our increased abilities and position in life until we are unable to remember where we really came from and what being alive on this earth really entails. All of my training made this vision so full that I began to remember having forgotten.

I understood then why old cultures like the Tzutujil reinvent the human being every year. You must renew the seeds all the time, feeding the Gods by initiating the people to remind them of who they really are and of the millennia of suffering and persistence behind being here as a human at this moment. Culture has to be reinvented, reinvested annually by ritually putting the tribe through the actual trials and experiences their ancestors went through. The human being as a race was remade each year and infused with the stories and particular sounds that make it all live. Essentially then, the tribe was "remembered" back to life each year. It was on the back of this constant reinvention of the human that our frail human destiny was carried into the blessing of being alive at this very moment.

It was nature, wildness, this undomesticated spirit that fled when it got enslaved, insulted, maimed, beaten, or scared off. This trespass on one's personal nature or soul is what Mayan shamans considered the prime source of illness to humans. People simply forgot that the nonritual inventions of the human mind insulted the human soul, which, like a deer, was frightened by the unnatural. And on a bigger collective level, the whole tribe, in order to avoid constant corrective healing, subjected itself to ceremonies of maintenance with the hierarchy that caused remembrance and the ritual mending of the holes we tore in the net of life while searching for our food.

The shaman was like the scout in old Westerns, the guy who had good relations with both the Indians and the cavalry. The Indians didn't trust the soldiers any more than the Gods in nature trust humans. But a shaman was a human married in with the spirits. Shamans kept the peace by being able to speak the language of both sides. These abilities with spirit language came to fruition through these exercises which forced the forgetful human mind to dance with the nature of the spirit. Nature doesn't need knowledge, because nature *is* knowledge, knowledge manifest. All knowledge among humans is taken from the investigation of that manifestation.

After a fashion, I would be able to practice being nature in my own village, being invisible to all my friends and enemies, to everyone except other shamans, who would just smile when they'd see me being unseen, and a few little kids. None of the village dogs were fooled exactly; they could see things humans couldn't, but, like dogs everywhere, having associated with humans for so long, they were unsure of what they saw and for the most part were afraid like most people would be.

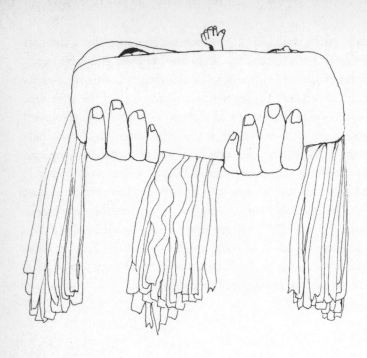

I 3

GOD OF
NORTH WIND,
BUNDLES OF DREAMS

Late one night a little boy came pushing into my firelight announcing how
he'd been sent by Yakix, Chiv's wife, to tell me, "Old man, almost dead,
come right now, he's calling for you." Jumping up, I ran over to his place
and swam through a crowd of whimpering daughters and grandkids into
the center, where Chiv lay violently trembling in his hammock, surrounded by his sons and wives.

"Old Martín is here, son," Yakix announced, then began scolding Chiv
about how he shouldn't have done this or that, or come in early, or how it
would've been better to leave such things to younger men, etc. Yakix was
an orphan herself, having no living relatives. Her only child had died in a

devastating measles epidemic years back; she was terrified that the old monkey-eyed magician was going to leave her alone with no one to look after, as all his other sons, daughters, grandchildren, and orphans had their places well worn in. Chiv was her whole life.

"*A Martín ach, kin cama anen ach.*" Chiv talked to me as a comrade instead of as an old man to a young man. "I'm going to die, brother, you know that? So many things you haven't learned. You'll never get it all, nobody has it except me."

He didn't want a cure, just to make sure his knowledge got passed properly, and now he was dying long before I'd even been able to learn anything all the way through.

So he said, "Son, go get one of those 'irons' that you talk into its belly and it speaks back what you speak into it," by which he meant a recording machine. He said he had seen one in use by an anthropologist back in the fifties, and he'd spoken a few things and heard his words again, played back.

Where was I supposed to find a tape recorder in those days in a village with hardly any electric outlets? One of Chiv's orphans said that the Catholic priest had something like that that he'd seen the priest try to use to learn to speak Tzutujil.

"Go get it, Martín, right away," Yakix said. "Maybe it will help old Father get well!" Then old Chiv started arguing with her about how he was already dead and the machine was for his words. But everybody yelled at me to get the blasted machine, so I ran with a couple of teenage grandkids of Chiv's, in our scav pants, sashes, and heavy sandals to the rectory, where an introverted middle-aged Oklahoma wheat farmer named Stanley Rother lived as the town's assigned Maryknoll Catholic priest. A theoretical enemy of all us traditionalists because of his profession, he was a friend to everyone as a man.

I burst in on him and blurted out that we needed a tape recorder, while he looked at me with a strange, quizzical terror on his pale bearded face. I realized I was talking Mayan. Even after this man's twenty years here, he still had a tough time with the language. So I switched to English, which felt funny and insectlike as it squinted and bumbled off my tongue. He dug around and got an old battery-driven, immensely heavy tape machine and a tape, and off I ran again to Chiv's deathbed.

Chiv was in and out when I arrived, but everyone was hopeful that the white man's machine might help, as machines were rumored to occasionally do in the white men's hospitals. Shaking, I finally figured out how to get the damn thing to record. When Chiv came around again, he began to yell all kinds of prayers and secret things into the machine, thinking that he had to speak up, that the very force of his speech would glue the words into the machine. When he'd gone out and returned again, we continued with a rain prayer and chunks of his life story, and just when he seemed pretty candid and alive and everyone was getting hopeful and relieved, off he went, his arms quivering and finally totally cramping and twisting into a locked knot. His eyes rolled back, his breath stopped, his heart was gone, and in ten horrible minutes he was immobile.

Yakix began beating his chest, yelling at him, and runners went out to declare his death to all his extended families. Hundreds of people came padding up to the doorway. Many men, big well-known men, showed up half-dressed, sobbing over Chiv, spilling out grief and condolences, while the women closest to Chiv began to pull their hair and beat their breasts, ripping their clothing in grief at the sight of the frozen figure of old Chiv dead at eighty-seven.

I was really down and weeping, having lost the best friend I ever had, and also because I'd been unable to learn all I needed to fulfill his old wishes to have a carrier and successor to his knowledge and ways.

After three hours of chaos and mass moaning and weeping, when all the body-binders had arrived and it was getting into dawn, Chiv's legs kicked out like a frog's and he rolled out of the hammock like a boulder and sat up wide-eyed and dazed. The first words out of his mouth were:

"Does anyone have a beer?"

And Chiv was back. The crowd went nuts. Yakix started beating him up again for having made her so sad, and she almost killed him again. I was weeping and laughing along with a thousand others, men who laughed, shaking their heads in recognition of Chiv's crazy life, walking to their cooking fires to gossip, drink some coffee, eat, and pack to wander off to work into the cloud-packed forests of the deep ravines of the surrounding volcanic mountains, where the corn grew and the hungry Gods watched. Accounts of Chiv's miraculous return from the dead went echoing up and down the deep ravines, as the Gods proceeded to disguise themselves into the trees and animals we always see when we go there.

Early every morning, all village families gather around the warm, fragrant open flames of the cooking hut's hearth. The old people warm their limbs, and the hard-working middle-aged men make ready their gear for their day's work. Women and teenage girls focus on warming clay potfuls of last afternoon's foods, reheating corn cakes or tortillas.

As smoke curls out of the dark hut into the cool of the pre-dawn air, each person begins recounting his dreams. By skillfully reading the family dreams every morning, a grandma or grandfather can help all the members of the compound navigate through the many dangers of this hard earth-oriented struggle for life. They may even be able to direct their families to some unseen opportunities.

No Tzutujil disregards his dreams. If the dreams are overly disturbing or more powerful than usual, or if they startle you awake, then shamans are approached for a ritual interpretation. To the shamans, dreams are the backbone of their way of life, influencing every decision in the most powerful fashion. Dreams are rarely taken literally, and must be read properly. Moreover, certain kinds of dreaming help Tzutujil shamans divine illness, allowing them to see inside a client's "wilderness body" into his or her spirit life, to find the true personality of their souls and thereby understand the nature of what has befallen them.

Inside the Earth Fruit level of creation, there are two simultaneous faces of reality called the Twins: the world where we dream, and the world where we work. To a shaman, a dream is not a creation of the mind, psyche, or soul. It is the remembered fragment of the experience of one's natural spirit in the twin world, the dreamworld. The twin world of dreams, like this world, never ceases living, forming as it does a parallel continuum to the waking world. It actually forms one half of the substance of our lives.

Although the landscape of dreams may seem different than the landscape of the awake world, it is actually the balanced opposite, reversed version, where our souls live out our bodies' lives reenacted as if in a complex kind of mirror. Like the two opposing wings of a butterfly, the dream-world is one wing and the awake world is the other wing. The butterfly must have both wings connected at the Heart in order to fly and function.

Neither wing—dreams or waking—contains all of life. Real life occurs as a result of the interaction of the two. The life is the butterfly's heart, and both dreaming and awake working life are necessary to keep the heart alive. Our lives, like the butterfly's heart, are kept aloft by two opposing, mirroring, twinlike wings. This heart is the third thing, the *Rukux* heart that all ritual seeks to feed and keep alive.

As novices, we shamans were taught to read messages from the spirits in how candles burn down, how birds sing, in animal tracks, in weather formations, in the twitching of our muscles, in goosebumps, in the sounds of crackling fires, in the forms of hot embers, in the daylight reflections in a bowl of water, the positions of tossed knuckle bones, the actions of dogs, the flight of meteorites, our own premonitions and gut feelings. But above and beyond all of these, we learned to listen and read dreams.

A shaman's bundle is essentially a bundle of dreams. One could inherit a bundle from one's teacher or a grandfather or grandmother. Very little inheriting of any kind comes from our parents. But all shamans' bundles start out as a dream bundle. Some bundles are bulky and large, and others are tiny and neat. Dreams are a direct, incorruptible expression of the mysterious nature of life and are considered to be free of human con-nivance. Because of this, people trusted dreams more than they trusted people.

The term for reading a dream was *n Tzikij*, the same word used for calling animals and weather. Dreams call upon life to move and live. Dreams read life back to us like a storyteller, reading life just as shamans read people's dreams! Some shamans' main aptitude is their quality of be-ing able to read life, to listen and interpret all that went on, especially in dreams.

Shamans want to be able to keep alive or recontact a powerful dream moment, because in these special dreams come prayers and songs from the very power who called him or her at birth to serve them as a shaman. It's very important, then, that these special dreams be remembered, and be ritually fed to keep the songs and prayers alive and strong.

Typically a shaman would find an object, previously unknown to him, exactly like one seen in a dream. Maybe a song or prayer would come back to him from a forgotten dream upon cradling this object in his hands. These objects are said to speak, because it is through them that shamans retain the special mysterious language of their power in the dreams. Such found objects become the throne or client for one's spirit. One's power would then have an actual physical place to sit, as the Tzutujil say. Spirits are given a home, just like us, the people. The spirits must have a home, or they become sad orphans or renegades. A person whose spirit has no home becomes depressed or a criminal.

The song or prayer has to be retained and formed from the dream, usually under the guidance of a teacher who knows how. Shamans are not interested in the meanings in these kinds of dreams and therefore do not want to preserve the meanings. They are after the heart or power of the dream. The song or prayer can then be used to call power into that holy object. When the power was in the stone, wood, glass, or clay, the shaman could quite tangibly feed the power by giving it liquor, copal, flowers, cigars, food, delicious words, and music. Invariably one's power had to be danced with, too. All of Chiv's did. Mine certainly do. Even the details and procedures of these offerings are determined from dreams.

Once a shaman has his or her spirit throne, then he or she could talk to the spirit, asking questions after feeding the spirit on its Dream Throne. The replies would occur in a dream. This back-and-forth dialogue between shamans and their power, from dreams, is a prerequisite and signifies the spirit's endorsement of a shaman's desirability. The people then recognize the shaman's power as a real possibility.

These Dream Thrones are usually kept in sacks or bundles on a shaman's altar, the construction of which came from his power's instruction in the dreams. Certain taboos and rules have to be observed in regard to these bundles. The main one is, of course, that no one but the shaman is allowed to touch them, address them, or speak of them. If insulted, these objects can make life miserable and bizarre for an entire compound.

Another rule common to all bundles is that a married couple or family is never to sleep in the same hut as these Holy Thrones. This is because the spirit bundle considers itself the first wife or spouse of the shaman. The shaman is essentially married to his powers. Because of this, shamans have to build special huts for the objects themselves. If a male shaman has his bundle residing in the house with his wife, his bundle will get so fiercely jealous of the human wife that it will use its power to drive her out of his life. The married couple will begin to argue about idiotic, trivial things until one of them gives up and moves out.

Like any man or woman with multiple spouses, each spouse has to have his or her own territory. So your bundle has to have its own little compound. The spirits are given little houses, shrine houses, sometimes trees or holes in rocks, where they live, depending on their preferences which were explained to their keepers in dreams. This way the flesh-and-blood wife could live at peace in her own house, each wife having her own domain. Likewise the shaman then provides for each spirit wife according to their own needs.

When a shaman got old, he or she might transfer one of these bundles to a new shaman, and the recipient would add his own dreams to the old bundle. But the new bundle holder would have to maintain the original feeding specifications and ritual taboos associated with the original bundle, on top of those belonging to the new shaman. When one of these old bundles had been passed for several centuries, then a lot of varied ritual had been formulated. Many privately maintained sacred houses grew up around a ritual reverence regarding these old bundles, which seemed to house the power of the old deceased shamans.

But a new shaman always has to find his own first spouse objects. Sometimes a shaman ends up with so many dream-given prayers and corresponding objects that he develops pet names for all his *qijibal*, as they are called. These names become abbreviations for long prayers and songs, and these shamans pray with long roll calls of cryptic abbreviations instead of long, interminable fluid dream prayers. In these cases, invariably the shaman affectionately calls his immense retinue of bundle items his herd, his little creatures, or his dogs, and so on.

Because shamans can read dreams and the nature around them, they are considered diviners too.

Though most shamans were diviners, not all diviners became shamans. Calendar diviners were diagnosticians, more like a priesthood, and they used prescribed liturgies and learned procedures to find out what kind of ceremony a person needed. Then a client could decide if they would find a hierarchal prayer maker to help them, or use an actual shaman.

Shamans always divined, some of them, like myself, with the old Tzu-tujil version of the Mayan calendar, with the little beans. But usually shamans combined three or four types of divination to give a fuller inter-pretative divination, which informed the shaman more than the client as to which approach he should take toward healing his patient. Experienced shamans didn't much use their own power to cure people but used their power to gain favor with the Big Gods who helped them with their clients. That's why Tzutujil people, when translating the word for shaman into Spanish for non-Mayans, call them *abogados*, advocates, spirit lawyers. We learned the language of the court, knew the channels, and had connections.

I didn't have my bundle objects yet, and so I eagerly awaited the dreams, figuring that when they did come, for me as with the bulk of Ati-tlán's shamans, the sacred object I would find would be the typical one-and-a-half-inch pre-Hispanic pottery head so commonly seen lying about in the village's tired old dust.

Finally one morning before sunup, I was jolted awake, shaking and sweating, having dreamt a powerful thing.

The little stone beings, about four inches high, with fat, crooked faces, were dancing. Some were of jade, and beautifully carved. A liquor brewed from clouds was being passed in a cup made of a curved whale's tooth. Each being drank in turn as he was presented with the liquid, just as we humans did in a ceremony.

With whoops and cries of delight, the little stones danced up to me, saying, "Axuan xin peta arja camic." "The Lord of Wind is coming to see you. We are his swallows that fly down in front of his storm." And they went back to dancing their own ceremonial song.

Soon a big God about twelve feet tall burst through the stone wall, accompa-nied by a lot of birds and wild animals.

His left hand was stretched fingers out, palm up, and his voice was pure windy thunder when he rumbled out the words: "Nix natí bá alá?" "Will you drink a little of this with me, child?" And out of his gourd, he poured me a tiny glass of liquor made from melted whirlwind hail.

Saying the right words, I tried to down the liquid, but it was filled with elec-tricity like painful lightning and a sourness beyond my capacities. He laughed and drank it for me, then another and another. By the third round, I could drink with him, but only with difficulty.

"I am going to stand with you. If you don't make my throne by dawn, I'll kill you."

Then, bellowing like Chiv, but louder, the Thunder God cracked through the wall like lightning, his stone swallows rushing away in front of him.

I woke with a start. It was still dark. I fumbled for some matches in a clay jar, and barely missed getting stung by a scorpion scuttling about on the jug, unable to escape.

After lighting seven candles, as Chiv had shown me, in a bird design like a T for the winds, I began gathering pieces of stone, wood, and stumps, carving and fitting together an altar befitting the Heart of Wind, Axuan, as directed in the dream. By the glow of early dawn, I was barely finished. I laid down a fine reed mat I'd mysteriously purchased the day before from an itinerant merchant from San Juan.

Normally a dream like that, if ratified by others having the same, would signify the imminent decision by the hierarchy to station the public bundles and effigies of the Wind and San Juan in one's care. This, however honorable, was totally unlikely in my still uninitiated state, and a terrifying prospect, considering the amount of responsibility.

What was the meaning of this? How would the wind come to sit on this throne? Chiv seemed secretive and pleased when he saw what I was up to. Almost every day I followed him as he made the rounds to four different Sacred Houses for his clients. The various Sacred Houses' procedures were very different from each other, since each housed a distinct group or Deity whose personality and power had its own procedures.

Chiv and I, with his clients in tow, would arrive, do our gesticulating, our shaman door prayers, kneel, kiss, and breathe on the Earth and above if needed, and address the Deities only after hailing the Keepers with the famous hierarchical salutations, *"Ex kola tidta, nutie."*

Only after a brazier of coals had been set inside for us did we enter. Once inside, we and our clothing, hats, called crowns or headdresses, were incensed with the ever-present copal smoke. Saluting the powers within, the saints, Gods, and bundles, we were seated. We let the old people talk in the formal, courteous etiquette that even enemies succumbed to in such formal situations. In due time, when our purpose had finally been announced, we distributed a little of our clients' liquor, which the Keeper chiefs would always pretend to refuse but were forced eventually to accept. This was all part of the ritual, repeated at all four places, every day.

Once our needs were explained and the Keeper and his wife were satisfied with our demands, they went to bring out the relics or bundles, depending on what we were doing. At this point, Chiv would make the ritual with me. During three years of this type of wonderful ceremonialism, I learned all of these procedures. The complexity of it rivaled the complexity of the world itself, and indeed all of these Sacred Houses stood for the powers contained out in the Earth Fruit. The houses were like sacred engines that were fueled by public ceremony, and by the private shamanic ones too, and the power that was fed flowered as a result, its Keeper always suffering to keep these special objects and places safe. The Sacred Houses were known as edges, mouths, hearts, temples, or umbilicals, and though they contained safeguards, they were also vulnerable—not safe without Keepers.

That morning after I'd dreamt of Axuan, I ended up in a ceremony with Chiv in the Sacred House where Holy Boy was kept. A wonderful fourteen-year-old boy named Aclax came running to speak to me. He gave the whispered message to the married daughter of one of Holy Boy's guard, who brought it to the chief seated with his *xuo*, woman chief, while they watched Chiv and me dance old Holy Boy during a ceremony to bless a Quiche woman and her son who'd gone crazy.

At an appropriate break, I placed my sacred headcloth around my neck and sauntered to where Aclax was respectfully standing, arms crossed. He told me that a man unknown to anyone in the village had come looking for me, Martín. He had a huge object weighing some two hundred pounds, wrapped in a reed mat, which had been placed on my new altar without asking. Aclax knew about my dream, and wondered if that wasn't sacrilege to the altar. To make things more interesting, the mysterious man had brought about two hundred fresh coconuts still on the vines and a hundred plantains just getting ripe. He really wanted to talk to me. I told Aclax that Chiv and I would be there as soon as we could finish here, and asked him to give my visitor some good things to drink and eat until we arrived.

By the time we arrived at my hut, the man had disappeared. We were told he was dark, with a black, wispy beard, and that he drove a blocky-looking car which, from what I could gather, was a beat-up English Land

Rover. I looked at the tire tracks in the volcanic sand and saw that the tires matched his tire-treaded sandals. But he was gone. No one knew his name, as he had refused to give that to anyone but me; no one knew where he was from, just that he'd come from the faraway coast to bring me this responsibility and gift.

Chiv gave his famous cry and went to gather coals and incense, putting up smoke, kicking me into action, clearing away coconuts and plantains to make space for an offering in front of the mat-shrouded object.

Pulling away the mat with fifty villagers looking on, Chiv revealed an extremely old stone carving of an indigenous warrior's head, four times life size, with his hands by his ears. This was being born out of a big serpent face whose nostrils spouted curls of steam, and upon whose head was carved the symbol of the *pop*, reed mat signifying king. The serpent was horned, and the warrior had teeth carved like a T. The T-shaped tooth of the wind.

Chiv and I knelt and prayed hard, recognizing that this was indeed an ancient throne of Axuan the Wind who, as promised, had mysteriously arrived from the ocean bringing coastal gifts. Chiv explained a lot to me then. I could feel the thrill, fear, befuddlement, and rightness of it all seeping into my bloodstream. Now I could truly begin my dialog with my own spirits.

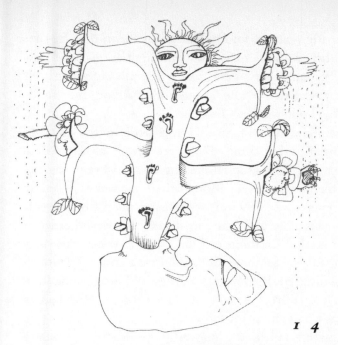

RABBIT FLUFF RAIN, DOG HAIR RAIN, ONE FOOT RAIN:

Chiv Sends Me to Hunt for Words

Rain.

Rain is to the Tzutujil like snow is to Inuit people. There are numerous words for types of rains, with or without different winds, falling at different times of year. Rain is so holy that all the Gods, regardless of their power or what they did, were generically addressed in the Respect Names Clouds and Mist, or Light Rain and Fog. These terms were synonymous with Your Royal Highness, or Your Majesty.

There was One Foot Rain, Rabbit Fluff Rain, Dog Hair Rain, The Breath of Mountains Rain, Northwind Urine Rain: all Gods of differing deified weather.

Rain was traditionally secured for the village in the spring by ceremonies held in association with the male and female initiations of adolescents into marriageable status. Raining was a male activity, but water itself was female. All water was owned by the Grandmother Moon, the grandmother of all life, whose body was the Ocean.

There were also rain priests and Sacred Houses dedicated to rain, but even then sometimes rain didn't come. There are people alive who remember widespread famine from crop failure due to lack of rain. During those difficult times, the people of Our Mother the Lake were blessed by the tule reeds and cattails whose tuberous roots saved them from certain starvation. These reeds are holy, and figure in all ceremonies and prayers. Their Respect Name is The Clothing of Our Mother. When the rains were late, the village made special rain-calling pilgrimages into the mountain shrines, led by the different Rain priests. In these old shrines, the Rain warriors were fed. These were the sons of *Rilaj Vinaq*, whose battles against dryness gave us water and plant growth.

If after three tries this failed, the hierarchy would begin sending gifts and courting certain shamans with a reputation for having a good relationship with the various God families of the Mountain Kingdoms and *Rilaj Vinaq*. This was one of the few circumstances in which certain shamans might work on behalf of the whole village. Nicolas Chiviliu was one of five shamans on the lake whose abilities had brought moisture in years past. Actually, Chiv was legendary for making rain, and Indians came as far as Mexico, from the Coast of Turtles, to get him to make rain.

Chiv had never taught anybody how he did it, including myself. But whatever reasons the Gods had for withholding the rains, old Chiv always found a way to get them to release water to the Umbilicus of the Earth, Santiago Atitlán. One day during the dry season, some time before the corn planting of "Its name comes out," Chiv sent for me, and nonchalantly announced that Holy Boy and the *Nawales* had said it was about time I learned how to make rain.

I'd been waiting a long time for this. After feasting on two chickens each, we smoked, and Chiv said, "I'll give you the last part of the prayer when you bring me the first part."

"How can I bring you something only you know, that you won't tell me?"

Chiv grinned like a weasel with a chicken's leg still in his teeth, delighted by my quandary:

"If I don't do anything else, I've got to teach you how to teach yourself, to learn how to learn without being given everything already learned, already digested.

"If God gives us life and we continue as we have, someday when I'm a pile of ashes and the smell of my smoke in your memory is all you have left of these days, then you will see situations and sickness never seen before. I've no idea what they may be; I have no way of recognizing them with our very old ways and traditional root. But you're the new one who's going to have to find special medicines to deal with them, instead of just using the old things because they're old. You must find new ways to do old things, and new medicines with old roots to cure the bad times made by new things. Does that stay lit in your head?"

Sounded beautiful. But I had no idea where I should look to find the first part of that prayer!

"You go tonight, and don't come back to see me until you've got the first part, *utz!*" And we smoked and joked some, and away I went, kind of sad since I had no way of meeting this challenge.

Ever since I was a boy, I've always gone out into the bush to look for answers. Understanding always came to me on the wild breath of the open land. Chiv taught me the same, and all the stories of the old Mayan spirit heroes, prophets, and so forth showed that all of them either lived in the wilds, coming to the village to visit, or they went to the wilds, to the Gods, to find solutions or venues for their people to survive the ravages of life and the pressure of external politics.

Meandering through the mountains, I went from shrine to shrine of the potbellied Gods, to the stone crosses, to the piles of stones on the ridges, to the tree shrines, until I got the idea to go down to the old canyon where the two ladies who had bought my paintings lived, to visit that new house on the cliffs above Chicacao. Powerful fog and mist beings reportedly had their homes in there in the thick tangled verdure, and they turned into birds: toucans, chachas, quetzales, trogons, mot mots, and cotingas. I thought I would sit and call the warrior sons, the mountain's initiate sons who brought the rains out of their deep canyons and ridges, whose fruit mothers watched in the trees for their welfare, suckling them on the breast like fruits of the wild foggy thicket.

I would call them with my heart as I'd been taught. Maybe I *could* find the words for Chiv's rain prayer. How had he gotten them in the first place? Maybe I'd fail. But at least now I would visit those ladies, two and a half years later, upon whose cash I still subsisted and whose generosity made my life as Chiv's acolyte possible.

When I arrived there walking, my string bag on my back, I thought I'd lost my way. There was no road at all, only a trail. When I reached the place where I could have sworn the house had been, a light-colored stone cliff stood, full of pale streaks and clouds of bats and swallows, going in and out of vertical cracks high up in the cliff. Instead of a road to the bottom of the canyon there was a tree-hemmed, narrow muddy path that forded a slow-moving creek where bare-breasted coastal Tzutujil women the color of tapirs moved along with their tumplines over their heads strained against their loads. They were surprised to hear me salute them in their native tongue as they rounded the trail past me and disappeared into the foggy forest.

Camping beneath the cliff that night, I dreamt that a big, beautiful wild mother turkey had two broods of baby chicks following her to the edge of the village. One group was all bright vermillion and fuzzy, and the other group was all bright yellow. With at least a hundred chicks in each group, they stayed miraculously separate, the red ones on the mother's right and the yellow ones to her left.

The old mother turkey was clumsy, and kept stepping on her babies, killing a couple here and a couple there. This disturbed me no end as I watched her close by, so I stepped in to help the babies survive but found myself killing many more chicks than she was, caught in the same predicament. When I lifted one foot up, the ground beneath it would fill with chicks, and more would be killed when I set my foot down again.

I was horrified, but I heard a strange and eerie chuckle, then an outright cascading cackle to my back, and when I turned to look, immobilized by my predicament, I saw Holy Boy, very small, wearing a hat and smoking, his legs bent over a stony ledge. Looking down on me, he was delighted with the absurdity of my so-called assistance to these chicks.

Blowing a cloud of smoke my way, he released me. Holy Boy had grown big and was wearing the same blue suit I'd use years later to disguise myself as I escaped the country in front of a price on my head.

He beckoned to me to get into a vehicle that looked like a kind of metallic grasshopper. When I entered, he drove the machine into the mountain, straight in. When we got out a couple of lonely, weeping women began to pester him about his face.

They fed me and gave me hail-water liquor and were extremely gracious, these two beautiful women. Though they were not Indians, one was dressed like an ancient Tzutujil matron, and the other in some other indigenous people's dress. Holy Boy said he had hundreds of wives, but these two he listened to. He then took me through the volcano to a land of people who sat in rows waiting for him to speak, like a TV show audience.

When he spoke, his face changed from wood to silver, then to jade, and then to gold, and he spoke in wind and thunder words that terrified the people, who all ran away. I remember his words very well to this day. Then he kicked me, and I woke up staring at the jungle lit by an intense flash of lightning in a pre-dawn drizzle in the dark.

Chiv was waiting for me when I returned to the village, smoking his old eye-glowing, bone antler deer pipe, my favorite.

He said, "I heard you got it. You did it!" And he elbowed me, more jolly than I and not at all perplexed. He was proud of me for something of which I had not an inkling.

I told him about my adventure down in that distant canyon where, a couple of years before, I'd sat eating breakfast in a modern house with picture windows and been given a lot of money by two pretty women. Where that house had been there was now only stone, jungle, ridges, canyons, river, fog, and birds.

Chiv roared his trumpeting laugh, his whole body a big tickle place intensely amused by the serious hound-dog–like perplexity on my face. "Forgive me, but the way you make your face makes my belly shake with a thousand snakes jumping inside. There you are with your hairs on fire, but you keep your face like a sad stone!"

"*Haya, hahi,*" he laughed, his whole body to the wall to regain composure. This didn't work, however, and with his face to the wall, he kept poking at me, laughing hysterically, until I started to go into fits of uncontrolled ebullient laughter. We both laughed till we cried ourselves dry, our souls well-washed in that freedom of release. It was always like that with him: Eat, cry, laugh, work, sleep, dream, being wild, brave, and friendly.

Then we got down to work, Chiv explaining, and I, Martín, remembering.

I began: "I saw a mother bird and at her feet roamed yellow and red chicks."

"Stop," he muttered, gently tapping my arm as smoke from his pipe inundated the murky room. "Now listen to me as I translate." He began smelting the prayer out of the ore of my dream with the heat of his experience and wisdom:

> At the feet
> At the hands [wings]
> The great nester, food bringer
> Mother of red life jumping clouds, yellow abundance clouds
> We your nestlings falling
> We your nestlings crushed
> Thunder in my chest
> Shimmering back
> Heads of yellow dawn,
> Heads of red dawn,
> At her feet
> The ones with heads of yellow clouds
> The ones with heads of red clouds
> At her wings
> Red-jumping life ones
> And yellow-abundance life ones
> The sons, the daughters
> Spent one by one at your feet
> The sons, the daughters
> Spent one by one as it dances,

and so on.

And on and one we went all through the night, sleeping and returning, forging a prayer out of the dream to meet a traditionalist format. The prayers were in all the dreams I'd dreamt since first seeing Chiv, and he simply showed me how to pull prayers from them. The miracle was that the prayers were traditional prayers exactly laid in the images of my dreams. When spoken properly with the right magical rhythm, physical offering, and incense, the power of my dream jumped into the words and things began to happen. There were other procedures, of course, needed to make the rain, but this wasn't important now.

Without the dream, words were orphans, parentless, uninitiated words with no direction, unpowered and scared, so that when used they actually took away power instead of instilling, calling, and inspiring the power. So simply learning a shamanic prayer without the spirit's endorsement in a dream was dangerous and futile. Chiv sat for days helping me memorize what I'd already dreamt, and then, as promised, he brought out the rest I had *not* dreamt, helping me put it all together as one.

This was the beginning of my shamanic initiation. I had to go out of earshot of any humans at the Rain God shrines and practice my oratory for rain and prayers, day after day. I chose a shrine, one up by Xecasiis, Under the Cedar, because I'd dreamt of little potbellied gods who brought me the wind and they were all living here, with the ropes of their servant status twisted around their necks.

Praying well as a shaman meant one had to learn to speak in a measured rhythm, beautifully, dramatically, with no pauses, and to breathe in such a way that one never lost the prayer or image being shot like bright-colored birds out of the heart. It was not enough just to say the words, since each had triple, double, or quadruple meanings. At any given time, you might be saying two to five polyvalent prayers simultaneously and they all had to make sense and beguile the Deities, while remaining within the traditional Tzutujil boundaries of form.

One began, of course, by learning a traditional prayer by heart, only after receiving the first part from a dream. But one had to practice and practice, until one could push sound into the rhythm instinctually with no hems or haws.

The prayers were accompanied by postures, gestures, and natural motions which had different meanings in themselves, effects which, when combined with the words, took on a new form of their own that devastated the boundary between here and there and echoed freely to the Gods and back. While one spoke, images had to be coming also in one's heart as they rode the prayer like a horse to the other world, pushed by shamanic gestures and ritual movements. At the same time, a supplication might be made mentally.

The prayer was the horse, the direction was the motion, and what you were asking for was in the mind. The heart carried all the images that corresponded to those contained in the prayer, like an armload of verbal flowers for the Gods. The Gods drink at the heart like a deer in a river.

This wasn't possible for all people to do; that's why shamans are a special breed. And even having the talent and the good graces of the Gods isn't enough; that talent had to be developed, and that took a lot of practice in the mountains. In the mountains, a novice shaman would begin a ritual by calling all the Spirit Dogs of the Deities into their shrines, where he had left offerings and explained his intentions and his predicament.

Then the novice proceeded to practice and fail. It was like being a beginner chef trying to get complicated recipes just right. When the recipes fail, the food is usually thrown out. With us novice shamans, it was the same, only we were working up to feeding Deities, and when we threw something out, there were always the Deities' Dogs to eat our failed recipes. There are also Gods who are satisfied with our failures as gifts; they eat and get fat like old dogs, and hang around for more, perfectly happy with our idiotic discourse.

After a long year or so, I was getting better at this. Chiv began letting me handle some parts of his ritual for him, and then more and more, until I could handle all the perfunctory blessings. By doing all the exercises that Chiv gave me, I was able to slowly learn how to learn, getting well-seated on my own word horses, finely tuned. When a shaman got good at it many years later, he could artistically combine images to alchemically create his own shape and style of beguiling and feeding the Gods. This was the task of recognizing, smelting, and receiving honorably the gifts of one's own prayers.

This was the real trick, what made one a shaman instead of a priest. When you got this right, you could soar. At this point, I couldn't, but I would. For now, I admired Chiv soaring through the atmosphere like a meteor.

Prayer-making couldn't be done frivolously or casually. It demanded great sacrifices, in order to ensure that the process wouldn't backfire in your face, killing you or you and your clients and family. We shamans have hundreds of prayers, each acquired in a long, strained, courteous fashion. They are as precious as a corral full of beautiful horses.

Anything newly created and as powerful as a prayer grown from a dream can leave a vacancy in the ribs of tradition. Death and tradition are very close relatives, and neither of these likes change. A shaman must fill that vacancy with gifts equivalent to the loss they felt by your creativity. Tradition wants to contain your creativity, and Death wants to eat it. The graveness of what was bestowed upon you was paid for heavily in sacrificial gifts guarded diligently thereafter. This keeps a prayer from losing its integrity and spiritual worth, and most of all maintains its friendliness to you.

A DRINK FROM
THE GODDESS'S BELLY:
My Shamanic Initiation

Everyone called me Matzejtel, or Fire Flower. Fire Flower was the name of the tree that Holy Boy was made of, and whose seeds shamans used in divination. The name Martín could have been the given first name of two hundred men in Santiago, but there was only one Matzejtel, me.

When a new shaman was made, it was done similarly to how the shamans remade Holy Boy, every year. In the beginning, twelve Rain Gods and their wives, Twelve Goddesses, had tried four times to make a named being, a human, but each time the human became self-involved, auto-cratic, and destructive to the environment he was posted to nourish and adorn. Each time the Gods failed, they devastated that creation, that section of time, turning their creations into stone, wind, wood, and water, adding each of these layers onto the next attempt, until the possibility of their fifth creation came into sight. The fifth creation was us, humans, represented by Holy Boy.

When my time came, I had wanted to be ready. When Chiv came for me, I tried to be ready, but I don't think I felt ready. I was as ready as I would get, though, and so we went to where we had to, to commence my shamanic rite of passage, my initiation. When initiated into manhood, you were with all your friends, most of your age set, the young captains and the chiefs. The whole village remembered you every day while they went about ritual preparations on your behalf. But shamanic initiation was between you and the Gods: between your spirit and the full deadly force of the Gods.

My initiation began by my getting an inevitable harangue in Chiv's old sacred house, under his old stuffed fish in front of all the myriad old Gods, the bundle contents showing again, which I'd not seen for three years since that first day he'd dragged me in here.

Along with Chiv's wife, two powerful traditionalist friends of his were there: MaCoy, an old fertility shaman who'd saved Chiv's life a couple of times when he'd stayed in the other world too long, and Ma Recanda Co, the famous shaman and musician. These three would stay here in the Umbilicus House to call Chiv and me back home. Ma Recanda Co would make the song of the Road in the strong, proud, and emotional way he always did. It was on this Road of Song that I should be able to find my way home from the otherworld place I was going. Like a mysterious beacon of sound, I could follow it back into this world.

Chiv had Ya Chep play the slit drum and guard the entrances to the house. We danced and presented ourselves ritually to every Deity Chiv maintained. Afterward he had me reiterate my personal magical prayers. Then I invoked all the Deities with the ancient prescribed words and gestures Chiv had so patiently taught me.

Chiv laid down protective ash and sprayed water boundaries, bathing me in rainbows and copal, and proclaimed our reason for calling to the Deities. Chiv talked to many Deities, with code names for Deities, and animals I'd never heard him speak of or to before. We smoked noticeably hard, and said a ritual good-bye to Chiv's two old friends, and we headed down the hill to the Sacred Houses.

Chiv had the hierarchical chiefs (*Ajauá*) and woman chiefs (*Xuojá*) in each of thirteen Sacred Houses receive us. I could only carry enough offerings for one House of Gods at a time, and so we had to refill my string bag after we finished at each one.

With arms outstretched and our heads gently cocked to the side, cloistered behind guarded and blanketed doorways, we were immersed in more than forty-eight bundles, ritually dancing them, holding them, being strapped under them. I was even placed under the woman bundles used exclusively by pregnant women, in the sacred posture of a birthing mother. What I saw in those opened bundles is impossible to tell, both because I was sworn to never divulge anything about them, and because the power and beauty of what they meant could only be understood after having gone the whole route of three years of patient training. Chiv had nudged me along like a mother deer with a newborn fawn, until I could hold the vision, and properly envision the bundle I held.

The Fire Flower liquor I'd been drinking had let me be many things by now. It must have been four days since we'd left home: the umbilicus beneath the stuffed fish in Chiv's house where two old men and Chiv's wife sat praying, keeping the smoker boiling with gift smoke for our success, and staring at the center of life, keeping the fires burning, the fires, called *Qáq al*, my firesoul. They would sit and and take turns watching, paying attention to our progress as I slipped deeper and deeper into the village's concentric spirit matrix, away into the Sacred Houses, hungrier and more inebriated. I was beginning to get rewired and to understand *nimlaj Achinag'* (Big Things) in my very bones, to become an instrument played by the Gods, whose very songs became my soul. My soul could easily wander off like a song into the mist, and possibly never return this time as it had years ago, when I was lost in the jungle. For this reason, the old men and woman kept up their holy repetitious sounds and songs to keep me homed in and to get me past all the challenges. Meanwhile,

I got to hold and see and kiss the Heart of Food and Water.

I got to hold and caress the Heart of the thirteen Holy Placentas.

I got to hold and dance the Heart of all the Wild Animals and their Keepers.

I got to hold and dance the Heart of Under the Water.

I got to hold and dance the Heart of Wind.

I got to hold and dance the bundles of Glass Blades and Thread Traps.

I got to hold and see and dance, and bless and understand and feed and be present as a son, a grandson, a father, a grandfather, a brother, uncle, keeper, and friend to many holy powers whose faces came to hold me. All the chiefs and woman chiefs had me bless them as I filled up with the accumulating fire of what I'd held in each of the thirteen houses, in all the secret bundles, saints, and images reeking with power and knowing.

I vomited outside the last house early on the fifth morning. I don't remember seeing Chiv, but he must have been there; instead a Tzutujil woman asked me to go up to the cave shrine close by *Choqóx Aqóum*, Medicine Mushroom, where Holy Boy was born to the twelve Rain Gods and Growth Goddesses.

I followed her up a tortuous incline past two camuc *or terraced slopes where, in the day's purple dawn, I turned to see if Chiv was keeping up with us, but saw three different people huffing and puffing behind us. As the sun got closer to dawn and we got closer to the Fire Flower tree shrine, I noticed that the three people, two men and a woman, were chattering and not keeping up well, and that they were white people for the most part, maybe tourists. How did they get here? This woman I followed was large for a Mayan, but was the most beautiful lady I've ever known, whom I've seen since many times. She was wearing old-time Tzutujil women's clothing but her* pot *(blouse) was solid purple, with dark purple stripes. A stripe of white was on her forelock in an otherwise long, shiny black head of hair.*

She told me to help these slow tourists up the hill, and she would meet me at the hut by the shrine, where we could all rest for the night. This all seemed fine to me, as I really wanted to help her and would have done anything for her. I didn't recollect a hut being way up there, but a rest sounded wonderful.

It took me all day to herd those chattering tourists up the hill, and keep them from falling into the ravine. The land was so old and beautiful—no airplanes, or signs of farms, just pure ancient land. At one point, the chubby white woman wanted to climb down a side trail to the left, claiming she was too tired, and the men were all too willing to agree, but I prodded and goaded them up the side of the volcano, fielding in a dutiful kind of way all their bitter complaints, until in the welcome evening, in the shade of a guanacaste tree, we finally reached the beautiful little thatched hut, just like the skunk-haired woman had promised.

"At kola nutie," I chimed, but there was no answer, and after investigating and finding the hut empty, I stationed the tourists in the northwest corner, where they promptly went to sleep. I slept with my hat on, machete and string bag by my side, awakening with a start at the sound of a crying whimper. Looking out at the pile of sleeping tourists, I noticed the lady and one of the men were missing.

In the pre-dawn purple, I heard the whimpering again and saw that there was another chamber inside the hut. I thought this very strange, as Mayan huts never have more than one room. I rose to investigate, figuring it had to be the tourist woman again. When I looked, I saw the man quietly sleeping on the floor and realized that he was me! He had my face. He had my hands. At first I thought it was my dad when he was young, but it was me.

I looked at my own hands, and they were dark and chocolate-smooth, holding my bone-handled machete. I couldn't find my feet. Each time I looked, they moved farther away, and I couldn't get a proper sight of them. The guy on the ground looked pretty immobile. I followed the whimpering, really scared, until I saw it came from the skunk-haired woman who was lying flat on her back in the dawn, her knees up and flexed, her huipil pulled up so I could see her beautiful breasts and sort of tired stomach, from many births.

I didn't know what to do, but she said, "Drink from my belly, son. Drink from my belly, Hummingbird." I couldn't speak well, so I approached her belly and as I did so, her belly button grew, filling with pure sky-blue water. When I drew back, it shrank to its normal size. "Drink!" she said, grabbing me by the hair and pushing me down toward her belly. It grew to a huge lake, our lake, and she cooed, "Drink from my belly, man," and I did.

The taste was something words can't tell, the taste of which is still in my mouth to this day. It's because of that taste that I live and continue to want to. The taste was beyond delicious—it was deep, clear, rich, and made me feel really strong again, and so I could speak well. She told me to go search for my Father's face in his house. I looked out the doorway and I could see far, far away, very detailed, every mouse, root, bug, cloud, raindrop, and every culture that had ever struggled to live in this Jade Leafed Flowering Mountain Earth, and I realized I was standing on the side of the woman's body, her belly the crater of the volcano filled with water. The flowery mountain umbilicus—this was it. I turned to ask the woman how to find my father's house, but her face was buried in mist and fog, and her breasts had turned to giant mounds of yellow flowers teeming with parrots and rare birds.

I drank as much as I could, then tried to climb down her belly volcano, so happy and full of her belly juice, but she was very steep. I came to the trail which the lady had tried to go down the day before, and the tourists' tracks were there. They'd come this way against the will of the Mother Mountain. Crawling down the trail, I came to a bunch of non-Tzutujil Mayan men in white, like Zunil men, weeping bitterly about how the land was to be destroyed on the other side of a little tiny creek in front of us.

Hordes of Indian women and millions of animals were fleeing from the other side, crossing to safety on our side, in desperate droves, killing some in the process, like wildebeests. I walked upstream to hunt for a better look, and there I saw them coming. A horde of Gods on horses with black velvet shirts and long hair, riding and thundering, making a world-wide loop through the land. One God had hair of white mist and swung a huge zigzagged blade in circles; all of them rode on colored horses at breakneck speed. Every time this man swung his sword, a subsonic thud was heard, and every plant and animal was instantly turned to ash in the intense lightninglike power of the weapon. All the land they touched turned to solid ash everywhere they went.

On my side of the stream things remained the same, the greenery, the trees, and so on, the water apparently protecting us. As the Gods came, I thought to hide, but then I thought, Why, what's the use to hide from such destruction? When the horde passed my dumbfounded eyes, the swordsman turned around and looked at me over his shoulder with two of his friends. He had the face of a skull, but he winked and smiled and nodded his head as Tzutujil friends do in foreign company. His friends were men I'd wanted to grow up to become, Indians of the old style with strong hearts and a noble sense of humor and duty. They nodded to me, which meant, "Just wait." They left fast, covering the whole world. The land was flattened of all life, just smoking ash. But a couple of spaces of time later, they returned with whips made of jaguar tails and lightning guns, and in a long traveling line of thousands of mounted Gods, they raised up the earth again, snapping their whips and shooting their thunder cannons. Greenery and trees, grasses and vines rose instantly behind them as they crossed over the land like a surging wave of instantly standing thicket.

They turned again, and this time the skull-faced one was young. He looked back at me and smiled, kind of melancholy, but went back to work, all the beautiful Horse Gods screaming, "Kit yik taja, ket kas taja," two phrases used by shamans to raise people back to life, ordering life to "stand" and to "jump back to life."

I returned to the crossing. Men were trying to cross back over the creek again, but kept falling in and disappearing. They wanted to exploit the Live Earth that had come alive on the other side again. They couldn't do it, because they kept dying, not knowing how to cross. They were drowning in that tiny stream, vanishing from sight until a great weeping was again heard, but this time on the other side of the stream. I watched myriads of men try to cross and fall off the little boulders into the driving water. Then like a flash a small light-colored rabbit sped successfully across the water in a zigzag pattern by touching a foot on each of four boulders in a specific pattern. He zoomed across unnoticed by the crowds who had given up trying and were returning up the mountainside.

Using the rabbit's method, I crossed the stream easily. Running, I pursued the clever little rodent for a long ways until he wriggled underneath a thick, impenetrable set of thorn-studded vines, and I was forced to go around. There were no roads or pathways here, as no human had yet to inhabit this new land. Scratched and bleeding, with my clothes in shreds, sweating hard, I was ready to give up on finding the Sun's House, my Father's House, when I heard the weeping again and I went toward it. A great egret, an animal of the Sun, rose flapping out of the thicket and flew toward what I thought must be the way. Looking up, I ran as best I could, trying to follow the beautiful weeping egret, but she was too fast for me, and I had to stop, lost, full of dirt and blood, bitten and cut, my lungs full of fire and despair.

The sounds of very pleasant waterlike laughter and singing seeped through the forest. I cut and pulled my way through the bushes toward them, until I saw, from my place hidden in the deep thicket, a group of gigantic people, gathered around a pool of water whose delirious fragrance I could smell from here. This was the same water I'd drunk from the Goddess's belly.

The woman with skunk hair was serving all these tall beings food and drink. They seemed noble and tolerant, of diverse appearances, and were chatting together. Finding me in the bushes, she coaxed me out like a little beast. She was wonderful and seemed large, like a mother looks to a child.

I came into the group. No one looked at me strangely or made any snide com-

ments about my indigenosity or my exhausted appearance. All were kind. I got a drink from my hostess and was instantly healed of my wounds. I could see that these were Gods, as they wouldn't show me their faces. I said to the woman, "That one there must be the Sun."

She tried to tell me something, but I wouldn't listen, and stubbornly insisted on wandering over to him. No matter how hard I tried or where I went, fast or slow, I was always at his back. I was horribly disappointed, because I had been charged with seeing Our Father's Face: the face of the Sun.

I began to wander off dejectedly, sure that my true father didn't want anything to do with me. Having no idea how to get home, I knew I must die lost in the jungle thicket. The skunk-haired lady, however, looking around to see if the others might notice, snuck up to me, held me, and whispered in my ear how she admired me, as did the Sun. Continuing, she told me that my father the Sun was nothing like I thought he was. He wasn't like a human and not like things on the earth, and in order to save my life he wouldn't allow me to see his real face, for fear I might be utterly destroyed by the power of its heat. He was simply protecting me from myself.

"But," she added, "if you jump into that pool there and swim around without coming out, then start spinning till he gets used to you being there, maybe you can look at him through that water. Don't try this out of the water, however, and don't tell them I told you how to do this."

Because the Sun was engrossed with many other Gods whose faces I couldn't get to see, either, I silently slipped into the pool by which he and his friends were standing. I did some turns underwater and noticed my feet turning into otter's feet. I became an otter, spinning sideways like they do. It was so much fun I forgot all about the Sun, but I began to run out of air. I realized that since I was right in front of the Sun, if I surfaced I'd be crisped. I had to look and die, either by water or fire; that was all that was left to me, so I took another spin and looked through the blue liquid and saw the Sun's enormous, magnificent face.

Everything was there. It was like a huge sunflower, each seed a face in a diamond window, each face changing into another face ten times a second at least, and his whole face was swirling. Every face was the face and fruit of every possible form of existence, swirling in a myriad of colors both deep and pale. Enchanted by what I saw, I breathed in water convulsively, prepared to drown for the beauty of this sight.

I found that I could breathe underwater. The Sun had burst into a gajillion *pieces, every man's face one of his, every spark and sparkle a piece of the Sunflower seeded into the day. As the skunk-haired woman pulled me from the water, choking, full of mud, facing the volcano of Chichuc, talking to that Elbow of the Earth, I thanked her for letting me see the Sun.*

When I looked again, however, he wasn't even up yet. The dawn was barely breaking, and a little severe-faced Tzutujil dwarf was gently pulling me out of the mire by God Rock, where I surfaced from the other worlds, chest-deep in mud, shaking in the cold.

Legend has it that this little four-foot Mayan man, dressed as an Atiteco but speaking in a falsetto in a strange accent of Tzutujil, saved me from drowning. True or not, I only remember crying and praying eloquently to the Chichuc Volcano, who, very much alive and listening, began telling me to rest. People say that when I appeared out of the quagmire in the purple dawn, those down at the lake getting ready to go to the mountain in their canoes and those returning from a night of net-laying say that I kept trying to reenter the lake by walking straight into it. Cajoling me with little chirps, the small man pulled me back to safety with superhuman strength, finally succeeding in turning me toward the village after wrestling me out of the mud.

Apparently I began to march in a beeline straight for the rising Sun, who was just cresting the crater of the Three-Boys Volcano in a dawn full of the songs of magnificent birds. It was up the side of this volcano that the woman had led me, but now the village lay between me and the mountain where the Sun sat squarely on top and the Elbow and the Lake were behind me.

Not bothering to walk the village pathways, and the dwarf unable to stop me, I simply went straight toward my goal, climbing stone walls, walking straight through people's huts where they gathered as families at breakfast around the cooking fires. I careened into one side of a house and charged out the other side; I sometimes even tried to climb over houses. The dwarf would step in, running alongside me to direct me as best he could. In my single-focused purpose, I couldn't be deterred, and I was moving so fast I caught the village by surprise.

I got my foot caught in a little lime pot, which broke. I don't know how many pots I smashed, taboos I broke, or lives I disturbed; I only remember knocking over my future brother-in-law and meeting for the first time my future wife, who was fixing her headdress as I pushed her aside in my fixated surge toward the Sun Father.

They say that after covering a mile of the village straight through people's early morning lives, I crossed the plaza and climbed the steps to the Catholic church, continuing to move at breakneck speed with the muttering dwarf at my heels, trying to keep me safe.

Covered in mud head to foot, my face fixed like a mask, I forged ahead. It was Sunday morning, and a mass was being prepared. The church at the Umbilicus of the Universe was filling up with people.

Past the window hole to the other world I stamped, making a perfect prayer for it as I passed. As I raced, I spoke the secret names of every road of the village, every place-name and its sacred correspondent name in the anatomy of the spirit world's body, and in the middle of the temple I really got going, apparently addressing every Deity at accelerated speed, but impeccably. When I hit the Catholic altar, I guess I climbed on, as it was in the way of my straight line to the Sun. There was no direct exit at the back of the edifice behind the altar, but there were animals there I remembered, and I asked them for a door. The crowd was scandalized by my altar-jumping, and more so when I begun to climb the thickly carved two-story tall colonial screen containing images of the Eternal Father and so forth.

I disappeared like King Kong behind this, somehow exiting the six-foot-thick walls through a little stone tunnel where Holy Boy was rumored to have been housed long ago. Off I marched, unhindered by any sense of amazement, dedicated to my cause, crawling through the church commission building co-op, saying "Hi" or "Bye" to no one except the Gods. Apparently I arrived at the place where I'd begun my journey, up the base of a volcano where Chiv and his assistants came out and caught me like a running horse, put some smoke for me to breathe, and bit me on the head above the hairline, which knocked me down, and then dragged my unconscious body into the umbilical hut, my starting point.

I remember none of this, but everyone kept telling me about it for years, humorously, of course. As shamans, we were always doing something mysteriously right and new that seemed oddly old and familiar.

I felt sick. I looked to my left where a beautiful, smooth-faced woman the color of a toasted tortilla lay sleeping. I looked again, and she was struggling to give birth to a child whose head was already crowning as she groaned and breathed and sweated. I looked again and there I was spread all over. My head was Chjuyu, a small mountain to the north, my feet were severed and scattered over the edge of the lake, my hands were far away, cut off, my body in chunks everywhere.

I heard a voice say, "If you really know a lot, put yourself back together."

I tried to move my hands, but nothing budged—neither my feet nor my mouth—nothing. It was terrifying beyond all imagining. Then I remembered thinking, If that's my head and eyes, then what's seeing me over there?

Then the voice said, "Call," Titzikisha, *and I realized I had to call in what made me live. I couldn't order it to obey or continue to march after it anymore. "Call what makes you live," the voice said. I called and nothing came, I wept and nothing came. I called—nothing came.*

I began singing a beautiful old song I'd heard in a dream, and while I sang, I heard a whining sound, a weeping of sorts. I got up and followed it and saw my baby son sitting in the dirt of a hut, his fat little thighs curled out in front of his angry, blubbering face. As I reached for him, I was under a tree, a massive three-way tree with no trunk suspended in front of me. It had three thick branches connected at a central knot.

Slowly a mask of Holy Boy was carved into life at the end of each thick branch. The three faces all began to smoke tobacco and speak above me. One was old, another female, and the last one was young. All three branches began to spin clockwise around what they connected, spinning so fast that finally all three faces blurred and became one central face around which the others indistinguishably spun like a propeller.

The central face began speaking words used to connect the body back together, the world back together, himself back together, life back together. On the left side women were weaving and on the right side men were chopping, each chop a phrase, each stroke of the jade axe a word, all carved and hammered into my bones, blood, muscles, nerves, and insides.

My intestines were made of stars with dark footprints of things that died to feed me in them; my lungs were windy caves where old people sat shivering; my liver was a beach of older stars where my fire sat on his throne: the little quetzal-tailed hummingbird, my new name, still trying to march toward the Sun. My heart was a lake of liquid jade where the Old Moon Lady sat underneath weeping

*yet; my knees were volcanoes. Lightning struck while I hid in the hollow tree of my
ribcage.*

*Three people looked down at me. "No, not yet," they said, and blew smoke in
my face, and I didn't remember until they were there again. "Nope, not yet." And
they blew smoke all over me. Then I sat up. I looked around. I looked for the
tourist, but he was gone. I looked outside and the world was so beautiful, I recognized nothing, I was sick; and everything was new and gorgeous like a baby just
born with adult eyes and ears. I just stared at things for hours, unable to speak,
knowing nothing, just seeing for the first time the true, complex beauty of all
things.*

Eleven days passed before I could remember life as it had been. Ever
since, a nostalgic mist of longing has hung over me that has never really
lifted. I've just grown accustomed to it and given it a home in my body.

I couldn't even remember my name when I returned, so Chiv, Ma Recanda Co, MaCoy and Ya Chep took turns warming my extremities and
pouring clay jars of cold water over my head to redistribute the spiritual
fire that, when it first breaks loose from the seed in your chest, sickens, be-
fuddles, and tends to rise in waves inside of the waves up to the head, giving an intense visionary confusion. This fire must be contained in the body
until it finds itself whirling smoothly inside an organ just under the sternum. It grows for a couple of years after this type of initiation, then solid-
ifies into a shieldlike shape, a flexible type of petrified lightning. I thought
that this was all in the spirit world, or a metaphor of one's spiritual
anatomy, but a couple of years later when Guatemalan Immigration required me to get X-rayed for residency papers, they kept doing it over,
asking me if I'd been in the war or had an accident causing me to have a
disk of metal under my sternum, which showed up as a silver-dollar–sized
mirror on the X-ray plates.

Well, I knew nothing about that yet. I'd spent seven days unfed, three
of those unwatered, and five more until I could talk. Though the beauty
I'd seen could never be invalidated, I was terrified for several days, as the
rest of me grew into my new shape.

Chiv looked small, as did the other men, and I felt sad about this, but
they were still my closest people. Chiv stayed close by me still when the
others had to tend to their fields, firewood, nets, and home life.

After the initiation, as part of getting used to my new body, I began to experience a painful and rapid swelling of my tongue. It got so big I could no longer talk or eat or breathe through my mouth. It hurt so bad it was like a thousand scorpions trying to sting their way out of my head. No one had a good cure. Chiv's didn't work, mine didn't, old Ma Tzapalu's didn't. In pain and near collapse, I went to an American doctor, who laughed at my pretty odd-looking face, shot me up with some antibiotics, painkillers, and vitamins, and sent me home, where I got worse. I was taken to a Guatemalan doctor, who tried some antibiotics guaranteed to kill anything, banned in the Free World (literally), but I only got weaker, and my tongue was looking like it might split open. It took on the size and color of a small eggplant.

So as I lay in the fierce April heat, waiting to die, my mouth open, my tongue poking out, a little man, the father of a man who was the neighbor of a one-eyed obsidian shaman who was my friend, showed up in a wry, humble, cajoling way, half naked, urging me, whom he'd never really met, to come down and take a *touj*, a sweat bath. He was not an herb doctor, not a prayer-maker, not a diviner, not a shaman, just a regular, small-town, poverty-stricken, grief-ridden little Mayan farmer with one grown son, a daughter-in-law, and a very malnourished grandchild. His last child and wife had died during childbirth the previous autumn.

Half awake and in horrible pain, I didn't believe this man could help. I listened, however, as he explained that he had experienced the same thing that was happening to me, and he would cure me as another old man had done for him.

Well, I went, and sat in the poor man's tiny ovenlike little sweat house with him and his whole family. They closed the blanket over the stone threshold and began praying as we always did in the sweat house and swatting me with sweet-smelling branches of *kixlanchie*. After ten minutes I passed out and woke up in their little leaky hut, face up on the wet ground; it must have taken all three of them to drag me there. The old fellow made me drink a concoction that looked like dream medicine, all red colored as any good Mayan medicine should be. I was so dry I drank the whole bottle before I realized I could do so—my tongue had come down a little bit. The old man threw me back in the sweat chamber, and off we went again, and out I went again, and when I came to I drank another carafe of that blessed plant medicine, then crawled back into the sweat. But this time I didn't faint, and within two days I was totally healed.

Mtmash Smaj was the man's name, and I owe my life to him. He helped me without being asked, simply because he knew how, and with an innate understanding of village economics, he wanted to pay me *before* he needed me as a shaman to help him live well. He was as good a healer as any ever was. Mayans don't expect their doctors to be illness-free or their lives to be easy. The people all knew how common it was for the shaman and his family to suffer so that everyone else could go free of problems.

Before my initiation, I'd been a skinny, frail kind of shy boy. But now I started to eat like crazy, and my muscles changed shape. I shot up an inch more in height, growing stocky and powerful. Becoming both gregarious and evocative, I was happy just to be alive!

As I returned from my initiation, I began to reflect on what it all meant to me. At first I wanted nothing more to do with all of this shamanism, now being able to understand why some other novices I'd known didn't make it through, having perished during their initiatory passage. They had expected that the sheer force of their human will, combined with their imagined knowledge and supposed power, would make it easy work for them. But they weren't prepared enough, patient enough, or lucky enough to realize how much their success in the other world depended on their animal awareness and on a courageous willingness instead of willfulness. These initiations were tests made by the Gods themselves and by the spirits of nature. No matter how adroit we humans thought we were, nature had no pity on us in the least.

Strangely, however, these spirits did offer us a way to survive inside of nature if we were willing to work by means of our nature soul. I saw clearly how this fifth world creation was not here to support us humans as its greatest production, to be lovingly and willingly fed by the Gods as their privileged children. We humans were more like a magnificent sacred adornment on an otherwise already beautiful natural world.

Tzutujil shamans called human beings in Respect Names the *Qop ruachuliu*, Earrings of the Earth Fruit. It was human grandiosity that carved, cut, hammered, and bent the earth into shapes it didn't ask to be in. How could that make us welcome here on this earth among the spirits? But our very ability to carve, bend, and shape should be used to feed and give gifts to what fed us from the other world. After all, they could kill us in a flash—why didn't they? Because the Gods were addicted to our beauty like an alcoholic to a delicious wine. They loved our poetry, our offering shrines, our beautiful clothing, the complex chirping banter of our village streets, and especially the expansive combination of all our abilities into ritual offerings and ceremonies. The Gods perceived us as delicious fruit. They loved our excesses as long as they were beautiful and the Gods got to eat a lot of them.

In a shamanic initiation, one could see the complex beauty of all life and nature in one soul-rewiring flash, recognizing at the same time the over-domesticated idiocy of humans and their persistent preoccupation with creating more and more spirit-insulting, life-killing ways. Humans had forgotten their function. It was hard for me to want to serve humans, now that I'd drunk directly out of the belly of *Rilaj Vinaq*, having spoken with Gods and been willing to die to see my Father's face.

But ironically, because of the vision this gave me, I comically realized that humans were part of that very nature they insulted with their prodigious amnesia. Even that forgetfulness was a part of their nature. To the spirit, the noise of the humans was just about the same size as a mockingbird's song, or a cricket's chirp; we weren't that big to them. I knew that the nature now bubbling alive in me, my shaman's soul, was a remembered thing. All humans had nature souls, they just didn't remember. Spiritual amnesia was the price of human cleverness.

Knowledge, when treated as a private possession, would like all possessions have to be defended to keep it from being stolen. But an initiated shaman, instead of hording, hiding, or defending what he knew, simply had physically *become* knowledge. Instead of knowing it, he practiced it. After all, it was all in the bones now; one didn't have to snatch at scarce crumbs of hard-gleaned facts hoping they would lead to a place of knowing and vision. A shaman simply had to become something worth seeing, a vision that inspired life in an authentic way.

Holiness for a shaman meant being a regular part of life, human and nature, where one participated by being oneself. Now that being oneself was infused with nature's way of going, just walking around, farming, fishing, splitting wood, laughing, and visiting was significant. This being alive with initiated awareness was the most elegant and exalted way of remembering the spirits you ritually fed to stay alive.

That which keeps you alive in an initiation is not your reasoning powers, or how much information you've gathered. It has to do with that spirit power that admires you. This relationship with your spirit power is not kept up by that power, but it is maintained by you. You must feed that very power, just like a magic horse, if you want to get back home—only your natural spirit knows how to proceed in the spirit world. You feed the horse, your power, and it'll find a way to get you home. You can't do it without the spirit power. But you use the products of your ability to think, reason, and create and the information gathered to feed to your spirit, like hay to the horse! This keeps your spirit strong and inspired to meet the challenge of initiation, leaving you with the power's admiration of your courage, your uniqueness, and an increasing awareness of a strange little ability to survive well as a part of nature and the fifth world.

Of course, none of this is thought out in a village. The Maya people are much more unencumbered and more sophisticated. They just did it. These thoughts are just the sincere ruminations of a man who could now stand and speak from both a white man's world and a Mayan shaman's as well. After all, you didn't need to be a shaman to live in a village. And you certainly didn't need to be a shaman to live happily. But if you were one, as I was, one had to relearn how to live in a village, and the village had to gradually concur as to how you fit into its constantly readjusting interrelationships.

Fully recovering from the shamanic initiation was like recovering from the physical impact of being hit by spirit lightning. The recovery time allowed it all to seep into you, infusing you with the valuable juice of what felt like illness. That very juice is what makes you realize your new or remembered nature. When it was done, your body became living tribal literature, a walking story, that had to be consistently employed according to its nature, not its knowledge.

A shamanic initiation did not make you a big man or a big woman in the tribe. You were simply a little, powerful piece of nature, strolling down the village paths, sniffing the luscious air of new life, small, unscratched, shiny, like a new tool just waiting to be used.

DANCING THE
SPIRIT TRAPS:
A Shaman's Honeymoon

Throughout all the time I spent with Chiviliu, I also had been participating in the village hierarchy, heading toward initiation there as well. I had become one of those heavily dressed, layered people who moved in procession with the chiefs and ladies, living a parallel life as a courtier in this Tzutujil theocracy.

To the matrons in the hierarchy, it was unthinkable that I didn't have a wife yet. The Tzutujil system of life was always male-female; except in special positions, all the hierarchy chiefs and ladies served as couples. There was no chief whose wife didn't serve as a female chief to the power they served together. The Gods also came in pairs. It was not that a man or woman was incomplete without the other; it was that the village was imbalanced otherwise.

I loved the women of the village, I suppose because they loved me. But old, young, middle-aged, or maiden, what was female in nature, in all life, in humans, was so strong and unintimidated in these village ladies that I was never seen as a threat or unwelcome in their presence. There were times when women I didn't know or had never heard tell of would appear out of nowhere to bring me cool water in a gourd when I was too hot in the sun, or working, sweating in a ritual. They knew they'd be blessed in the ritual for their help, but they also worried about how thirsty I might be. Little girls would tug at my knee pants to have me hold them up, so they could give me something or talk about the wonders in their lives.

Old, old, old bent women with tiny bones and more wrinkles than meat would stop in their gradual progress to give you a blessing as you passed them, saying some words of encouragement for your task. All over, men were blessed by women and women by men. Not that they couldn't kill you, too, because these women were not ignorant, delicate, or docile, but they knew well how to be friends, how to fight, how to bless, and how to laugh beautifully and often. If the truth be known, I wanted to marry them all, but at the time I could barely feed myself. So I tried to wait until I could pull together some funds from my painting sales, at least enough to court a bride properly.

Sometime before I was initiated, Chiv had taken me aside and asked me why I didn't paint what I was learning. The reason was simple: my experience with traditionalists all over Native America as a kid had taught me that representing sacred things into salable art went against tradition.

For truly traditional Native people, what modern people called art was never sold. Such things were reserved for the sacred. All painting and carving could only be seen by designated people at certain times in specific sacred environments. This sacred art was infused with the same creativity that the Gods manifested. For the Mayans, the Gods actually coveted the beauty humans could create. They could make an artist's life miserable if they didn't get some or all of it. On top of this, if the creation of the artist was a real thing, it must be fed. Thus all the Gods were fed ritually through their forms. This gave natural forces a place and a face where they could be nourished, adorned, and addressed. Everything that an artist created out of this imagination gave form to a previously unseen force. Mayans did not think it was necessarily a human right to give form to every conceivable image.

By the same understanding, if artists made multiple images of sacred things, then the Deity force represented in the singular original form was diluted in half again as many times as it was copied. Permanent multiple copies of any unique thing weakened the soul of the original instead of strengthening it. This insulted the Gods.

But Chiv said I should paint what I saw and learned, not who I learned it from. He said, "Paint a lot, son, but there are three things you must never expose, depict, or allude to, and the rest will be fine." Once shown what the three things are, I always respected them. I had given up painting when I began my shaman training, thinking I was not good at it, for one, and that Chiv would've disapproved. He was always complaining about three of his enemies who were painters and Christians who were always bugging him to let them do his portrait. There also just wasn't any time left in a day to paint, since I was both a hierarchy initiate and a student shaman.

But I started to paint again at Chiv's suggestion, and I became a kind of painting champion for the old traditionalists to counter the Christian painters, who claimed to paint native customs as reminders of their ugly heathen past, which they had successfully transcended. We thought this was kind of ridiculous because everything they painted was happening right before their eyes, not lost or forgotten. They just wished it was. Their paintings made the elders mad, which made the Catholics and evangelists happy. They sold millions of their strange little paintings to tourists, and those painters who became rich felt it was because Christ loved them. Now the traditionalists had me as *their* champion!

Chiv loved to watch me paint. He'd sit in the back smoking his crazy-headed pipes, supporting me as I slopped paint onto gypsum-sized salt sacking. Often he'd show up at my hut with as many as fifteen black-jacketed old white-haired guys with wide knee pants, wrinkled feet, and canes. Then after a couple of months, watching me became the main sport of the retired hierarchy, the council of chiefs, who were the real power among the people. They were like a crowd at a soccer game, squinting at my works which must have amazed and baffled them. They figured it must be a sacred activity, because out of cloth, hair, sticks, and earth I made things they recognized from *my* dreams looking back at them.

A round of approving grunts would rumble behind me when an ear or head would appear on the canvas. The old men murmured to each other, nodding about the greatness of their "*chulaja a* Martín," their "ingenious old lusty Martín."

They got to their feet and canes, cheering when an eyeball came along, staring back at them from the living canvas. Sometimes they'd pray to it and give offerings, or tell me to do so, to feed the being come alive within it. If the eyes were especially convincing, sometimes they'd run out and call in everybody washing their clothes in the lake, all the passers-by, and anybody in the village who was in earshot. My little lakeside hut would fill inside and out with enchanted admirers of this thin painted cloth looking back at them.

The old boys took to telling me how to paint after a while, which I'd known was only a matter of time, shuffling up behind me whispering in my ear while pointing: "I think it needs more red on the sun," or, "Don't you think his teeth should be bigger?" and so on.

But they were all unanimous about the eyebrows. You see, Tzutujil people love eyebrows. The main complaint about the woman I'd declared an intention to marry, Yalur, was that she had no eyebrows to speak of, though she was pretty and smooth with long black hair.

These old guys hated it when I didn't put eyebrows on my figures, so I took to doing it as best I could rationalize. But it got really crazy when they decided that a horse and a deer I was painting needed eyebrows, too. "But horses don't have eyebrows, and neither do deer," I bitterly complained one morning to the gallery of stunned old chiefs. "Yes, but don't you think they'd like to have some, so they could see us better?" The villagers knew that good eyebrows not only made men and women handsome and better-looking but also allowed them to see better. Well, it was hard, but that horse got an eyebrow. The clincher was when they wanted a frog to have eyebrows, with lots of hair.

The stages of a shaman's training are very much the same as the steps young Tzutujil men went through while courting young women. A shaman's initiation was essentially the marriage between himself and the spirit he'd courted ritually for three or four years. I'd felt very much like a young boy in love during my training; I was fully immersed in a cloud of anguished longing and deliciousness while I tried to develop a relationship between myself and my nature spirit. Like all young Tzutujil men, shamans had to dig deep into their ingenuity while tempering their heroic hearts with traditional ways of going about it.

The Tzutujil people approach living in general with a sense of courtly behavior. This meant knowing how to approach a spirit of another's soul without scaring it away, and still present one's true natural self unaltered. There were boys and novice shamans who were very good at touching the hearts of ladies and of spirits. They had inborn abilities and a fierce affection for what they were courting. Still others were successful because they loved the age-old courting process itself on whose back the whole ceremonial Tzutujil culture survived. The panache, fine stories, beguiling songs, offerings, and love-drunk attention to what they loved, either woman or spirit, were all part of this. The people knew that young men and women and shamans were feeding the Gods with beauty when, through their excellent speeches, heroic gifts, and serenades, admiration was created for what each loved.

One of the major differences between a regular person and a shaman was that a shaman's first spouse was a spirit power, represented by a bundle, and largely invisible to everybody else. This spirit wife was considered a shaman's first love, while his flesh-and-blood wife became his second wife. Very few women would understand this, much less desire such a situation even if they did comprehend it. Only a brave and extraordinary woman could be happily married to a shaman. Shamans were always suspected of using their powers to gain a young lady's affection. People didn't approve of that. This was on top of the fact that no family wanted their daughters knowingly married to a shaman.

Shamans fought witches, captured dangerous ghosts, dealt with powerful Deities of illness and death. Plus every time a shaman succeeded in pulling off the hardship, bad luck, evil, sickness, witchcraft, or debt of a client, the people believed that the evil might run amok in the compound, causing sickness and hardship among the shaman's people. Shamans believed the same thing, but they were well trained regarding how to capture and turn to dust, or send back, the bad things that had been released, thereby protecting themselves and their people.

Villagers knew full well that shamans, especially able ones, had to deal with witchcraft sent to their compounds in retaliation for healing a witch's enemy, usually by sending it back to the witch. Shamans had to prove they could save their families from spiritual attack, because those witch enemies attacked what the shaman loved, killing friends, relations, and loved ones in order to cause suffering to the shaman. The more popular a shaman became, the more clients he had. The more clients he had, the more he had to deal with evil and problems, until his life of great fame was essentially a relentless state of siege. Not infrequently a shaman died protecting his people.

People respected a good shaman enormously for his work and courage, but realistically no parents would subject their daughter to such a life. Therefore, a shaman was hard put to find a girl willing to share his precarious existence. A shaman's wife had to have a great deal of traditional knowledge, as she'd end up being at least as important as her husband, since in the most ideal of marriages they worked as a team. A certain air of First Lady-ness came with being a shaman's wife, and that meant preparing feasts, welcoming visitors, and so on. Her compound would be like a combination hospital and embassy. Chiviliu himself was on his fourth wife, and it was in Ya Chep that he was finally able to confide, secure that she was on his side, strong enough in her own spiritual right to do what needed doing and dodge the spirit arrows inevitably thrown the couple's way.

There was a certain amount of glamor in shamanism, and there were many beautiful daughters of hierarchy chiefs who liked me enough to marry me, but it would have been hard for them to get their parents' endorsement. The wife of a successful shaman would be highly respected, and at the pinnacle of all the village issues, aware of any crisis. This appealed to Tzutujil women, who loved to originate news and gossip instead of being the last to hear. Shamans' wives also dressed well and ate well for, unlike the hierarchy, they were well compensated.

But I, *Ma Tzejtel*, had hardly any redeeming qualities. For one, I was an orphan by Tzutujil standards, meaning I had no parents present and lived in an adopted situation, with no land, no farms, no real business, and one leaky canoe (some men had five or twenty; I knew one old childless couple that had 110 canoes). Plus, I was larger than everyone else, making it more difficult to weave for me, and I ate more food than the other small Tzutujil fellows. Worst of all, I was a shaman with no clients. Though I did have an income from my paintings, thanks to Chiviliu and Holy Boy, nobody really understood how that worked, so they all figured it was some kind of magic.

It was my old heroic attitude that finally got me married. While I was casually talking to a woman, her seventeen-year-old daughter Yalur forgetfully plunged her little hand into a big, furiously boiling pot of wild greens, severely scalding herself. The girl had been staring at me in wonder, and I felt very responsible for what had happened, so I cured her hand. As I came by her house day after day to continue the treatments, I got to know her, and we became sweethearts.

One day as I was coming out of the bite, the trancelike effect of an intense three-day public ceremony with the hierarchy, I made a threatening wager with Yalur's father, who liked to beat her. Yalur had had frequent epileptic seizures for many years. Recently she'd been returned to her parents by her brand-new husband, a lazy, uninitiated rich boy. She'd been unfairly branded as unfit by this man, who demanded his bride price be returned. This was a real problem because her family, in their poverty, had long ago exhausted what little of it there'd been.

Though I was infuriated with Yalur's father, I told him that if he promised me then and there that I could take his daughter to wife whenever she chose, her seizures would cease magically. He laughed at me as if he thought I was a fool. So I challenged him with my spirit power. This was totally wrong of me, but I was trying to be a hero, and I couldn't stomach the way he beat that sick girl.

Yalur's father was no one to trifle with. He was a Christian convert whose sect openly preached against any and all ancient ways. Once I saw him slice the head off a running dog, and the dog went headless for two steps before he died. He'd also killed two men back in the fifties, which is why the shamans said his child was afflicted with epilepsy. But I stood up to him. Yalur's mother loved my offer and was all for it. As many Tzutujil women know how to do, she independently proclaimed that we had a deal. I should have Yalur as my wife if she got well because of the promise.

She did. And what she and I thought of each other, what we did, and how we made our life together are best remembered by us. To me, she was *Rilaj Vinaq*, the spirit of the land, beaten and rejected. She was all the village women, smiling and durable, the deliciousness of the people's soul and a strange, brave little Mayan girl. To this day, she has only had one more seizure.

When we married, in accordance with Tzutujil tradition, I moved out of Chiv's hamlet-sized compound into my in-laws' tiny compound. There I commissioned a traditional *bney jai* family to direct the construction of a four-star thatched *pach jai*. Such long huts had become increasingly rare in recent years and were being torn down and replaced with tin and stone supplied by the Christians, who pressured their flocks to abandon use of these fine old-styled dwellings because of their association with traditional Mayan belief and the remembrance way of thinking.

Ironically, I, an outsider, was fast becoming one of the village's most successful and stubborn upholders of remembrance rituals and *Ojer Tzij*. *Ojer Tzij*, Original Words, were the ancient myth-stories that connected Tzutujil everyday existence to the visible and invisible landscape around us. Since all creation in their past history had actually shaped these mountains, the villagers could only find their present position on the earth and in history by living among those histories of their past that surrounded them.

When a villager no longer lived among the stories, because he or she didn't know them, then that person ceased to be Mayan. He or she became a Guatemalan citizen. The missionary Christians and almost all wings of political entities had no true awareness of the value and richness of old Tzutujil understandings. For the most part, these influences, foreign to the village, were consumed with getting their own way.

The Peace Corps, Agricultural Programs, Guatemalan plantation owners, revolutionaries, religious missions, business developers, and tourist advocates were all equally frustrated by the traditional villagers' strange preoccupation with amassing money, corn, food, and goods, only to exhaust them all in one week in high-visibility public rituals and feasts. When these took place, the whole village would be sustained off the backs of a few families for a short couple of days. When a chief got a new layer, or position in the hierarchy, he would be leveled economically of all his wealth in a ritual fashion until his family were back to the normal level of poverty of the rest of the village.

Providing such rituals usually signified passage into greater prestige and public importance and eventually renewed the Village Heart and furthered one into deeper positions of knowledge or remembrance. So the whole hierarchy of chiefs was composed of people who'd regularly and ritually distributed all their wealth to the village as part of their rites of passage into deeper layers of remembrance. That the self-impoverished theocracy represented the ideal of what a traditional Tzutujil should be at his height horrified all the Christians, businessmen, and politicians, who couldn't imagine how this Mayan aristocracy didn't base its power on prestige or amassed wealth or personal well-being, but on knowledge and giving away. Traditional Tzutujil loved to get more than someone else, just so they could dress fancily and give it all away to be big. To get anywhere in traditional Mayan society, you had to work really hard to get wealth, get appointed to office without campaigning, and then give it all away.

We had a hierarchy of chronically poor people who knew things, and hundreds more trying as hard as they could to be just like them. But all of those judgmental external observers, the missions and businesspeople, saw this feasting and giving away as ignorance and waste. To them, it was an archaic relic of lesser-evolved times. Truly, it was archaic; but it was exactly this archaic feeling we tried so hard to reassemble in the village throughout every year in the ancient cycles of public rituals. Mayan tradition is not concerned with progressing to a glorious future. The Gods had already achieved that, and we were living in it! We were concerned with maintaining a glorious present dedicated to feeding what gave us this life in a remembering way. Because the culture was old, this remembering way was archaic by nature.

New things or ideas were fine once they got old. That's how traditionalists thought. They always waited a long time before adopting a new idea or method. By then, of course, it was old anyway. New ideas were like a young person who was still tender and inexperienced, but sure that he knew everything. If put to hard work too soon, he might just break under the strain of life, so the old traditionalist adults always waited for a new notion or invention to more or less grow up before putting it to use. They'd never adopt anything just because it was new. The word for *old* in Tzutujil also means "great," or "strong like a tree." Oldness, archaicness, meant that a long time ago a new thing had lasted and was now proven to be good because it was old.

The old-time Tzutujil Mayan way of being was firmly lodged in the culture by means of the sophistication and uniqueness of their indigenous Mayan tongue. The secret of my own ability to survive and thrive in this beautiful, stormy place could be directly attributed to my early recognition and delight in the fact that Tzutujil has no verb "to be," and therefore no real future tense.

Tzutujil was a language of carrying and belonging, not a language of being. Time, for instance, did not exist, it had to be carried. The language has no word for time. This is interesting in light of how much Mayanists talk about how all Maya culture is based on time. This might be true in a way, but time is not based on existence, but rather on the carrying of Dawns on our backs by remembrance. There are no "isms" in the language or any idea of something being absolutely this way or that. If two people argue, they are said to be split—like firewood, they say—but both sides are still of the same wood.

Some of the idealism, rights and wrongs and so forth, that whole nations and populations have fought and died to defend or obtain are not even relevant concepts to traditionalist Tzutujil. This is not because the Maya are untutored primitives, but because their lives are not built on the anxiety of absolute states or permanence. With no verb "to be," permanence becomes a comic hypothesis for most Mayans, who don't believe anything will last on its own. That's why everything in their lives is oriented toward maintenance instead of creation.

"Belonging to" is as close to "being" as Tzutujil thinking gets. There are no generic nouns for people or things; all words have to belong to someone. There is no word for just "mother," for instance. Obviously to be a mother, you have to have children. In Tzutujil you can only describe a mother by saying whose mother she is.

Nobody could say, "He is a shaman." One says instead, "The way of tracking belongs to him." A person traveling is called "belongs to roads." Because of this, the present nowness is everywhere, and the future blends mysteriously with the past.

In a culture with a verb "to be," one is always concerned with who one is. To determine who you are implies a possibility that there are things you are not. To find out who you are, these other things must be determined. In Mayan culture one defines oneself by belonging. To belong, you must bond yourself with gifts. You are defined by where you stand, and who you are standing with. Without a verb "to be," you can't invent a car, a nuclear missile, a shopping mall, or a one-God religion, because in the strictest sense you don't create things because that implies being. For Mayans, everything grows and is defined by the fruit or form that belongs to it like a child to its mother. Since Mayans belong to things, they don't really make them; they maintain life, take care of things. In the past when they cut, carved, bent, and built big things, it was not, as in modern culture, to force things to be friendly or to take them somewhere, but to feed the world something monumental that they couldn't otherwise use in proportion to the immense gifts the Gods had given them. Mayans don't force the world to be what they want it to be: they are friends with it, they belong to life.

In order to get their own way, those frustrated religious, business, and political entities finally learned that they first had to undermine the language in the young. Language is the glue that holds all the layers of the Mayan universe together, the eloquence of the speech, the lifeline ancestral connection of the mythologies. The Speech of the Gods of the creations is in our very bones. Force the verb "to be" upon our young, and the whole archaic Mayan world disappears into the devouring, monster jaws of the modern age. That's what happened to the old Maya: an unthinkable thought came and ate what held a culture together; it was eaten by its own children.

That's what was happening in Atitlán. It was a traumatic time against which Chiviliu and the traditionalists had braced themselves. They saw me as a kind of secret knight against the confusing forms melting their world. Being an outsider by looks and birth, to these outside forces I appeared to be one of them, yet I worked day and night vehemently to keep the old world glued together, well remembered. This mystified the missionaries and politicians, who saw what the villagers and shamans did as vacant and to no purpose, and wanted every Indian to forget about it. After all, you can't sell heaven and modern business practices to a people who think they are in heaven, and who insist on giving everything away in a grandiose way to prove it!

Half of what they gave away went to something neither the Christians nor the businessmen could even see or rationalize. We in Santiago knew that we were doomed, that old world of eternal Now, the Earth Fruit, would have to begin to be in our minds, meaning soon enough it would have to cease being and die. But we also knew that as long as the archaic language was kept talking, there would be a trail to carry the Village Heart to sanctuary in the sixth world. We wanted all the beauty and speech to outlive us, their keepers. We couldn't know if we would succeed, but we had to try.

Yalur and I took to visiting the different Sacred Houses during the post-ritual hierarchy feasts, when all the *Ajauá* chiefs and ladies came together informally as couples, elegantly dressed to eat and dance to the marimbas. These feasts and music went on until the host chief had run totally out of resources. These were the happy days for us, our honeymoon times.

When a shaman first marries his power, he also goes through a kind of honeymoon period. For a year or two after initiation, a shaman has an extra amount of juice, of fire and ability from his spirit wife. This allows him to survive what is a very vulnerable period. Like a molted animal, whose new form has outgrown the old, the shaman stays unarmored until his new form has solidified. Honeymoons of both types are called "swellings" because, like a deer in heat or the head of a cattail full of pollen, we swell up with erotic deliciousness to solidify our new forms. During this time for the shaman, the spirit is stronger than it will ever be again. Sometimes very magical things happen.

After a year or so, one's power settles down, adjusting like a married couple to the equally wonderful continuance of compound life, life as a contributing hard-working adult. Being an adult is highly respected in the village. Strangely enough, both my honeymoons coincided. During this period, one delicious cool October evening, Yalur and I strolled regally attired back to our old-style house after two days of dancing, eating, and being happy with all our hierarchy friends. As we turned into our sandy pathway, I saw a ropelike streak of purple light stretching from my big longhouse to a huddle of young merchants gambling the corn dice game on a blanket, their backs to us, intent on the game. I yelled a greeting, hoping they would turn and face us, but no one did as they answered back.

The power was rising in me. I could see clear as neon where an enemy had laid a spirit trip-rope. Zigzagging along the purple streak was a little curling erratic green line, meaning the enemy had brought an "uncooked" friend. Most likely I'd come here earlier than the enemy had planned, and they had ducked into that intent knot of happy gamblers to hide. The purple faded, as did the green, but I crossed the compound from another side, took out my sacred tools, and captured the trap into a gourd, my power getting a workout for the first time since my "cooking."

The next morning I awoke with a start, lying beside my wife, who was a hard sleeper. My image of Holy Boy had leapt three feet to the floor, and was still standing. This was miraculous. I knew he was helping me and that something was wrong.

Through the cracks in my hut's walls, I could see deep orange light, and when I craned my head out the door without crossing the threshold, I could see hundreds of candles melted together in curious witchcraft array, burning, completely circling my hut. My power hadn't warned me, so I knew this might be the work of one of those powerful sorcerers who could make the victim sleep while he worked his mischief. Technically, if I crossed the line created by the fire, I would doom all the others in my compound, even though I myself would most likely survive. A witch always tries to hurt you, not by killing you, but by destroying what you love.

But I knew how to fix things, and I did. By the time I'd completed my work, a crowd had gathered outside, and the sun was up. Wanting to help me, the neighbor men and women knowingly kept all the curious children far away so that nothing bad could jump onto them. As I worked, I finally cleared a safe roadway, and Yalur awoke totally unaware of the morning's adventure, horrified and enraged by what she saw. She was going to cross to her parents' part of the compound when I held her back and pushed her little sister back with a staff to the other side of the seemingly safe walkway. I thrust my machete into the earth beneath all I'd cleared, and to my delight I uncovered a row of witched old metal money in the shape of a huge crescent laid out like little land mines under the earth. I salted, ashed, liquored, and rainbowed them, when I saw an orange lying in the rows of fine tall blue corn growing between my in-laws' place and mine. A little kid was grabbing it, so I grabbed a *matazano* (a custard apple) from my baskets and traded the hungry baby for it. The orange was full of spike holes, denoting the entrance of poison or an infusion with illness taken from someone and laid there like witches do. Whoever grabbed the orange would take on the sick person's illness, becoming sick in turn and alleviating the original illness. I suspected worse, and my fears were vindicated when one of the turkeys pecked into the orange and was stiff in ten minutes.

This was why a woman with good sense and no power of her own rarely considered taking a shaman for her husband. The witchcraft wars were always on you. I had to be constantly alert without being paranoid. Every day there was some occurrence, some subtle attack from one side or another, in the day or the night.

Finally I resorted to using my divination bundle to determine the source of the attacks. But before I did, I consulted old Chiviliu, who was now in his nineties and getting more creatively old all the time. He welcomed me to my place on his bench, and we ate and then smoked hard, laughing about things that weren't that funny, to make them bearable. He told me his life story for about the thirty thousandth time, adding a few new details about his own initiation story.

"If there is a good thing born, a beautiful thing born, a wonderful thing that becomes apparent on this earth, then there will be three things that come to test it to see if it is also strong, to see if it has what it takes to live." Being beautiful meant having strength and wiliness, without losing the vision of the initiation, and the ability to remain beautiful. There was no sentimental thought among the Mayans about a place of peace finally reached in this earth where you could rest on your accomplishments, or where for loveliness life would pity you. For regular people, the community was a place of identity and rest, but for the shaman it was a place of challenge and work. Though a shaman might be favored, he was never free. If he was good at his work, he'd get the grace of friendship with the Earth but no immunity to its foment.

When a shaman was initiated, as a continuance of his initiation he would be tried and tested by enemies attracted through jealousy and the curiosity of hard-hearted people already consumed by the unintegrated power of ancient devouring ghosts. These witches were sometimes shaman doctors, too, but because of their natures they couldn't help but test out your shields. The test for me and my kind, of course, was not to strike back but to find a way to turn the poisonous arrows into a fertile dust that wouldn't hurt anyone, and would actually make something flourish. I couldn't shoot back at my enemies except in a situation of emergency when my back was pushed against the wall. If I retaliated out of self-preservation and survived, I still failed in my task, which was to capture the assailant's volleys and transform them into something useful.

I was automatically at a disadvantage because my witch enemies wanted me or my loved ones dead and had no rules or scruples as to how this could be accomplished. But I still had to dance with what they threw at me, obeying Chiv's rules because of the excellence embodied in the style of shamanism we both represented. That style had to retain its basic principle of naturalness and growth, neither of which would survive if I became witchlike myself and began manipulating phenomena for selfish interests instead of promoting the "food and water" ways I'd been initiated and sworn into.

Chiv said that if I could pull off this next stage, my newly enthroned spirit would admire me a lot and I would get proficient at many things on account of this spirit helping me. I was doing really well, he said, but I'd better never be tempted to pity my assailants, even to the bitter end. I was to keep my head down and my eyes open, ready to creatively jump at all moments and learn how to make decoys, which he taught me and which I still do to this day.

One day when I returned to the village from a hierarchy errand in the capital, I was met by the yelling and sobbing cries of many of my married-in female relatives. I found Yalur rudely detained in the muddy cell of the municipal calaboose with an unpaid fine hanging over her poor, bruised seventeen-year-old head. I paid the fine to a contrite Tzutujil substituting for the white government-appointed mayor, who had been so afraid of my wrath that he'd disappeared for a few days. Yalur grabbed my chest and wept, explaining through her tears what had happened, along with thirty or so of our relatives simultaneously. We walked back to our hut at her mother's compound a mile away, as the village gathered watching from their huts, issuing formal salutations, nodding their heads respectfully, wondering how this would all end.

Yalur had a black eye and a pretty good lump on the side of her head, which I didn't like on account of her history of epilepsy. The hierarchy had called me to an errand, or I would never have left her. I was very angry at myself. I had asked all the compound not to leave Yalur alone at any time while I was gone, since I knew that our enemies were yet planning something. Yalur was pregnant with my child; she should be watched over well anyway.

When this incident occurred, her father had been out cutting wood in the mountains, her sisters and her mother had been at the edge of the lake washing clothing, and her brothers were all out working or playing, leaving Yalur strapped into her backstrap loom, weaving me a scav, a pair of Indian knee pants with purple stripes.

While she was alone, a bitter local Ladina lady and her three strange unmarried adolescent daughters had come strutting into my end of the compound lobbing fist-sized stones, calling my wife a filthy Indian whore and saying how they were going to beat the bastard out of her belly and so on. Well, Yalur was pretty feisty, to say the least. Though in a poor position, pregnant and tied into her loom all alone, she took a nearby piece of oak firewood, and with her famous deadly aim, threw it like a Mayan duck club and hit the mother square on the head, knocking her out like a hammered cow. The girls, screaming and weeping, dragged off their casualty while Yalur continued returning the rocks they'd thrown at her. Yalur ran for help, but by then, the girls, presuming their mother had been killed, went and rallied the white government officers, who sent their boys to drag Yalur struggling wildly to jail. She saw that as wholly unfair, since she'd been attacked in her own house without provocation. The old lady came around, paid some people to lie as witnesses, and Yalur was convicted of the attack. When she tried to leave, the guards beat her.

I was really steamed, and I wanted to do somebody some real damage. I was mad at Yalur's father, her mother, and at her for not keeping aware of the danger still around us. This in turn made me angry at myself for having compromised these poor people by bringing enmity and hardship upon them. I was a shaman being tested by life, and they were in the line of fire.

The truth was that the Ladina lady was unable to marry off her daughters. Her husband was a likable drunk but useless, and she was livid that I had married a poor sick Indian girl instead of one of her more civilized girls. To add insult to injury, I enjoyed the love and acceptance of all the Indians, wearing their clothing, eating their food, and speaking the language, instead of, as she put it, civilizing the dirty barbarians. I was becoming one of them, egging them on to continue in their backward, inhuman, animal ways!

After thinking it through, and seeing that Yalur would recover, I sauntered over to the Ladina lady's house and reviewed the story from her end in Spanish. She made no apologies about attacking Yalur and reiterated how filthy and proud the ignorant Indian whores were, and how could I let my bastard ride in that rotting animal's belly, etc. But toward the end of her tirade, she looked at me, scared, and inquired, "Are you going to take me up to the department court?"

"Not at all," I replied, biting hard on my molars to release a little rage. "I'll leave it up to the spirits."

"You're going to witch me then!"

"No," I said again. "Simple justice, in whatever way the spirits so deem, that's all. What do you take me for anyway? I'm a respected *ajcun*, not a lousy candle salter."

I laid my case to the spirits in the mountain shrines and stayed home out of the way until their struggle was concluded. By the following morning, two of the people the Ladina lady had bribed to falsify their testimony had come to me to beg for mercy. Since they were evangelical Christians, I replied as I had done to their patroness, adding, "Let God handle it."

The next night, the first witness's hut burned to the ground, and the occupants had to move back to the husband's mother's compound. The second witness's canoe caught on fire on the shore, and the wife left the husband for having betrayed us. Three days later the Ladina lady fell off her roof and broke her back. She not only survived and wasn't paralyzed, but mysteriously became friendly to everyone, including Yalur. One of her daughters got pregnant, nobody knew by whom, and the others had to take care of their mother, giving her something to do besides hate.

At the end of that week, one by one, my witch enemies wandered into my house and took back their challenge, proclaiming me the winner. This made me nervous, since winning was a term foreign to the food and water ways of Chiv's teaching. All my enemies came in except one, and I accepted their gifts and surrenders, if not the lame reasoning behind their attacks. But the most adept of the three stayed away, continuing to throw corpse dust and skull pieces into my place, to create false beetles out of toe bones to infect us, to send moths with enchanted dust on their wings, or to throw spiderweb magic on our compound threshold. But I fielded it all, and we survived.

After another three weeks, my last enemy came in ostensibly to lay down the sword. He was a peculiar little fellow who spoke unabashedly in a high falsetto. He had curly black hair, odd for the village, and wore a white man's short-sleeve cotton shirt, no shoes, canvas slacks like a Ladino, and a small straw hat. He twirled his fingers like a cat does its tail to keep your eyes off his eyes as he spoke. They called him Pithy Gourd for his small size and hollow ways.

Pithy Gourd came in to congratulate me on my abilities and to add that, even though he did not fear me, he was calling off our war. To show his sincerity, he'd brought a liter of good beer and a large cigar for me, both very traditional, honorable, and proper gifts for a shaman.

I removed the top of the beer, using my left elbow, and spilled it out on the ground in a particular ritual design taught me by Chiv and others. At this, Pithy Gourd bitterly complained and urged me to drink to show my confidence in him, of which I had none. Hitting the bottle square on its thick base, I dislodged three long poisoned glass spines that I tumbled into his unwilling hands, saying, "I believe these must be yours," which in Mayan is a pun meaning, "This witchcraft belongs to you." In all probability, they were tipped with a strong poison from some venomous tree sap.

Then I pulled out my little knife and cut open the big, good-smelling, handmade cigar he'd given me and there they lay, just as Chiv had warned me years back, like a maggot in the meat, a long set of datura leaves and worse, rolled into the tobacco. This combination would have set the smoker of this cigar back a bit, creating madness before death, a madness that wouldn't pass if death refused to visit.

A crowd was gathering, and they weren't happy about this man's ways. The adroit witch dropped to the ground, grappling my feet, weeping tears on my toes for mercy. The rule in the village was that any person actually able to drop tears on your feet must be listened to at least, and should be shown mercy. At the same time, an ancient Mayan custom is to kill a witch-sorcerer, who is just as much a thief of lives as a bullet-wielding killer. I'm sure that, after all the preceding months of bad things called down on my family by this jealous witch, anyone in the village would have suffered me to take his life right there. I pulled my machete to add a little pressure, and he began to scream and beg, terrorized, though anyone who knows me knows that's not what I'm about. I told him I'd spare him if he'd work for me without remuneration, reserving the right to set my relatives on him if he resumed any witching.

"What do you mean, work for you?"

"I know you can extract illness as easily as you shoot it in and lay traps for it. So now you'll suck out any illness that's been shot into my clients by sorcerers like yourself. That's my offer. You can work for yourself, too, but you must accept and help anyone I send to you for free in exchange for your life." Of course he accepted, and for a couple of years he did work well and I actually got almost friendly with him, until someone less tolerant of his venomous ways shot and killed him in the Cakchíquel Mayan town of Solola across the lake.

But now my witch wars were over. We'd danced the traps and weathered the hate and had good friends pretty much all around after that. It wasn't even good for me to try to go anywhere on the village streets anymore, as everyone kept pulling me in to talk and give me food and drink. I never got where I was headed.

BECOMING USEFUL TO THE CANYON VILLAGE:

My First Clients

My mother-in-law came trundling into the compound, her solid, bare brown feet thudding through the volcanic sand, resounding in the hollow, basaltic shelf over which our end of the village was situated.

"*A, Martín, nkibi jie vinaq iko pkibaal xinki peta rmial Alin Tacaxay rli ya marchant stoy awxin!*" "Martín, all the people over at the open market are saying that the daughter of the famous shaman Alin Tacaxay is going to come to see you to petition a baby."

What was this? I knew nothing about fertility. Chiv hadn't taught me how to make a woman fertile. Where would I begin? This would be my first actual client, and I didn't want to fail right out. I would simply turn her away, that's what I'd do.

Besides, this young woman's father was the most famous and adept fertility shaman in the village, whose power resided in the breadfruit tree, or *Ixim che* as the Tzutujil called it, the corn tree. This tree gave old Ma Tacaxay the ability to bring down the buds of a woman's snakelike coiled womb vine out of the spirit world. Yet his own daughter, after being married for seven years to a well-off merchant named Ma Acabl, Ceremonial Gourd, had been unable to bear a child. And one night after petitioning his own Spirit Dogs, thrones, and keepers, Ma Tacaxay had dreamt that I could give his daughter a medicine to make her have kids.

They were coming tonight, with three workers bearing gifts and sacrifices, to convince me to do them the favor of petitioning their case to the Deities. When they arrived with her family and workers, my in-laws and extended family were very cordial to these people who were like royalty in our village. The daughter's merchant husband wore a hundred-dollar brushed beaver black felt Borsalino hat to the side, solid gold teeth that nevertheless did not outshine his scav that was so thickly embroidered with birds that none of the original handmade white and purple cloth was even visible, and a sash of solid gold and silver threads. He had seven-colored inlay sandals, and had brought cases of liquor, flowers, candles, threads, fruits, cloths, and pots to give incentive to my in-laws to pressure me into service.

I hadn't the slightest notion of where to begin besides doing a divination for them. I thought to stall by asking them to come back at another time in a day or two; meanwhile I'd run up to Chiv's and ask him to take the case and pull me out of this one, just this one time. But after I proposed that we make a divination, first the daughter, Corn Silk, said in her attractive and dignified way, "Father, don't trouble yourself. It's already been thoroughly divined by Ma Tacaxay my father, who says you must take us to ask 'Mothers' and 'Holy Wombs' for the child."

I knew where the Mothers were and the Holy Wombs, but I'd never seen the ceremonies that went with them, or how to even approach such a place. I finally just blurted it out: "I don't have the knowledge in me to carry out what you ask of me. I've only been recently initiated."

I figured I would lose face and just fail right there, but Ya Tzimai, beautiful, happy, childless Corn Silk Girl, said, "Oh, we know that, Father. We heard that you've spoken to our Father [the Sun] and are in good relations with his mother [the Moon] and defended your child in the womb against multiple assailants, so we want you. Someday you'll have the wisdom, but it's not your wisdom we want. We want you because it's been dreamt and divined by several people that you can do this. We need to proceed to the 'Keeper of the Herd,' where the thirteen holy womb hearts and the Holy Throat are kept, and then we need to do a bundle transfer with the male rain side."

I was utterly astonished—she knew every detail of what was necessary, having been at her father's side as a child, watching him work. She knew more than I did. She was four years younger and had the knowledge I didn't have, yet she and her father wanted me to do the ceremony because I had initiated power, not knowledge. You couldn't get the knowledge unless you had the power, but knowledge without the power, no matter how extensive, didn't make you a shaman.

Dumbfounded, I sent them away after they corrected my suggestion by telling me what time the rituals should leave the shaman's house and where they should begin. My clients were telling me what to do and teaching me.

As soon as they'd left, I swaggered into the sweet night to Chiv's place, only to meet an angry, half-dressed Yakix, who told me he was not to be bothered, as he was still in the sweat house. But he heard my voice, and told me to get naked and come in the hot little *touj* with him.

It felt good, all pitch-dark, hot and snug as a fox's womb, scented with the aromatic branches of wild jungle plums. Having heard all about my first client, Chiv chewed me out, telling me that under no circumstances would he step in; the people wanted me, Martín. If they needed Chiv, they'd come see Chiv, and if it was Chiv they needed, Chiv would already know and would probably have already seen them years before! So that was that. But I said, "What do I do?"

Chiv said, "Just do it."

"But what?"

"What do you mean, 'what'? Just do it."

"But I don't know what to do."

"Just follow instructions. Then you'll know!"

"Shouldn't I know what to do?"

Chiv said, "What the hell should an inexperienced baby chick like you know? You're just a new shaman. What does any new shaman know?

"Your success as a doctor will not depend on your knowledge until you've gained experience. Until then, the power of the 'honeymoon' of your marriage to your spirit will carry you through. When the honeymoon is over, then the work begins, because then the spirits will hold you responsible for what you know when you do know it. Right now you have the tremendous leeway of their grace and favor, because you are still beautiful and inept."

After realizing the humbling comfort and truth of this, I had to laugh, and we both laughed hard. Yakix didn't like it because she couldn't have any children either, her only pregnancy having ended tragically, and no more ever again. We remembered how bad she felt and prayed in the dark for her and all things, just like old times.

After coming into the hut and regaining our composure after the heat, we ate cold perch cooked in peppered lemon with hot, reheated green corn tortillas.

Then I asked Chiv, "Where do I begin with these two people?"

"Oh that," he said, as if it were nothing. "First, remember that old hierarchy rascal Ma Mishiya? Well, at midnight after the normal leaving procedure, you and your people [clients] arrive there and wake him and the *xuo* up and tell him what you're up to with the 'big language.' Then follow what he says. That's all, you'll see." Chiv kept on eating and finally went to sleep and I went home, prayed to the moon for a dream, and slept.

Just as Chiv said he would, the old man, Ma Mishiya, woke up. When he heard what I'd come for, he told us to wait a while. He roused the *xuo*, the female chief, who got a fire started for the incense pots, as every *xuo* always did. Fire was male, but it was in the charge of the female in the house.

We sat, then danced the beautiful and powerful contents of the ancient Herd bundle, containing the spirits of all young unborn things, the spirit fetus. The husband transferred the male power to the wife, and the wife handed the child bundle to him. Then I had them both dance the Herd as a baby to the strong rhythm of the slit drum played by the *xuo*, and our elegant dance echoed through the village district called *Xe Chivoy*, Under the Armadillo, where we were.

The complexities of the ritual stayed with me, as well as the prayers and the order of things, just as Chiv had promised. At the end, after all the ritual tobacco and drinks had been distributed, and gifts given by my clients to the old man and woman chiefs, the old keepers asked me where I was going next, knowing full well that I had no idea. "To the next part, as I believe there are four more parts. What do you think?" They agreed and imparted the directions on where and what to do next.

"Go to Panul to the house of Axep [Spotted], wake him up with the ceremonial greeting, and tell him you've just come from the Herd and what you're up to. Follow his instructions."

That's what we did. This next ceremony was very emotional for Ya Tzimai, as she could actually feel the babies in the baby bundles. This next Sacred House procedure was almost entirely female and had four kinds of babies to dance and ritualize and make offerings of a certain color to. I learned all that in one shot. The slit drums here were tiny and made very haunting little sounds as they were played with antlers.

When we'd finished with that, we followed yet another instruction, arriving after dawn at the Sacred House of the wild animals and the heart of food and water, ending at the house of Holy Boy, of course, and making our last stop at the umbilical hole that led to the other world.

Every movement in the village was synonymous with a ritual edifice where corners and doorways, insides and outsides, were inhabited by the Deities. If you knew how to speak, offer, and move, there were myriad doorways of different styles, and each opened onto the world kingdoms of different Gods and their families. Even if they lived far away at certain times, God places were dangerous, so shamans learned courteous ways to approach these things.

Out of one of these places appeared the woman with the skunk stripe in her hair, carrying a huge basketload of hens' eggs, hundreds of them. She passed us around midday as we, slit-eyed and fatigued, finished up our prayer to the middle hole, as instructed by the Holy Boy keepers. She smiled at us and said, "Well, you do very well." Ya Tzimai was ecstatic. She knew the woman was the Moon, and she had come and now disappeared. We left a lot of offerings and magic for her.

Ya Tzimai did get pregnant. Though her father never got to see his granddaughter, his wife did, and she became a solid client and supporter of mine all the way through.

Chiv breathed down my neck for the next two years off and on just to make sure I didn't walk off a cliff in the dark, supervising, stepping in when I endangered myself unknowingly or was making a bad decision with a cure.

People came for everything you can imagine and more. I cut bony calluses off the backs of hard-working men whose work-thinned blankets couldn't prevent the rubbing of their heavy loads from building up calluses as thick as your thumb and wide as your heel on each shoulder blade. I'd cut them to the bleeding quick with a piece of freshly broken glass or obsidian, cauterizing the wound with boiling tallow and plants mixed with beeswax. Those guys would start up a terrible hollering, but they'd sure get mad if you stopped pouring on account of it. They knew this was the only way they could keep working. Their families depended on the backs of the men, on which all sustenance found its way home. It was pretty much hand-to-mouth for your regular Mayan family, and the men had to stay fit for work.

We did the same on the heels and feet, because if you neglected them, the calluses on your back and your heels would eventually crack open and break straight to the quick, vertically into your flesh. These wounds just kept opening and opening, never really closing unless you didn't work for three or four months, which was impossible given the desperation among some of our villagers. So they kept their calluses trimmed, and a lot of shamans were entrusted to do this, as we supplied plant medicine and prayers, too, that kept the men protected and healthy.

Many barren women came to me for help. I was also good at curing intestinal ulcers from parasites and malnutrition, and got pretty good at curing all kinds of diarrheas and vomitings. Most epidemics were called white-man diseases. They came and affected large numbers of people, having originated with the Spanish colonials, each wave of settlers bringing in some new illness. But there were indigenous diseases, too.

All the illnesses had code names and secret names; the secret names were descriptive and were the actual names of the Deities of that disease. All disease was Deified, meaning that the Deity itself carried the nature of the illness. This did not necessarily mean that some angry Deity came to give you illness, although that might happen, but not as an epidemic.

We had typhoid, dengue, cholera, measles, mumps, and influenza. An epidemic Deity might come to visit and when he or she was done, they moved on to the next house. Like a bad relative, this friendly visit made you ill! There wasn't much a shaman could do about these guests, because, just like your relatives, you couldn't turn them away or throw them out because they just got worse. So epidemics were considered just a part of life, something that somehow kept a balance with things.

Some Indians were actually against curing certain epidemics for fear of insulting the illness, which then might kill you for vengeance. In many cases, a family member, usually a child or one of the ladies of the compound, would dream that "the old people," or the Lords of Hot and Cold, as they were sometimes called in respect, were coming. A little ritual was thrown for them. A feast, candle, incense, and some flowers were placed at the *mu xux jai*, umbilicus of the house, to welcome the disease in hopes that he'd eat and become quickly full and happy, making a light case of whatever sickness he was.

Non-epidemic illnesses were the specialty of the shaman. Shamans were most often resorted to for intense, atypical, and unexpected illnesses. Most families had some relative in the compound who knew various simple cures and for the most part, as anywhere in the world, these did the trick. But when that didn't work, the relatives were sent in their misery to a shaman or diviner.

After divining the cause of an illness, a route was determined and ritual offerings were gathered. A ceremony or series of rituals was performed depending on the kind of sickness, and then the *Ajcun* went to work on the sick person and then on all the family members, doing what was necessary to make it all good again. Usually some magic being was left behind to watch over the family while the cure took place.

One time a man, a woodcutter with a small family, almost died spitting blood from his lungs with TB. The TB treatment was free, but the man couldn't afford to take the time off necessary to get well, which was at least two years. What would his family eat in the meantime? So I blessed all his pills and injections, gave him medicines made from plants for the side effects of the streptomycin, PHS, and INH, and divined him. We made ceremonies for him to realign the spirit of his dead mother on the other side, who was caught in his chest.

That done, he got better. But while divining, I saw that this man should not be cutting wood, but dyeing threads instead. This was traditionally a woman's domain, but he did as I told him. I gave him a grubstake, and he became after a while the finest thread dyer in the village, developing many new twists on the traditional ties and dyes. As a matter of fact, he recovered altogether and got so arrogant we couldn't even breathe the same air! But at least his children ate.

Another time an old widower with no living children, from whom I learned a lot of the old God stories, was seen walking around with one arm held straight out to his side. When asked about it, he just grunted, until one day they pulled him in, burning up with a fever and hardly alive.

When I stripped off his shirt, I could see that his armpit was swollen with pus. I cut open and drained the abscesses, filled them full of a root powder, and sang him back to consciousness in the way we know, by grabbing his wandering spirit after going into the geography of his anatomy and pulling him home to us. He'd fallen off a cliff ten days before and cracked open several upper ribs. But he'd bound up his chest and kept working day after day, until his wounds festered and infected so much that he couldn't even lower his arm. The tough old curmudgeon survived and kept on going.

There were epidemics during which my compound looked like a hospital with forty to eighty groups of people lying all over the place, following my instructions on what to do for their dehydrated children. There were epidemics where even the hospitals closed, when I was really overrun. At such times, hundreds and hundreds of groups and kinds of illnesses poured into my place along with most of Chiv's traditional clients. Those I couldn't deal with I sent to someone who I thought could. People with ailments I knew doctors could easily fix I personally took to one of several doctors I'd befriended over the years.

There were many magical problems, too, and these I liked the most. Once a little girl, whose grandfather had been a great shaman, though I didn't know him well, continued seeing him after he passed away in doorways and where she slept.

She was a very little girl only five years old and pretty shy, but her grandmother took her everywhere she went. All the other grandchildren were big and she was the only girl. One day while out with a group in the mountains hunting cactus fruit, the little girl began yelling, happily pointing to a figure just beyond the flinty, basaltic flats that shimmered in the very hot midday sun. The figure was wearing a black *paquan* (jacket) and scav knee pants, and just stood there and didn't budge. The little girl charged through the heat waves toward it, calling out the name of her deceased grandpa. Up until then, no one else had seen any of the figures the little girl had cried about. One of her aunts, the daughter of Aming Xbalam, grabbed her niece just in time to prevent her from falling off a cliff, and the little girl passed into an unconscious state in her arms.

A general alarm was raised as the womenfolk, the girl's mother, her sister-in-laws, both grandmas, and several of her aunts (her father, a merchant and Christian, was gone to the city) came rushing to find me through the village streets. Off painting in my new little hut by the lake on the cliff, I was found by my little big-faced brother-in-law who came pushing through the orchids and coffee bushes, out of breath, to tell me.

Striding back to the compound, I saw the child, and found her very slow, faraway heartbeat. On a song in a trance, I went to her in that land, then sent my dogs to find her. She was traveling fast back to the land of the dead, probably in her grandpa's arms.

I took her in my arms and redrew the road she was on. I called the Lords of Death, who came ringing their clashing gold bells. People could hear owls, the whir of beetles and moths, and came to see the altar. I challenged the Lords of Death to a gambling game, and they accepted. I rolled and won with a roll of a pair. And off they went, taking the girl's old grandfather with them.

She woke up vomiting so hard she almost choked, but we got her back. I laid ashes around her, put her in a bath of warm herbal tea, and gave her traveling medicine for fright. The young mother was happy, but I wasn't, and neither was the grandmother. Why was this old guy returning? It was typical that he would try to grab the tenderest of his relatives to take along with him. As nice as he was when he was alive, his niceness made him dangerous in death, because until he was integrated into the ancestors, he was in between and still a ghost who should be traveling toward the Land of the Dead. For some reason, he needed the living juice of the little girl to get him there.

I made a big divination, pulling out the calendric bundle, and after an hour or so was able to determine that the problem was that the crazy old man was missing some of his shaman tools! When a shaman is about to die, he must either bequeath all his bundle objects to his apprentice in a ceremonial way or leave instructions to his descendants on how to feed and take care of them without disturbing them, until someone is born into the family who, without being coached, recognizes the names and functions of the spirit tools that he or she has inherited years or centuries after the old one has gone. If neither of these conditions prevails, then every single tool, sacred object, and piece of divining stuff must be put in the grave, so the deceased will have them to show as he passes the many territories and weather kingdoms and portals. Otherwise he can't get to the ancestral land of the dead. If he bequeaths his tools to someone, then the ritual feeding of these holy relics frees the dead person's passage.

If some of the tools are missing, pieces of the shaman himself are missing, and he must come back to get someone to put them where they belong in the grave or to feed them properly so the deceased can leave this world and go to his real home in the other world.

In this case, my divination revealed that several of the old man's objects were still around. There being no student or chosen caretaker, they all should have been put in the grave. But his elderly wife, a severe but thorough and sincere woman, was positive that they had all been buried with him. She personally had put them there, knowing best from her closeness to her husband what they looked like. I insisted that she look and find the objects. If not, we'd have to do a big type of ritual that was very dangerous for me. We all knew the ghost would return soon, and take somebody with him this time.

Six hours later, toward sundown, the little girl's grandma, irate and disgusted, surmounted the raw basaltic boulders and breezed into my hut, chirping out the requisite greeting of one her age, gender, and accomplishments in relation to mine. She opened her shawl, where clutched in her fist were seven objects that I incensed and put into an ancient stone incense bowl with the face of a water monster. "I found these in my son-in-law's house in a salt sack under his reed mat!"

I talked to my divination bundle again, and it said there were more. "There's not one place I haven't searched," she said, "completely and everywhere!" But I divined some more, and sure enough found that the son-in-law in question was busy selling the objects a few at a time in

Guatemala City to collectors to finance his new immense stone house with a tin roof! He was a Christian and had been told by his pastor that these shamanic things held nothing sacred and that he should turn them into something good for his family. In the meantime, his daughter was going to be hauled off by the ghost of his father-in-law, and the objects were gone.

So I had no choice but to do a big ritual to capture the old man and give him a new start, redraw his road to the other world, and feed every stage with a great deal of fire. In the middle of the ritual, which I did in the son-in-law's house, I had going at least a thousand candles made of kidney fat, and when my songs began, the house's roof began to shake like an earthquake. It got so violent that everybody ran out except me, the old lady, and the little girl. A cold wind came and knocked the light out of the candles, and when I got them relit, the seven shamanic objects were gone and the house had stopped rattling.

After that, the girl didn't see any more ghosts, but she was depressed, as she missed her grandpa. This was understandable, and I gave her a grief medicine for her sorrow.

Other syndromes, conditions, and sicknesses come directly from Deities, ghosts, or nature, who are insulted through human arrogance or forgetfulness. The personality of the irritated Deity, tree, rock, wind, or animal "jumps" into a person, causing terrible pain and sickness. A cure is brought about by reestablishing the Deity in its rightful house through corrective ritual. Again, these rituals are very complex and are the exclusive territory of the shaman. Some illnesses are inflicted upon the villagers by other people. This is accomplished either by calling foreign powers into your body or by bad thoughts being thrown or shot into you. These are all considered witchcraft. To cure this, a shaman must intercede.

The north wind blew hard, raising the poisoned dust of coldness that made many villagers ill. The north wind also buried seeds and matured the fruit and corn and cooked souls, and released the babies from the womb. As the grand maturer, the wind whipped through our village, unpopular but necessary, the bringer of dry cold and the rebirth of our Father the Sun and his little brother, the Deer Star, Venus.

For the Tzutujil, most maladies are considered a natural part of life and described as weather phenomena. The weather patterns in your body account for how you feel, just as the weather outside is the emotion of the

Earth. And as each emotion is Deified, these Deities can be dealt with ritually in a person's body as a micro version of the Big Weather. As most weather comes about through dealing with the absence or abundance and differing forms of water in the air, so most symptoms in the human body are delineated according to kinds of different weather bloods. I can't repeat their names here, because when called they are given form, and the force, when conjured, comes, and comes hungry. If you're not adroit, trained, or a shaman, you have no way of knowing what each weather eats or demands. If these forms' desires go unrequited, then the speaker of the names becomes the food, and you yourself will become ill.

I don't know why people in modern life want to be shamans. There's nothing romantic about it. We just go around capturing monsters, resweetening the earth, and making people's memories taste good again.

There is an eloquence in negativity that quickly becomes evil. We see evil as a form of negative creativity with a vengeance. Its parents are simple, natural desires who, because they have gone unfed, become frustrated, unnatural hungers. These hungers begin to put together things that don't go together, creating monsters, which are personified unnatural hungers that eat everything and never get full. This dynamic is identical to the bent way that some modern people breed animals to fit the same distorted and deformed pattern that their own overdomesticated natures may have fallen into.

We, the shamans, can be thought of as spirit dogcatchers; the pets we catch are these composite hunger monsters. Unlike the dog pound people who kill what they catch, we shamans break the monsters back into their component parts, thus sweetening the earth by allowing each thing to flower back into its own original shape again.

True creativity doesn't just make things; it feeds what feeds life. In modern culture where people are no longer initiated, the spirit goes unfed. To be seen, the uninitiated create insane things, some destructive to life, to feel visible and powerful. These creations are touted as the real world. They are actually forms of untutored grief signaling a longing for the true reality of village togetherness.

The result of this uninitiated approach to life is violence, spiritual and otherwise, where the hoarding of wealth, street violence, the soul-curdling banality of popular television, and the creation of weapons of mass destruction are all considered status quo.

One morning during the dry cold-wind time, I was dreaming hard when a very strong, glaring-eyed God pulled me from my bed. We flew together to the top of a *Par ki* plant, where the God turned me into a little bird. He was an owl, and when I looked at my feet, they were tiny hummingbird feet. We soared up there in the breeze for a long time together, looking over the sleeping village.

The owl had a long sword made of rippling lightning that sizzled. He said, "I'm going to come and kill eighty-three people with the necklace of Holy Boy soon. You pick them right now."

The necklace of Holy Boy meant typhoid, referring to the swollen knots of lymph nodes around the base of the neck. In an effort to seem egalitarian, I began pointing to friends of mine. The owl slapped me in the face, almost killing me.

"Buzzard greens, do you think I'm that stupid?" he yelled, echoing in my head. "Choose now!"

So I started pointing to my enemies. The owl, turning back into the God, but with bird feet, whacked me again. "Do you really think we care which ones have to go? Do you think you have anything to do with all that?" And he slapped me right back into my bed, where I awoke with a start next to my pregnant wife, while my mother-in-law snored, competing with a neighboring woman who snored harder still in the doorless, sleepy village.

Typhoid came. And we didn't lose eighty, but we lost forty-three, mostly old people. Cholera tended to kill more adults, typhoid struck the old people, and the children most often died from the next epidemic of measles, which always left a lot of kids blind. Measles was the number-one killer of Mayan children.

During this particular typhoid bout, the villagers brought me a guy who was losing his hold on life. The clinic was closed because all the staff and doctors had typhoid, too, and had left the area to find recovery elsewhere. My compound had long rows of people's families who were nursing the sick ones as I made the rounds. This particular man had been receiving treatments before the clinics closed, and they had tried everything, including drugs banned elsewhere like chlorofenicol. In spite of all this, this man just wouldn't get well.

With typhoid, every day your fever hits around the same time. Your body feels as if it's burning up and then you get chills. Afterward the fever sort of relaxes, but it returns at the same time the next day, going up a notch. After five or six days of this, people sometimes go stark raving mad. They become disoriented. These symptoms, plus the debilitation and dehydration, make typhoid a disease hard to keep up with. Nevertheless, I'd been successful so far, holding down everyone's fever and keeping them well-hydrated and strong.

This new man, however, wouldn't respond to anything I tried. As he shook and fried, I prayed hard for a medicine that would help him. He had no relatives to look after him. No one actually seemed to know him, but he was an *Atiteco* (Atitlán villager) for sure.

I did my ceremony and fell sound asleep for a few minutes. I dreamt about a beautiful full-figured coastal Tzutujil woman with very dark skin, dressed in a short, bright yellow *uk* (wraparound skirt) and a loose yellow pot and a head ribbon with big yarn balls hanging down, all of the attire of coastal Mayan ladies. She approached me and scolded me for not sleeping with her sister, who felt abandoned because I wouldn't make love with her. So I said, "Where is she, your sister? I'll be hers right now if you both wish it so." At that point, I heard a rustling in the woods, and out came a smaller, younger version of the yellow woman, only she was wearing the same clothes in solid white. We went off together and made love in the river. Waking up sweating, I knew that the key to this unfortunate man's suffering lay in this dream.

I consulted my creatures, my ritual objects, and realized that the main plant medicine I'd been using to calm the typhoid fever had a yellow blossom and grew on the coast where the Tzutujil maidens all wear yellow hand-wovens. But farther down the Nahualate River lived women who wore white and were as shy as the woman in the dream. I surmised, having learned how to learn from Chiv, that since the first lady was the medicinal plant I'd been using for typhoid and the two were sisters, that there must be a second kind of similar plant with a white blossom that would fix up our sick man.

I sent a runner to my mother-in-law's brother, who lived about three miles from us, knowing that he spent half his time working down on the lowlands since his wife's father had land there. Abuxtol, Little Bald Tortilla Gourd, was his name, but everyone just called him Boosh—Bald—though he wasn't at all. But he was undersized, very pleasant, and a tremendous joker. Never was there a better man born for gratitude and dedication.

When he arrived, I asked him if he knew of a plant that approximated the type of yellow-blossomed sensitive plant I used to cure typhoid, but which had white blossoms and grew around Cunen. "Oh yes, Martín. I was so scared, I thought you were going to ask me for a loan!" He was the most poverty-stricken man in the whole clan, so this was his constant joke. "Of course I know the plant. It curls up when you touch it and has white blossoms. It's called Jaguar Whiskers, and the coastal people eat its tendrils for food."

I gave him a couple of quetzales for the bus ride, and off he went, to travel the fifty miles and obtain some of that plant I'd dreamt about. He didn't return until late that night, tired and with a big old string bag full of the stuff and a big long story about how hard it was to get. We loved hearing him tell stories.

I boiled up some of the dark vine, since that's what I made love to, the girl's body, not her clothes, the plant's blossoms. I drank a cup to see if it would kill me, but instead it gave me the symptoms of a fever. So I cooked my patient some, and made an offering of a lot of gifts, fat, candles, flowers, tobacco, jade, and liquor as a sacrifice to the plant's keeper and its fire-soul to pay for the gift of her timely appearance and the gift of her "giving" herself to me. Now I was married to another plant, which brought the total to about sixty-one.

The man recovered, walking out of my compound in two and a half days, and still nobody knew much about him.

DAWN ROADS, ABUNDANCE ROADS:

No One Trusts a Skinny Shaman

One day after I had taken a stroll through the coffee terraces under the *jocote* trees, past "Turkey Eyes'" house, past "Velvet Leaf's" hut, past "Ears'" hut, past "Boy Head's" hut, past "Monkey Horn's" house, past "Hotspring Man's" hut and I had returned to my own hut, saluting the mother-in-law, my youthful brother-in-law, my wife, and my sister-in-law, we heard a rasping, melodic male voice asking to gain entrance into our compound.

I kept eating while the womenfolk fielded this man's intentions, but their polite ministration began to escalate into an insult war. The man, a young merchant with heavily tinseled knee pants, a snap-button shirt, an expensive felt hat worn to the side, gold teeth, and a pockmarked, smart-assed face, demanded to see me, Martín. When quizzed about what he wanted, he wouldn't tell anyone. The girls told him that if he wouldn't tell them, nothing could be done because Martín was busy.

That wasn't one hundred percent true. No one really wanted to help him, since he had once been an abusive suitor of my sister-in-law, he had no courting instincts, and he was an uninitiated, Christian merchant who thought everyone should do what he said. As the Tzutujil say about businessmen who don't farm, fish, or work with their hands: They think each of their eyelashes is worth a dime. The girls also figured this guy had VD, which I'd only seen in merchants who made a habit of visiting the bordellos so handy around non-Indian marketplaces.

What I didn't know at the time was that the man was irate because he'd been turned out of the compound by our unmarried girls several times before when looking for me. When I went to meet him at the entrance, he handed me a transistor radio. "Ah, Martín, you have to heal my radio!"

"I don't heal radios, little brother. I don't know anything about that."

"Don't say things like that to me. You know perfectly well how to fix everything with electricity. You fix people with electricity in their throat [TB], electricity in their blood [arthritis], and the people of Green Lightning Death [epilepsy], don't you?"

It was abusive and discourteous of him to be using these terms in full view of the public, as the names themselves conjured illness if not received with ritual food. My sister-in-law, miraculously a traditionalist in spite of her Christian father, was watching over my shoulder, listening horrified to this man's words. I nodded to her and she went and got the smoker full of embers and copal, and put up a lot of candles for me at my altar until I could get to fixing the results of this thoughtless character's words.

This man, like other modern Tzutujil, figured that since illness was a kind of body weather, and lightning figured heavily into it, disease was mostly a displacement of electricity, which was toxic in the wrong places. "No, I can't fix radios," I said. "Wherever you got that thing, you take it and ask them. Forgive me, I have no idea."

Well, he lost his stirrups with me then: "You just don't want me to have what you have!"

"I do not have a radio. I don't like the ugly noise they make." And that was true; I had no machines at all.

"Yes you do, and you go where they are every day. I've seen you."

"Your mouth's not making words, brother. They're coming out of the flames standing on your head. Speak the real words from your belly."

"I see you go with those rip-clothesed greens-eaters whose patches flap in the winds of their putrid speech that cracks out of their asses, and I've seen you take them to that long stone place, and you disappear and go to the Land of the Dead around that stone, and you come back right away. Why don't you take my radio over there and bring it back in a couple of days when they got it fixed? I have plenty of metal to pay you with. Do it, man. Why don't you? I'll pay you a lot."

I didn't know whether to laugh or to cut his useless throat for heaping insults on my poor, sick clients. So I laughed along with a lot more of the crowd who had gathered round to listen, until he stomped off. He returned to harangue my compound for several more days until he just finally gave up and bought another miserable radio in Guatemala City.

It was beneath all of our dignity to get mad at him. Like most of the villagers, he believed that since things made of steel and plastic—for which they had only one word, *chich*—were obviously not from the center of life, then like all wealthy, incomprehensible machine-made things, they really must come from a Demon World. A great deal of what merchants thought was great, such as watches, sunglasses, radios, cars, and so on, actually came from the USA, a place generally considered an unclassified spirit realm, unvisitable by regular Indians. Since shamans were notorious for going to other spirit places and returning with magical things from other worlds, this guy figured that since my specialty was with lightning-based illnesses, as my medicine was based on lightning animals and things that flashed, that I must spiritually have relations in the land where electric things were made, the United States. And, of course, I did come from there!

A shaman had to move around a stone stele in a special kind of dance, in order to enter another world. The merchant figured this was just like catching a transport to the USA. He assumed I could leave his wretched little radio for repairs in America, pick it up the next day, and then return to the village from behind the stele. But nobody in that world I went to knew how to fix radios, not that I ever knew.

It was heartening for the elders to notice that, for all the obvious erosion of this man's social skills by his contact with the orphan culture of business, he still had style and took notice of what traditionalists like myself did. "Poor boy," they said. Someone knew his story and told it to me, and what had made him the way he was. We never liked to forget people even if we disliked them, because they were still part of the village.

After a year and a half of practicing as a shaman, three-fourths of the people who sought my services were epileptics. Yalur's generation seemed to be plagued with this condition more than any other age set. I laid this at the feet of American-supported cotton growers on the Guatemalan coastland that we called the Female Earth, because it was the most fertile, wet, untamed land full of animals, delicious fruits, and mysteries, next to the Grandmother Ocean, and where all the Growth Goddesses lived.

But after the fruit-growing people put in the rails and highways, the cotton people flattened the land, pulled down the trees, and planted cotton and sugar cane on huge tracts. They shanghaied thousands of indentured Indians to plant, hoe, and pick cotton at ten cents a sack. As with the coffee industries at higher altitudes, in the fifties and early sixties landpoor Mayan farmers ended up working on these sweat farms.

The growers unscrupulously sprayed the fields with chemicals from airplanes, sometimes with the workers still working the land below. They sprayed the workers' camps and their food as they cooked on open fires at the edges of their fields. Herbicides, pesticides, and fertilizers were inhaled and ingested in toxic quantities, and pregnant Indian women gave birth to a generation of children with all kinds of genetic problems, one of which was an odd appearance of neurological irregularity in girls going into puberty. At least five percent of all the adolescent girls in our village alone became epileptic at age fourteen. All their parents had been sprayed in the fields, trying to make a living, while their mothers were pregnant with them.

Other villages were equally affected. Of course, many children died of complications at birth; many parents gave birth to asthmatics, and some of the parents themselves died. I remember that one whole village up by the Motagua River died *in one day* because a farm company just dumped its extra chemicals upstream of where all the people got their cooking water. Nothing was ever done. No non-Indian ever cared one way or another.

I found a way of dealing with my clients' epileptic seizures to the point where over eighty percent stopped having them altogether. If we caught the condition early enough, then the girls and adolescent boys usually outgrew the condition by the time they were in their mid-twenties, if not earlier.

My medicine was so successful that many modern doctors sent all their epileptics my way. Sometimes the client was so severely damaged that I had to use a modern drug to get the person to a place stable enough to work on him or her with my own traditional methods. Various international health organizations also came to observe my work in order to study my method for curing various sicknesses. I did well with amebiosis, shigelosis, and other illnesses. But, unfortunately, they were unwilling, and probably unable, to comprehend and utilize the route I employed, which depended in large part on a network of people maintaining a traditional system of monitoring an epileptic patient over a period of two to three years, during which I kept tabs on them on almost a daily basis. This network was the village. Also I refused to teach anything to anybody connected to the fraudulent pharmacies that sold Indians fake and untried drugs for very high prices, or marginally useful medicines for prices beyond their reach.

In the case of epilepsy, this was especially harmful. Ten phenobarbitol pills of fifty milligrams that a pharmacist bought in bulk from the drug companies cost about a Guatemalan penny. Ten thousand pills cost about ten quetzales or ten American dollars. It takes three to six of these pills a day to control untreated grand mal seizures occurring three times a month. Even if this treatment controlled the seizures, the patient was indefinitely stuck taking this heavy barbituate, without which the seizures would most likely resume. The pharmacies sold these pills for a dollar apiece. So young Mayan women or men, who still worked at the side of their father or mother cutting wood, hoeing, weaving, or hauling water, would cost their parents a minimum of three dollars a day. This was $1.50 more than both parents made to feed the whole family, if they had other sons and daughters, which in all likelihood they did. Nobody could afford the medicine.

Although I didn't like all doctor medicines, some were useful for emergencies or for calming down certain symptoms until saner and more natural, traditional ways could be employed. I would trade my paintings to certain medical companies for drugs and sometimes give out medicine free in appropriate doses. The pharmacists hated my guts, but not as much as I hated theirs. They killed a lot of good people, including several friends of mine, with bad medicine. This is not to say that here and there a good-hearted drugstore person didn't exist, but it was a racket, I tell you.

Anyway, the Americans were angry at me, too, because a couple of charitable organizations had told their donors that the money they gathered was going to give free medical treatment to poor people. But in our village they sold phenobarbital pills and Dilantin, etc., for about twenty-five cents apiece, but you still couldn't get enough medicine to treat anyone for more than a week. Even seventy-five cents a day was too steep for most families, since that left only seventy-five cents to feed and clothe the whole family. For these reasons, when the organizations came to observe my methods, I told them that unless they exposed the pharmacies, clamped down on the charities' money-grubbing and cultural interference, and most of all lobbied against the reckless use of chemicals banned in all the countries that produced them and the indiscriminate spraying of the people in the fields, these organizations would have to study *that*, because I refused to tell them anything! They were all too politically and economically intertwined with all the culprits, and they chose to do nothing.

Nevertheless, I continued in my little tiny ancient way. Nobody ever actually died from epilepsy while I lived in Santiago, but three people had previously died because of what happened to them on account of seizures. The local terrain was rough, and people struggled hard to coax a living from the stone and water, plants and fish. One lady had had a seizure while alone, and she burned to death in her own cooking fire. Another drowned in the lake after cracking her poor head on a rock underwater while washing her brother's clothing. Another man had a seizure and drowned while pulling his fishing nets into his log canoe. Another lady's feet were burned off completely in her cooking fire during a seizure, but she survived and continued to function pretty well. All in all, epileptics were almost a tribe of their own, having in common certain physical traits unrelated to their illness and the same attitudes.

I remember one poor fellow from the neighboring Cakchíquel people, who had no living relatives save his old skinny aunt. For some reason, this thirty-year-old man had never grown up, remaining childlike even though he was huge for a Guatemalan, at least as tall as I am, about 5'6", almost a foot taller than his sixty-year-old aunt. This boy-man had so many epileptic seizures that his aunt had to take him everywhere she went as if he were a big pet bear, leading him by a handmade cotton rope she tied under his arms. This fellow had as many as three seizures a day, spending more time "out there" than in.

I guess his old aunt had heard about us Atitecos and Martín, so she started walking to me, carrying a lot of gifts in her poor little hands, dragging her nephew behind her as if he were a cow going to market. She walked up over the Black Coyote Mountain, down the White Talc Hills, to Palopoj, to San Lucas, over Pacaman, past Chijuyu, and down into our town, an overland journey of over fifty very rugged, trailless, and mostly roadless miles. She came on bare feet, pulling her nephew and carrying her load.

It took her a while, but she finally arrived. They lived at my house for about five weeks while I treated the nephew. The old lady was so great and kept trying to give me everything she owned for payment. In my house, the boy spoke for the first time in ten years. He was still pretty simple, but our culture hero, the *chp*, was like that. Maybe it was him coming to test our hearts! I got the boy down to a seizure or two a year, and then he became completely well. Thank the spirits.

One morning, an old fertility shaman named Qwa, Hotspring Man, whom I didn't really know but whose middle sons were underwater shamans with whom I was friends, saw me walking past him and saying nothing. This was very rude and untypical of me and mine. A minute later he saw me walk by again. When I greeted him this time, he ran out of his hut and grabbed me hard, telling me not to leave my hut once I got there; he would show up in a little while. Good, I thought. Although my compound always talked surreptitiously about this fellow, I knew it would be good to get to know him.

So I obeyed, arriving at my house cold, dry, shaking, and terrified of some unspecified thing. In a little while, Qwa showed up with a good bunch of herbal medicines in old nineteenth-century bottles. He told me to drink one all the way down, which I did, breaking into a tremendous fever and sweat, and then I slept. When I awoke, he gave me a different bottle to drink out of, and I slept again. When I woke again, it was night, and the old fellow was still there. I was soaked head to foot in bad-smelling sweat, so I went to the lake and bathed and returned.

He explained that he'd seen me in two chunks, shot by an enemy with fright, as they say. This attack had shaken out my spirit, which always arrived before or after you did. If your spirit arrived before you did, you could be easily cured, as Qwa did for me in this case. Arriving too late usually meant death.

This man really helped me out. I'd been overworked and exhausted. I had let my defenses down and had gotten hit by one of a client's enemy's volleys, which had been meant for him. As payment, Hotspring suggested that I promise to take care of his youngest child, a son of fifteen years old, in the event that he and his wife Ya Ca, Grinding Stone, died. I'd seen the boy in the village. He didn't seem to stray very far from his father's home. He was a mute and an epileptic, and these people's *chp* or last child, his parents being in their sixties.

The old man, unable to help the child with his seizures, thought maybe I could help the boy to live, for he was unable to work, they thought, and needed someone to provide for him. A little chunk of land came with him, but his many brothers would be in charge of what to do with it. I accepted, of course, and told old Qwa and Ya Ca to start bringing him over to get accustomed to our compound, so that when his parents passed away he could feel all right about living with us.

The boy was funny. He followed me everywhere, copying me, to the great delight of all the villagers who'd all run out of their huts as we went by. The kid started walking like me, wore his hat at the same angle, and so on, with a big goofy look on his face, though saying nothing, of course.

Over a period of weeks he started drawing pictures while I painted, so I gave him a big bunch of papers and brushes and paints, and he started doing some pretty wild things, especially images of Deities and spirit things I myself was banned from painting. He had no seizures at all while he was with me, and after about three months he began to talk. His parents had thought he was deaf because he never responded to anyone, but he could hear just fine and now he was talking.

Well, it didn't take but a month before he was a total pest and wouldn't shut up. His people were really happy and surprised when he decided to sew Indian pants and shirts for a profession. The village named this boy

Cabracan, Earthquake, because he got things shaking, and was never still after that. He seemed really well, and we didn't have to worry about him anymore, except that he liked to grope the girls. He made up for all his years of silence with nonstop yakety-yak. We all figured he'd catch up with himself somewhere along the line and even out, which he did, but it took him a long, long time, and we knew he was enjoying it.

We did an evil thing with him once, though, I must confess. A pushy anthropologist was demanding stories and information about old things and wanted us to supply it to him, acting as if we owed the scientist our precious intellectual property.

Earthquake's dad was a masterful traditional storyteller, but he only spoke inside ritual contexts. Earthquake, however, had been *listening* to his father's style for sixteen years and could imitate him perfectly. The only problem was that he didn't know the stories at all and just made up endless nonsense, which went on for days unless he was stopped. He loved to try to be "in" with us older guys when we all competed to tell the most traditional tale the most thoroughly and creatively. But Earthquake was a runaway mule train with nothing in the packs, talking as much as he could, with nowhere to go and happy to go on that way forever, just happy to be able to be heard.

So we told the arrogant anthropologist that if he gave the shaman's son enough good stuff, he'd probably spill all the Tzutujil secrets of the ages. About three thousand miles of tape later, the anthropologist, who still had to find someone to translate that drivel, thought he had it all! Old Earthquake got a lot of drawing supplies, pens, radios, shirts, and threads of all kinds, and the scientist got what he paid for. Earthquake was deliriously happy.

Life was going well. My clients were getting cured, Yalur's belly was swelling, and I had no big personal enemies. Though there were rumblings of warfare and revolution on the wind, none of that had particularly touched us here yet.

Satisfied with my life, listening to the wind, my mother-in-law snoring, and the waterfowl and the grebes calling in the lake, I drifted off into the Land of Spirits and Dreams . . .

. . . when *crash, blam*, someone put his foot into the lime pot, smashing it, then hurled a dog-headed stool straight into my bed. Soon enough I found myself jerked to my feet with tobacco breath puffing in my face, carrying hard phrases:

"Why do you do like that?" *(Natzraga Naban cavrá?)*

"Why don't you receive your food?" *(Natzraqa majun na cam awey nkiyá?)*

It was Chiv, of course, never one to wait until daybreak, busting in on my life, crackling mad about something.

"You mean the pots of food my clients leave? I receive those."

"Don't make jokes with me. What you do bites hard—because of you I can't sleep. Don't be funny with me. I want to stay mad till you tell me why you refuse the pay people give you."

"Old Grandfather Ma Clash, it has to be that way. I have lots of cash thanks to your teaching, and the people have nothing. How could I take what little they have left, when they could use that money to feed themselves and stay healthy?"

"Do you think my charging the people is no good?" Chiv blasted.

"That's different. You're from here."

"What? And you're not from here? You don't want to be from here! What kind of poisonous beast has bitten you [What's the matter with you, to act so strangely]? Is your head being disassembled [Your head is a house and the thatch is removed and this is disorienting your brain] or what? Are all the years and roads and wisdom I've passed on to you worth nothing, that you give them away, like no one had to die or suffer for hundreds of generations so that an ungrateful boy could have them to toss around and throw away, as if he would never exhaust them?"

"No, it's not that, Papa, just that so many people have so little, I don't want to make them have less."

"Listen, your skull is thick. What about the power of the spirits? Don't you know that the power of these things will run away if not fed by the honor of the people's payments? And if that happens you will have no abilities to help them anyway."

"Oh yeah, *catzijwa*, that's true." I began to see a little what he meant.

"That payment contains some of the origination of the illness, which you must burn off to the ones who eat the illness and who give your self-centered belly the ability to help at all. Then you go around like some lazy guy acting like they belong to you, instead of you belonging to them, and to those past keepers like me and thousands of dead ones who are your acquired ancestors who need feeding, *catzijwa*.

"You have to use large chunks of the payment you receive to feed them, because you are only the visible fruit on the tree, who looks unique enough, but whose secret, which you know well, is rooted in a thousand-year-old trunk filled with their suffering and well-stabbed faces; whose roots need the food that you, as their most recent 'fruit' and 'horse' [bearer], must give them as you're here in this world, translating sour, twisted words [illness] into delicious words, turning manure into fertilizer, monsters into tools and food, which you feed back to the roots that gave you the power to do so! Does this stay lit in your head?"

"Yeah, *catzijwa*. But what about the poverty of the people?"

"You make them poor by not accepting their gifts! When you try to keep them rich by not accepting their payment, all they see is that what they have is not good enough for you, much less the spirits you serve, which makes them hopelessly poor! Does this stay lit in your head?"

"*Jie ta catzijwa.*" "Yes, Father, it's true."

"Take their payment to honor me, Ma Clash Chiviliu Tacaxoy, to remember the people of the Umbilicus Deep Canyon Village, to remember the Flowering Mountain Earth Navel Valley Lord and Ladies of all that moves near and far, before and now, who never forget. You're doing very well, *Tiksajachoqá*. Wear your courage, wear your wisdom, long life, honey in the heart, keep up the excellent work."

My eyes were blurred with tears. Old Chiv, my friend, my father, my crazy friend, who never let me drift, kicked me back from the canyons' edge even when I insisted on going over it.

Mayans love fat. They love fat people, and they are envious of a skinny person who gets fat. But in Santiago, because of the honest and non-mechanical nature of the village way of being, the economic landscape was stark and the margin between having enough and not having enough was very thin. There were people who starved to death; many, many children died of malnutrition. Most babies were the most beautiful, chubby, sharp-eyed lovelies you could ever desire, but all children came into great peril when they began to eat solid food, either for lack of protein or because of diseases and parasites.

If you made it past age five, chances were you'd make it to forty. The average life expectancy was forty-two years. The hard, unyielding labor men and women had to do to survive and the slim diet they had to share in a family made starvation a gradual thing. This made it such that a little abundance wouldn't cure forty years of starvation rations. No one died from not having enough food for a couple of weeks, but rather from not having certain kinds of food for many years.

But if you made it to forty-five, you could probably make it into your seventies. Anyone still alive in their eighties was like a legend, and some, like Chiv, who was in his nineties (he claimed in his early one hundreds!) were close to God in stature.

Fatness was rare and looked upon as a sign of happiness. People said, "You can't expect much from a skinny shaman," or "Don't trust a skinny shaman," and so on because we shamans were, in a way, like the Social Security system of the village. Every family or individual that a shaman succeeded in aiding somehow was then related to you in much the same way as a midwife became a relative to the children she helped deliver. Children were coached to hug you and kiss your hand as they grew, remembering when you had saved their lives. Village custom had it that every time a cure came good, the people would deliver large clay pots of traditional kinds of stews, depending on the nature of the illness.

Most were *pulic*, a kind of dish with a couple of big one-to-five-pound chunks of meat cooked in a beautiful, tasty broth of wild greens, three kinds of native peppers, and toasted squash seeds ground on the grinding stone with a local variety of tomato. Another dish was made of turkey meat cooked in a wild mint and a kind of toasted corn gruel. Sacrificial meats were offered in some kinds of ceremonies in order to eat away an illness, turning the illness into food and bringing the client back to fruition by eating. Whatever was given away was gained spiritually. Food was also sacrificed to certain holy places representing the part of the client's body affected, so that the illness could eat the food instead of the client.

There were many kinds of food, and people felt that they had to present a shaman with them three separate times in order to be fully cured.

When they brought food, they brought enough to feed your whole compound, too. Each client's people would send over four or five gallons' worth of food, accompanied by the most well-made, tender, lovely, unblemished tortillas, a big warm stack of them wrapped in a new brightly colored handwoven tortilla cloth, which you sent back with their cooking pot as a sign that you'd received both and treasured the experience.

But on certain village feast days, all clients felt obligated by custom to send the shamans the same kinds of sacrificial foods plus basketfuls of avocados, jocotes, zapotes, mangos, and many other kinds of fruit from their family fields. Of these feasts there were about twelve big ones a year, and fifty-odd smaller ones. So if I'd worked on two hundred groups that year, then I'd get that many five-gallon pots of stews and meats, and tons of fruits. It was *xjan* not to eat of each, so one ate a little of each, and I confess I ate a lot of some, because you couldn't beat these dishes for taste (and that's when I knew I had married into the wrong clan!). So if a shaman did good work, he could not and would not stay slim. He'd put on weight, and the Indians loved to say that they were the "people of such and so fat shaman." You wore their honor and their willingness to keep you alive on your belly. The Tzutujil were all very proud of that.

By feeding his compound, a shaman was a big hero, too, because when he was present, all of his relations ate well on a regular basis. But the greater part of these offerings was divided among the most honored elders; your teachers; people such as Chiv; those who'd made you a canoe or a well-embroidered scav or a headcloth; and families of the totally orphaned, widowed, and indigent, who got most of the food and who needed it the most. There were stingy shamans, of course, but that was not the rule, and without refrigeration what good is a bunch of rotting stew all to yourself? If you didn't get enough food to distribute, it was because you didn't get anybody well. Rows of clay stew pots were your credentials, not a piece of paper or a position supplied by some authority, but the opinion of the village itself. If you did good work, you were fat. If you didn't, you were skinny.

People coming from outside the villages, often Christian officials and political idealists, saw only a stream of badly needed food coming into the courtyard of fat, greedy shamans. They never stuck around to see how the indigenous system really worked. And so shamans got a bad reputation for impoverishing the public. Maybe some deserved it. I don't know. But I know that Chiv and I never did, though we lived like barbarian kings. Like real Mayan kings, however, we were responsible to the people whose lives depended on distribution and interconnectedness instead of on private handouts or enforced egalitarian flatness.

I had trouble accepting further payment beyond the food. Payment was sometimes given *before* I even started to work, sometimes in the form of cash or expensive gifts. This is where Chiv stepped in, showing me that these gifts were hazard pay and were to be distributed among the spirits just as the food was distributed among the people, with a little left over for oneself.

Shamans walked their talk by living the fat exuberance that Mayans consider the blessings of life. Holiness doesn't show itself only in the holy. I didn't consider myself holy, but a lover of the holy. The blessings of that holiness were the joys of practical everyday life, full of food which we saw as peace, and little suffering, at the sides of our peers and our blood. This was holiness, and the goal of holiness was this blessing. Anything else had to have this golden moment as its goal, or to the Tzutujil it was witchcraft, folly, or the destruction of war.

TURNING BULLETS
INTO CORN

Their well-sculpted oiled brown feet padding through the cindery sand of the village paths, not yet cracked or calloused by years of toil and travel into the painfully gnawed chunks of armored bone with rawhide grapes for toes like their grandparents', strong as jade, their backs as promising as an unpicked field of corn, these two fifteen-year-old grandchildren of Ma Cu Xbalan came coyly, sparkling and flashing into my compound after my first son "made his dawn" (was born).

Like little stuck-up nervous deer, these two smooth-skinned beauties oozed into our compound. Pushing into each other, they walked as if I lived in the underworld or something. Raising their expensive tinseled shawls to their lips, the young girls spoke sideways of how their grandfather, Ma Cu Xbalan, had sent them to fetch venerable Martín to his deathbed to determine by divination what day he should plan on dying!

A crowd had gathered, and the girls felt self-conscious, as they were being scrutinized by our people. Of course they were little rich Mayan girls and the prettiest ones I'd ever seen. Old Ma Cu Xbalan's wife, The Merchant, had known well to send the youngest and best to get me, as I could conceivably have refused.

When we arrived at Ma Cu's home, I was humbled to find two other shamans already there, one inside with the old fellow and the other being kept separate from me by one of Ma Cu's numerous sons.

Over our shoulders, all of us diviners held our string bags containing our *Qíjijbal*, our divination bundle or Sun tool. When Ma Cu's family heard that I'd come, they admitted me into the long dark hut where I found the noble old duffer propped up in a hand-carved Guatemalan bed under a sacred *pop*, a reed mat covering.

"*Xat peta la?* Did you come, venerable Martín?"

"Yes, Brother Father, as soon as I heard. The two shimmerers brought me."

"I want you to see what day I'll die, because it's near now, I think, and I have to divide the land, the cattle, the houses and all so as not to have an evil war ensue among the youth over these things. Don't tell me nonsense. Give me a message straight from the bundles!"

When I'd finished my layout and counting, and returned from my trance, I told Ma Cu that according to what I saw he had two choices: One was to live nine months more, then die walking the village streets. The other was to die here in seven days at midmorning.

"Good," he said. "Pay him, Venerable Woman," as he called his wife. "Wait outside please."

The other diviner, Malvish, came in after I left. I really admired Malvish, who was in his forties. He had a great style, but was always standoffish to me, probably because of Chiv. His father's wife had some reason to dislike the old man. I don't know what it was, but he and one other shaman were the hope for the future as far as good shamans went. He had a fine face like an ancient Zapotec chieftain crossed with a fox, a flattop crewcut, and flashy traditional clothes, both hip and archaic, a perfect Tzutujil.

Anyway, Malvish and I emerged triumphant, for without having consulted each other we'd come up with the same answer. The other diviner, Amendoza, whom Ma Cu had on retainer, had failed him and was given money and sent away to brood. So Ma Cu had sumptuous gifts carried to our houses as he consulted further with both Malvish and myself in tandem as to how to spend his last days.

Being a rich man, he had crates of bad Guatemalan orange wine and liters of better beer, and tons of bad uncured rum. He sent runners to all parts of the lake region to invite people to come over and help him die. The great old man drank and danced and chatted with hundreds and hundreds of people over the next week. It raised stock in both Malvish and myself when he died within the hour of our predictions.

I hated to see him go, because I'd only known him by fear early on, and at a distance later. He'd been very powerful in the village and an old acquaintance of Chiv, who was actually his only rival in the hierarchy. Ma Cu was not a shaman.

These old Tzutujil Maya knew how to die. They didn't just get sick, they had style. Of course some didn't get the chance to leave so elegantly, and there were some awful deaths, as happens anywhere, but death from old age to the Mayans was considered a blessing and a goal. Death was never hidden from the village, and it wasn't considered a shameful event. It's important, the villagers say, for children to know people who die, but not good to see people killed by other people. To the Tzutujil, death is not violence; killing is violence. Killing only makes ghosts that get into somebody and must kill again. Death is peace, the final rent payment for our time on this flowery earth.

Old people in our village laid down the tracks that we ran on. They were the reason we went forward into our own uniqueness; the subtle, wonderful shine that issued from the ingenious ways they lived their lives gave us a beacon to stretch toward with our own creativity. They showed us something hopeful to live for, making the courageous struggle to get old in this hard landscape a reward instead of a penance. Grandmas and grandpas called their grandkids *N Cixel*, meaning "my replacement," or *Vi nu mam*, "that which makes me prominent." Grandchildren called their grandparents collectively "my greatness."

We addressed old people in the streets as *Nim che, nim caam*, "Big Trees, Big Vines." Old people called anybody younger *Ca tzej, ca jutay*, "Our Flowers, Our Sprouts." We young sprouts took root in the shade of the elders' old branches, which protected us from the very things we would need later on to grow our own branches. They allowed only a certain nourishing amount of sunlight to reach their sprouts, and kept the harsh wind, hard rain, and killer hail from the younger people, taking the brunt of the storms and gently distributing the water and air in good, useful quantities to the tender flowers and sprouts.

The village hierarchy was accountable to the ex-hierarchy who was the trunk of the tree. But the existing hierarchy was the shading branches, which ritually flowered to make sure that the ancestral faces kept returning on the tree, that the village remained fertile. The branches protected our children from direct exposure to the same powerful truths and forms they would need later to grow into and spread out from to become true adults, providing shade themselves for the next crop of young beings.

Our old were not in nursing homes, and our young were not in day care. Our parents and peers were not working to get away from where they were, to go on vacation or retire. They worked to find food to be well where they'd always been. Life was not to be improved, but renewed and maintained.

In order for this to happen, the old had to be with the youngest, the shade tree with the shaded sprout. We knew that the grandchild was the grandparent, and as the old tree died and dried, it fertilized and fueled the bright, fiery flowers of the new tree as it matured into life. The word for "to live" was *n kasea*, "the ember yet glows." When a grandparent died, a grandchild got filled with his or her excellence and inherited the grandparent's face or way of being.

For this to happen, the very young and the very old had to be together while they were still alive. They had to teach each other, licking each other like cats or horses did until each had the other's face.

My life in the village had become delicious. I felt very complete in my daily routine of sacred usefulness. For the first time in my life I was truly welcome and at home. During this time, a sort of habitual ecstasy of everydayness saturated every villager's life. The people felt somewhere between delirious and able as they went about their lives.

Such honeyed lulls in the village foment, however, were like the undertow of a great wave of disturbance soon to arrive. It wasn't long before strange and unfortunate events began descending on the village from the outside world.

One afternoon, after I'd returned from supervising the transfer of some ancient shrine posts back to their keepers, my hut was invaded by five out-of-town blue-uniformed cops with lots of guns and frowns.

Already sitting in my hut were two shamans awaiting a bottle of medicinal herbal tea I was cooking over the fire in a clay pot. The older shaman's daughter had hemorrhaged badly five days before, due to an early miscarriage, and he and his son-in-law had come to seek help for her. Although she seemed much better, I'd insisted that she continue to rest and drink plenty of good medicine plants to ensure that she healed well and that there was no lingering infection, or bite, as we called it. These people lived way out of the village on the road to Place of Cacao. They were terrified when they saw the police.

I told my clients to act normal as I handed them the very hot bottles of red tea. Mayans think all medicines should have a red color, so we always had to put plants into the water to make them red, no matter what color the operative plant made it. Guessing that the cops couldn't understand Mayan, I spoke to the two village men: "Get up, shake hands, don't look scared, and go on your way. Once you're outside, go quickly to your homes and tell everyone you see to keep away from my compound until I give the sign in case something bad happens here. I don't want it to escalate, or for anybody else to get hurt." They did what I asked.

Once these villagers had left, the head cop ordered his boys out to the street and began talking to me. In Guatemala, when underpaid policemen showed up at your house, it meant nothing good and was a sure sign of one of three things: 1) They wanted a bribe against hauling you to prison on an imagined charge. Guatemalan prisons are worse than dying, which you can also do there. 2) They were sent to haul you off under the pay of a private party to batter, rape, rob, or kill you. 3) To get information on some-body else for whom they were planning numbers 1 or 2.

The power of spirit works deeply, and a shaman's courage is always being tested by the precarious onslaughts of the outside worlds and their jealousies. The cop asked, "Was that moonshine you gave those men?"

"No, it was a medicine to help their people."

"Then it was illegal drugs."

"No, it was a good medicine to help them get well."

"Do you have any moonshine here in your possession?"

"You know I do. By tradition. I have to give liquor to all visiting digni-taries, chiefs, or their families."

"You know, I could put you away in prison for seven years for having only a cup of that stuff."

"Yes, I realize that, but I have a writ from the governor of Solola stat-ing our exemption from the stigma in the interest of village tradition. Would you like to taste some?"

"I guess I could, just to make sure."

So after a couple of cups of the best illegal liquor available (I had fifty-five gallons of the stuff), which should've been diluted four times before drinking, though I gave it to him straight, he began: "Well, I've been watching you for two weeks now."

"Yes, I know that, too."

"Uh ha!" Surprised, he continued: "You'll know then that I've been sent to find something wrong about you and to haul you off and drop you in a volcano somewhere. But I personally can't find anything to complain about. I have watched people going in here sick and coming out cured and no one has a bad thing to say about you. So I got to thinking."

This guy was a very portly man, obviously a hundred percent Indian, but descended from people who had given up or lost their traditional ways. He didn't look so mean now and he was actually almost likable, but he had four "white" Guatemalans with him outside with guns and cowboy atti-tudes, one obviously of German ancestry from eastern Guatemala, proba-bly Zacapa or Zanarate, where there was a cattleman culture, like there is in northern Mexico.

"I've been thinking. You see, I've got this horrible pain in my back," he explained, grabbing his kidney, "and I've been to doctors, healers, chiropractors, and hospitals. I'm taking codeine now and Valium and Demerol, yet nothing helps. I'm in constant pain. Do you think you could help me?"

The spirits were at work here testing my abilities, while my own dogs and enthroned spirits began to work converting this man's violence into curable illness. Here you could see it: a man sent to frame and assassinate me decides that I should heal him while four guards outside stand sentry duty on our "consultation."

"Of course, captain. I can try, but there's no guarantee. Take off all your armor, please, your guns, uniform, and so forth, and lay down on this *petate* (reed mat)."

He did so, amazingly enough, and then there was a mostly naked policeman with all his junk and weapons hanging from my doorpost, lying in my hut. I ran an avocado pit up his fat, aching back until it jumped, to locate the affected area; then I did a divination right on his back, using it as a table.

"I see very well, my friend, what's wrong."

"What is it? It's killing me down here."

"Well, Mr. Choy," I said, using the officer's last name, "you've killed someone and you feel bad about it. The soul of the killed person is stuck in your hips."

Choy tried to leap to his feet and go for his gear, but his pain impeded him, and I was able to grab him, talk him down, and get him to explain. Obviously, I'd hit upon the truth.

"A vendor in the open bus market in Mazatenengo on the coast sent an urgent message that they were being robbed at gunpoint. Rushing down there, I saw a boy running away, and the vendor said it was the robber. I yelled for the boy to stop, but he kept on going, so I pulled my revolver and told him I'd shoot. At that point he turned. Seeing he had a gun, I shot him in the head and killed him. But he'd only stolen three grapefruits, and his gun was just a painted piece of wood made to look like a gun, and he was only fifteen. . . ."

Cesar Choy began to weep, talking through his bitter tears about his own sons, one of whom was only fifteen years old, and how bad he felt about the killing and how he'd been promoted to his current position of killing enemies of the State.

As I cooked him a lot of medicine over my open fire, I let him weep, then made him drink the teas until he fell sound asleep on the reed mat, looking a lot like somebody from the village and even more like somebody you'd be happy to know, maybe even a friend. It took a couple of hours to bring to life all the words and songs we shamans do to remake and re-member a person's soul back through the layers. The guards outside were getting hungry and curious, so I gave them five quetzales and told them to get drunk and come back later.

Cesar slept thirty-six hours at least, waking up at dawn a day and a half later. When the danger seemed over, my family and compound returned to our homes. He'd slept so long and peacefully we thought maybe he was dead, and we kept sticking our ears to his back to listen for his heartbeat and breath. He was very much alive, and finally when he awoke, he thought he'd just slept the night.

Hurriedly donning his uniform and strapping on his leather and guns, he said, "I feel a lot better. I haven't slept more than fifteen minutes at a time till now. What did you do?"

"Señor Choy, you have to drink a bottle of this plant medicine every day for a couple of weeks." I gave him the plants and instructions on cook-ing, and I went on to say, "You have to give up being a policeman. You're not that kind of person; it'll kill you in the end. You must stop. As far as payment goes, you've given me my life, the highest payment of all. You didn't kill me, so that's all there is to it."

He went on insisting that I be paid, however, he was so very impressed with the cure. In his euphoria he even started talking about his ancestors, one of whom was a *curanderoa*, etc. Some young villager associates of mine had this man's very drunk police accomplices in tow and disarmed. Choy looked at me, and started laughing and marched off with his chums.

For weeks after that, every couple of days or so, we'd find big baskets of mixed eggbreads and fifty-quetzal bills on the threshold of our com-pound. Since these things were foreign to our town (and very high-priced), we supposed it was Choy who'd left them in appreciation. One night weeks later, as one of my children's great-uncles was wandering the village, a huge dog belonging to one of the few resident Ladino families rushed him and took a piece out of his calf. The uncle, alone in the dark and desperate, killed the dog with his machete and very nearly bled to death himself.

This uncle was sent to prison by the white owner of the animal for killing his dog. No mention was made of the uncle's injuries, but after only one day in prison, Uncle was sent back to the village, free of charges. This sort of miraculous release was unheard of. No one ever got out of prison without years of petitions, bribes, and red tape, much less bussed home. Indians in particular were never treated this way. For the next two years, however, every one of my friends or relatives who had had run-ins with the government or police was immediately exonerated, released, or never brought to trial. This treatment included myself on two occasions when the powers that be tried to use the system against me.

This good fortune was all very mysterious, and it not only raised my stock considerably in the village but also gave a lot to think about to those recent converts to evangelism who had converted in order to get more things and favors out of life, as promised by their pastors.

One day, while on an official mission out of the village to straighten out a tribal boundary dispute, several of the village headmen and I had to change buses in Mazatenengo. As we waited, we wandered in the open market there. This village was the entrance to our sister tribes, Samayac and Santo Domingo, on the coast. We were very restless and careful here, because the place was crawling with shamans with female power. We had only male power, all except me, on account of old Chiv, who'd passed on to me the female power he had gained in his enforced early wanderings.

As we perused the stands, I was delighted and astounded to see Cesar Choy, fifty pounds heavier, wearing overalls, planted on top of a crate behind piles of pears and mangos. Flanked on either side by two pretty little sons, he beamed beneath his little straw hat. We all shook hands as he started loading us up with fruit. "I took your suggestion under advisement," he said, pretending to talk like a military bureaucrat, "and stopped being a police officer. I waited for two years, though. Did you notice?" Then he became the warm village man he was really meant to be and addressed me.

"Don Martín," he said, squinting and smiling through his beautiful, comfortable bulk, "you know, all your people who didn't get fined, beaten, or jailed? I worked to let them go, and many others, to do what I could do to help unseen before I resigned. That's how I got to pay you back! Now I just sell fruit."

Right here, two years earlier, in this very market he'd killed a boy. Now he sat selling and giving away fruit, in the midst of his family, poor but at home, proud of the realization that the pain in his back meant he wasn't dead or numb. He had turned his hurt into life by releasing my people back to life. This was a shaman's crowning victory, when he could turn hatred into breath, and bullets into corn; killers into fruit sellers, death into life.

Our compound was now continually flooded with villagers and Mayan visitors from other towns and tribes. Camped in little groups with their own cooking fires, or sitting elegantly in long lines, they waited to see me for alleviation from one problem or the next. Sometimes I worked from dawn to dawn, not noticing at first that my compound had mysteriously taken on the appearance of Chiv's when I'd first been hauled there by him.

Ever since my initiation, old Chiv had begun staying away from what I did little by little in these last two years, letting me take the rudder all the way. But, too, I was also slipping deeper and deeper into the heartwood of the village hierarchy, having greater and heavier positions of responsibility wrapped around me. I was continually being asked to feast the village and flatten myself economically.

During these intense, inspiring times, my oldest son was born to Yalur. It had been difficult to keep him alive, and this was no surprise to anyone. Shamans were the target for problems, often unable, like midwives, to find in their own lives whatever balance they might be able to bestow on the villagers' lives. So, although Yalur and I finally succeeded in keeping our first child alive and healthy, the second boy died as a baby during a terrible typhoid epidemic.

The sorrowful memory of that little creature gone cold and stiff, after his mother had worked so hard and long to bring the tiny being into this fifth world, will never stop haunting me. For years to come, I'd wake every night to check my sleeping children, bothering them to wake as well, just to be sure that they were still very much alive. Now through this terrible happening all the Tzutujil counted me as blood kin in the village. For to be truly alive in this Belly Button of the Universe, one had to be related to someone who had been born and died in the village, of village blood. Now I was a direct relative, with both my blood and Yalur's Ratzaami clan blood buried together in one seed with all our common ancestors. Those few people who hadn't wanted me before now accepted me as a child of the Canyon Village. At this point Yalur and I began to live the harsh, grief-soaked, bittersweet lives of all Tzutujil parents, just as burdened as we were respected.

I'd always sent lots of food and gifts to Chiviliu and his compound, but being big in the village did not mean as much to me as having been small with Chiv. I'd see him once in a while, but I missed him breathing down my neck with all his messages from the Gods and his zany solutions to life. So Yalur and I took to visiting him and Ya Chep on a regular basis.

The time of monkey pods and wild jungle plums was returning, and Yalur was pregnant again with our third child. Despite a threat of war and violence on the horizon, a short period of delicious peace set into our lives for about five months. My clients were getting well; my boy was a little prince in the village, happy and spoiled; very few people were dying; the world of the village was peace-filled and balmy. For once in my life, I had time to visit Old Chiv again, and I enjoyed being alive, knowing that I belonged unquestioned to a people.

Chiv, Ya Chep, myself, Yalur, and a group of old hierarchy *Ajauá* Lords and Ladies regularly met and ate together. Sometimes we'd load up our dugout canoes and row out to the base of the magnificent Elbow of the World, the Volcano of San Pedro. We'd disembark on a sandy beach below the forest, cook our food on a fire of fragrant woods, smoke our pipes, and make fake divinations with the clouds that drifted over the mirrorlike lake, and laugh hard. We listened to faraway thunder and the distant sounds of the village we all came from, enjoying being humans from such a beautiful place, the Canyon Village at the Umbilicus of the Earth on the verdant edge of the Flowering Mountain Jade Water Earth.

One clear moonlit night, Chiv called out the guard! He shot out of his hut, already running like crazy, half-dressed, down the rocky hill bellowing at the top of his lungs, "They've stolen the Heart! They got the Heart of the Village, just like they took the bell!"

The young men initiates out on their nightly patrol came hauling up his cliff. Men piled out of their huts with machetes, and women held babies in doorways while we all tried to keep up with old yelling Chiv, who, with only his long handwoven red shirt on, was scuttling and trotting toward the lake.

"Grab them! They've got the Village Heart, there they go! See?!"

He looked straight into the murky shadows beneath trees and rockpile walls, perceiving something no one else could see. Sleepily assuming that the others could, we all headed steadfastly on our mission to pull down the culprits who were stealing the village heart, the ancient bundle that gave its secret vitality to the place we called home. Then, running like a deer, Chiv shouted, "There they go! It's our last chance. They're going into the water!"

Two centuries before, demons had stolen a bell, and then, at the turn of the century, they had stolen some sacred artifacts from the village. Each time they had disappeared into the lake. Our ancient Prophet had wrestled them and gotten the bell back, but the artifacts were lost and reputed to be in a neighboring village, a village of strange people, some of whom turned into demons at night, I was told.

Right up to the water we ran, following Chiv, who jumped into the freezing night lake, plopping into the water, while about twenty of us youth bravely tried to follow him underwater. The rest just walked around on the moonlit shore, staring into the water and at all the villagers gathered up on the little cliff above, wondering and chattering about what was actually taking place.

Finally we young guys resurfaced, having lost the old man. Chiv was gone a long time, but finally he walked out of the water a hundred yards farther down the shore. "They got away" was all he said. But then after a couple of shallow, shivering breaths, he added, thrusting his hand in the air, holding a big bundle, "But I got the Heart!"

Relieved, everyone cheered and dispersed, darting back to their huts to make hot water, coffee, or hand-ground hot chocolate to warm up.

While he and I dried out at Chiv's cooking fires, Chiv turned to make sure no one was looking. He leaned over to me and whispered, "*Tistá!* [Look!]" What Chiv had retrieved from the water was a smooth stone he'd wrapped in a cloth he'd brought along in the pursuit. "I just wanted to see if the village still cared enough to rescue her own heart. It's a good thing I'm still here to do that for them!"

Not long after that, another man came rushing into my compound one day, using the appropriate terms of new hierarchal relation. Gradually, though desperately, he got to the point.

With a whole crew of workers shouldering sacks and ropes, Old Chiv had shown up out of the dust at a piece of disputed land on the edge of the village where this man's boss, a Ladino from our village, had a sizable orange grove. Chiv swore and swore to my new in-law noble that his initiate Martín had purchased this orange grove, and that the land now belonged to him. He, Chiviliu (now ninety-seven), had been sent by me, Martín, to harvest all the oranges. While this poor man looked on, Chiv's men proceeded to do so.

Because of the intense nature of village hierarchy etiquette, if this man, newly inducted into a hierarchy relationship with me, had refused, it would have meant a feud. To refuse Chiv would have been even worse. Chiv was like my father, and that relationship demanded ten times more respect. Chiv had his workers harvest all the oranges immediately, while he loaded them into rope nets. Then he disappeared over the ridge like a grinning possum with his marauders in tow, while this man came panting to my hut to see if what Chiv had said was true. As the hired guardian of the Ladinos' grove, he would be in big trouble if it wasn't.

"*Wachali*, Lord Witness, I tell you, I'm not even sure where this land is, and I know I didn't buy it."

The *wachali*'s face went deep, and he began sweating. "No, but you did buy the harvest, truly I'm sure as the Old Bark [meaning Chiv] related to me?" He was smiling like a hopeful fox.

"No, I've never had any dealing with this Ladino. I don't really know him. Did Old Chiv get all the oranges?"

I tried not to laugh, but Chiv and this Ladino hated each other, and Chiv had been cheated pretty roundly by this guy off and on for the better part of this century. The owner of the grove made it his business to even up scores by confiscating anything he chose out of Indian huts. So I guess Chiv was getting back at him. But this could escalate into a dangerous situation, and I thought I'd better go see what the Old Man was up to.

Arriving at his old familiar compound, my home for years, I found everything looking pretty normal. Blurting out my *exkopajay*, I entered his sacred house after hearing some rustling sounds, knowing Chiv could be selectively deaf sometimes. The whole roomy chamber was brimming with big handmade nets packed full with green and yellow Valencia oranges stacked six feet high, wall to wall. Chiv peeked out from the back, his long wispy gray wiry hair sticking out. He had on his favorite voluminous bright yellow bumblebee jaspeado handwoven shirt, and a raggedy pair of scav.

He held a piece of fruit out to me, and said with his big old toothless smile, "Would you like an orange?" We both fell down on the orange pile, kicked our legs up, tickled by his nutty caper, and laughed until his wife came in. Almost laughing herself, she told us to have some shame.

"What'll he do to you once he finds out?" I asked as soon as the laughter had cleared out a little.

"Well, he thinks you ordered it!" And we started laughing again.

"Oh that's really good! Just what I need, an angry old white man coming after me!"

"He beat up old Ma Yel badly for not paying a debt this morning, but no one could do anything to him because he's got *cuello* [connections] with the government. So I took his oranges! We'll sell them after we decorate this sacred house of mine, and I'll give the money to Ma Yel without telling anybody. Then they can pay that crazy man back and have enough left over to eat. When I die, I'll take that evil fellow with me!"

Chiv was always fixing something, and he was very dramatic—sometimes badly melodramatic—but I was no better. And it turned out just like he said.

2 0

TO CARRY THE
VILLAGE HEART

An angry wind was churning up the lake. All the canoes had been dragged to safer ground. The sky was gray, but there was no rain, just a raging April dust storm. I was painting in my new hut at the south end of the village between Xechiboy (Under the Edge of the Armadillo) and Panaj (the Place of Cane Reeds), where the ancient *pov*, the paper tree, stood.

This place was on an inlet, perched on a cliff overlooking the bay of Santiago. It was here that all the youth liked to swim, jumping off the big flat black boulders into the very deep, cold water. Like a deep turquoise velvet mirror, the water was clear here, as this place had belonged to A Plas, the ancient prophet who'd arranged Chiv's birth. No women washed here, and no men parked their canoes here out of respect and fear, but the boys used it to swim far out into the Mother Waters.

On this day, the lake was deserted, choppy, dusty, and gray. Even the birds had hunkered down. No human had ventured here, save myself, alone at my painting, trying to have a moment of peace, responsible only to my sense of color and the deliciousness of not having to paint eyebrows on everything. Suddenly I heard old Chiv at a great distance, howling my secret name in the raging tempest. At first I tried to insist it was my imagination, but the Doppler effect of the wind on his hornlike voice was not the product of my mind, and I peeked out my stone hut's little door. Down the shore a quarter of a mile, old Chiv, togged out in his best handwovens, was balancing on a large, slick boulder that towered twenty feet out of the lake, flapping and bellowing in the wind like a shaggy seal with legs. If he slipped, he'd crash into a soup of cold water and craggy rocks and die for sure. I couldn't figure out how he'd gotten out there to begin with, but he was calling my name, and I had to respond. I'd come to his rescue!

Crawling and curling my way past basaltic columns and chunks, I slipped and pulled myself high to where I'd last seen the old man. But when I got up there, he'd disappeared and he was nowhere in sight, nowhere. I called and called to him, but to no avail. I searched the crashing spray along the boulders beneath for any sign of him, but he wasn't there. A feeling of deep loss came over me, and in desperation I began moving back toward my painting hut to put away my tools. I planned to head to the main village to get relatives to search and see if Chiv hadn't reappeared somewhere else. Or maybe this was a vision after all.

After entering my stone hut, I commenced to nervously fold up my precious brushes and colors, when I heard a fierce bout of growling and snarling, which sounded like some wild beasts unhappy with one another. A gnashing of teeth and some high hissing made me guess that one of those unfortunate ownerless village curs was taking on the old oppossum mama who lodged under my stone hut.

Straggling through the doorway with a stick to break them up, I saw nothing, and the growling instantly left off. Then, whomp! I was knocked facedown to the hard, cindery earth, with a heavy weight on my neck. A hand with a thick fistful of curly hair pulled back my head while Chiv's familiar voice bugled in my ear:

To Carry the Village Heart

"I thought they said you were an awake and clever boy! I'm leaving all I have and know in your charge, and this is how you plan to guard it? Tomorrow I'll be gone, and you will have to wake up by then."

He let me up and dusted me off, having outmaneuvered me. Chiv had slithered up the deep cliffs from his stranded position, onto my rooftop. While I searched for him below, he waited for a chance to topple me over and teach me again about awakeness. Ninety-seven years old, he was still full of that thing that makes us jump up and live. I invited him in, sat him down, and cooked him some coffee.

He was dressed in a new wide-brimmed Italian felt hat, a new handwoven black paquan jacket, a new jaspeado shirt in his favorite black and yellow bumblebee pattern, a solid bird-embroidered scav, and a long, tinseled sash. He looked every inch the resplendent Tzutujil king God made him. Then, pulling out my favorite deer-headed pipe, he loaded it with a half-penny cigar, lit up and began telling me his life story for maybe the two hundred millionth time. This time, I actually found details I'd never heard before about errors he'd made early on in his life and some regrets over unfinished business.

Congratulating me on a part I'd played recently in getting old Holy Boy relics returned from some Paris museums, he told me that he felt this time he was finally and truly going to die. Life without Nicolas Chiviliu in Santiago Atitlán was not even imaginable. My life, without Chiv, was not livable. What would I do without him? He didn't even care. So I chose not to believe him, assuming that this would be like the last time he tried dying. All this was soon overshadowed, however, by what he came out with next.

"Plas, you know how every day before we ceremonialize I yell and plead with the *Ajauá* and *Ixoc Ajauá* to take me to the other world. I say I'm done here now, I have someone to carry on my ways, and the relics are being returned, and I've done my job and am ready to go and die now. You know what I mean?

"Well, finally last night the old prophets and *Nawales* came over and told me that tomorrow was the day and to let you know. So tomorrow midmorning I'll dance my central bundle, and they'll come get me, and you'll have to catch the bundle before it hits the ground as I die. Do you understand?"

"You're not dying tomorrow, Father, but yes, I do understand."

"Anyway," he continued, blowing plenty of smoke my way, "I will die, so don't wait around. Just get on with the wake. You're in charge of the others; my unbelieving Catholic sons and evangelist offspring will attempt to commandeer the whole affair. You will keep the peace, right? You're powerful enough anyway, just do it so it goes right. Okay?"

"Okay," I said in disbelief at the horrible possibility of the burden of having to keep that many factions at bay.

"Then before I'm buried, make sure none of my *Qíjibal* [shaman tools] get buried and that none get frittered away or sold or stolen. Right? Good! Then don't let any of those shamans lay claim to any of my *Qíjibal*. You'll have to have a contest to see who they speak to, and whoever wins that contest will take them and feed them. Of course, the only one who will win will be *you*, and so you already have them as yours as far as I'm concerned. And if you catch them before they hit the ground, there'll be no problem with these tools helping you. But to keep the gossipers at bay, you must hold a contest of shamans who lay claim to my stuff and that contest must take place thirteen days after I'm buried. If it happens too early, you'll not have my support from the other world, as I'm still traveling. You know perfectly well what I mean, don't you?"

"Yes, sir."

"Also, I'm making you the executor of all my lands. Make sure everyone just keeps what they're already using, because they are the ones who deserve to get what they've been taking care of. My body is the land, and these children who've used the land have fed me well from it. Be certain to get Ya Chep her share, and don't let anyone swindle her, and don't let some Christian grandchild of mine push her out of our house. That's hers! Okay?"

"Yes, sir."

"Then when you've accomplished all that, you have to leave the village."

"What? Leave the village? No way will I do that, Father, no way!"

"Yes, you will leave the village, because if you don't they'll kill you, and all we've done together will be lost. Do you understand? A big stormy war is coming, just like in the 1930s when I was jailed and tortured with all our shamans and chiefs. Back then I had to leave for a long time and then return. But in the meantime they auctioned off and burned many of my holy articles. I worked forty years, and even you did, too, to get back what was lost in those bundles. Now they'll kill you and burn those bundles, so you'd better believe me. I spoke with the *Nawal Achi* and *Aii*, and Plas, Maxcop, and all of them, and they say our ways will be disassembled and thrown away, and that you will be killed if you don't leave.

"Take this bundle, take all of them—yours, mine—and guard them like babies. Take all their rituals and knowledges and keep them firm. When things are bad, depend on your divination kit. Don't ever, ever disregard what it tells you. It will save your life and the life of what we have and have kept alive so long if you listen. So take these bundles and don't show them around. You've done well with them here so far. I congratulate you on that, but now you will be in this alone. Other people are taking their teachers' chunks of the whole to where they must, to replant each piece where they are directed in hopes that it will grow and ripen there to keep the seeds regenerative and viable.

"Each part of the body of the Village Heart is carried by a different being and you will carry the part I've always carried, which you know perfectly well. You know the words; you know the songs; you know the rituals; you know the food; you know it all—but most of all, I hope you know how to listen and in listening you know how to learn. You see, you must return to the Land of the Dead, to the land where you came from and keep this bundle, its seed, and its knowledge safe and viable until truly signaled by me from the next world to bring it with the other pieces to its home to reassemble and bring back to life what no one person, or people, can do. So you in the Estados Unidos will have to continue doing this work over there, because only that way will the fire soul of the bundles' seed stay alive and viable. In the USA you will see sickness we've never seen, be asked to fix things we have no cures for nor names to ask for cures. In all this, the bundles must be listened to, and if you are the person I've known you to be, you'll be able to learn what we haven't by listening to what we have! *Xacaxaj*—you hear and comprehend?!

"Also, if you see your friends and relatives killed, your village burned, our womenfolk split and raped like stepped on fruit, do not go to fight on one side or the other. We know you; I know you; the Gods know you; the *Nawal Achi* know you; and we know you are a good warrior, capable of destroying the enemy. But the real enemy cannot be killed that way. You must carry the baby [bundles, knowledge, songs, and ways] without pulling out your machete, without drawing your weapon, because to win against what you hate and perceive as the enemy, you will need all your power, and in the instant you draw your weapon, you'll have to drop the baby, and that baby must never hit the ground. If you drop the bundles to fight what you hate, there will be no justifiable reason for your battle, because you will have lost the reason for the fight, which in your case is to keep this living thing, the baby, bundle ways, alive.

"Men who are cowards must be made to fight, and most will lose their lives but gain their courage. Men like yourself with ability and the warrior spirit in their blood must, like all of us, make a sacrifice in these desperate times that are beginning already, and your sacrifice will be having to refuse to fight, though every fiber of your being says you must. When you see your friends and loved ones cut and killed, it will be so hard for you not to retaliate, but you mustn't. You must carry what gives us Mayans life. The true enemy is not in a specific people, but is a force that takes these people over and makes them powerless, then offers them revenge over what their primitive minds think is killing them.

"The baby must be carried by you through the rain and hail of bullets, through the hoop of fire, to be planted to make more of itself, beyond either one of us, so that the enemy cannot kill what gave all things their lives.

"*Ajoj vinaaq xincoquina nka kamsaj kí, sjaura nuya kaslem chqa majun nka kamsax rmac ju vinaaq.* We humans can in our conceit kill each other, but that which gives us life will not be killed by any human being. The Earth Fruit contains what makes us great, and humans can't kill that.

"Will you honor my death by doing as you must? This is what you were born for. Are you the man I know you are? Will you carry this baby away from the fire to plant right in the heart of the killer, maybe fix up the killer's heart, in the land that abandoned you, the land that you dread? Promise me. Please!"

I had no intention of leaving a village with hundreds of relatives, friends, houses, huts, a position, a way of life, where I was loved and where I belonged in as deep a way as possible, where I had one child buried and plenty of land, and where I even had enemies of the village sort. Who could go back to a land of anonymity, to a place that never had any love for me, much less itself, with few if any true ancient customs, to the land of unhappiness, to the land of the dead, to the very land whose unhappy policies and parentless individualism had caused it to throw its own communities, native cultures, and immigrant identities into dishonor? To a land whose people had little awareness of the depth and excellence of people like us and that in all probability was funding the very bullets, shrapnel, helicopters, and torture squads that tore at our cultural shores like the waves outside? To a land whose materialism had poisoned its own native people and now was beginning to destroy this Native American people, the Maya, from within, with missionaries and money? To this land I was to proceed, abandoning all I loved, to live with the uneducated enemy of our Mayan souls.

Better to die here in the village where I was loved, I thought, which if I stayed would surely be the result. What of my children being raised in a culture that wouldn't know them for who they were, would subject them to the generic label of "Latinos" or "people of color," with no inkling of the deep cultural wealth of their people? What would they do? They would be flattened and told that they were not the sons of kings and chiefs, but the sons of a poor, unknown half-breed and a displaced mother from a land of tropical peasants shunned for their brown skin—not the sons of knowledgeable leaders with well-placed, highly schooled shamans, chiefs, woman lords, and initiators. They would have to be unproud of me in a land where I couldn't save them with my power because away from the Umbilicus, I would be unplugged, depressed, disempowered, back to being nobody in a land of people dedicated to being somebody by beating each other out in competition. Americans probably couldn't believe or care about what we knew.

I thought of many, many things, but realized, after Chiv told me how I would be hunted here in Guatemala, that I could become a liability for those around me and that they might be killed by association. I certainly had no desire to bring disgrace and more suffering upon the people who loved me. They had no idea what was coming. Though I knew somewhat, I had no personal experience with being an outlawed human being. But I would soon.

For that, and for Chiv, I would leave all that I'd ever loved, leave the place where I'd seen the Gods and learned to be a human being, the land of my friends, deep friends, deeper than deep compatriots in the community spirit of initiation, ripped from my beloved home of so many years because that hungry, culture-killing thing wouldn't let any village people anywhere on this earth continue in their gradual, unmarketable beauty.

I recognized what was coming to destroy my culture as the same heartless force that sent two-by-fours marked "Board of Education" crashing into young ribs and cracking little girls' heads open for speaking their mother's native tongue. It was that same numbing, uninitiated madness that boasted about its ability to threaten and utterly destroy the fifth-creation world with nuclear weapons. Like a wild animal, I could smell that same insatiable force grinding in toward us here, over this last horizon, that same thing that had terrorized my childhood, killing my mother, stealing my first village away and grinding my family to dust. I couldn't believe that even here where I finally had a home, and was loved and accepted by thousands in the Canyon Village, that I wasn't going to be allowed to bite this thing on the neck. We couldn't fight and win our village remembrance back because, Chiv knew, by fighting this monster we'd become its allies by learning hate.

This time, however, I had something to hold on to as I fled, a world of remembrance to rescue to safety. I had a mission this time around: I carried the Village Heart, and it carried me. That would make all the difference. Over a decade ago I'd blown into Santiago like dust in the wind, but I'd leave now full and weeping, carrying the Village Heart, my baby, just like the mother jaguar from long ago had carried her precious kit firmly in her mouth, putting her revenge aside for the moment, struggling from the sanctuary of the jungle to save her baby. That was me. If it hadn't been for this, my jaguar baby, the Village Heart and I would have both perished in the jaws of the monster, trying to fight it. Chiv knew.

Chiv died right on schedule, having danced his bundle for three quarters of an hour while we played the slit log drum for him. He stopped, stared, stumbled a little, and crashed to the floor of the Sacred House, deader than a shot deer, his age-blued eyes glazed and slit, gazing motionless toward his old fish swinging in the breeze.

This was the same exact spot where, years before, I'd knelt the first day I got hauled here by Chiv. Now I knelt here again, his bundle in my arms. I wailed and wailed, mad at the world, and wept for the privilege and the loss of Chiv. The older people in the hierarchy filed in for hours until the whole courtyard was full, and they built fires through the night as everyone agreed to wait a full twenty-four hours before beginning the funeral proceedings, just in case he came alive again. We had to make sure, because with Chiv you never knew.

All the women were insane with grief, ripping their clothes and pulling out their hair, hitting and scratching themselves and sometimes us men. The men wept and drank as always, grabbing each other's arms and arguing to tell the most painfully wonderful thing they could about the old fellow. Men borrowed each other's chests to weep on, held by their peers; then they'd change places while the other shook and shed water and sobs, myself not the least among them.

Things got said that nobody really meant, but we had to take it. It was a time of grief, and Mayans know that mourning tears help the spirit on its long backward trek to the other worlds.

Musicians melted us into a tearful ooze of wailing friends, relatives, and cohorts. All the women had woven Chiv special burial clothing. A person in Chiv's position had to wear at least three layers of funerary clothing to pass all the thresholds in the other world; otherwise you wouldn't be recognized, and you wouldn't be allowed to pass, or you'd end up as a lost ghost. Chiv had enough clothing for fourteen hundred layers, so at least twenty women had to carry massive intricate bundles of new burial clothing to the grave along with his body.

This time Nicolas Chiviliu Tacaxoy stayed dead. Everybody had known it, for as promised, his old archenemy, the mean white man with the oranges, had died within an hour of him, and this meant that Chiv wasn't coming back. But we simply didn't want to say good-bye to him or his era. Ya Chep kept hitting me, furious in her drunkenness and grief: Since I was such a great shaman, why hadn't I saved him? I felt the same way.

When we finally carried the old chief to his hole in the *Nixtie*, the Place of Cactus, the burial ground, it was as if the whole world went to say good-bye. The funeral procession wound around the base of the forested humps and skirts of the Little Boy volcanoes for over a mile, twenty people wide, even though it rained. Rain was a good omen, as the Rain spirits liked Chiv.

We had to dig three extra holes to accommodate Chiv's clothes, gifts, and belongings. Everything is buried with the deceased, though I succeeded in keeping back his bundles as directed. Teeth of old chiefs, inlaid with pyrite and jade, came up with the earth as the men dug, and we scrambled for them, rubbing our gums and children's gums with them in hopes of getting some of their ability to speak the delicious words of the layers and live a long life; then we threw them back in with old Chiv, knowing he'd been the master of all time, before and now. Ya Chep wanted to jump in with him, die and follow him on, but we caught her.

Nicolas Chiviliu Tacaxoy was the last great bastion of traditional Tzutujil culture holding back the tyranny of twentieth-century civilization. Without him, we lesser holders of the wall would soon be washed away and the village drowned in the unbelieving rationalism and self-interest that seem to arrive with missionaries, marketing, and myopic politics. The spiritual disassembling of the layers of ritual and the subtle magic of the village was only a matter of time, now that time existed. What we knew about carrying time would soon cease to be. The village would become just another beautiful part of Guatemala, remembered for once having remembered what soon would be forgotten by most.

Five hundred of us hierarchy with our long red headcloths untied and worn loosely over our heads like hoods and our black blankets draped over our shoulders stood en masse, praying and doing what we do that's never been told. And then we buried the Old Man. The poor rich white man, Chiv's enemy, had only a few relatives to mourn him; Chiv probably had pitied him in the end and taken him home to the next world, like he'd taken me home in this one.

Kiil, Utziil, nimlaj taq kaslimaal, saqbey, saq colo, qan bey, qan colo, ajaual ruachuliu majun loulo oxlajuj matioxiil. Long life, Honey in the Heart, white roads, white ropes, yellow roads, yellow ropes, magnificent mask of Earth Fruit, no evil, thirteen thank-yous.

EPILOGUE
IN THE FLIMSY
HUT OF THE WORLD:
The Indigenosity
of the Human Soul

More than eighteen hundred villagers were killed in the next seven years in Santiago Atitlán alone. They were either shot to death, beaten to death, tortured and shot, tortured to death, poisoned to death, chopped to death, starved to death in holes, beheaded, kidnapped, or disappeared. Not one family was unaffected, and at least two or three people in every family had cuts, holes, or shrapnel wounds. Before 1979, most Atitecos didn't even know what a gun sounded like, much less what it could do, and less than a dozen slayings had occurred in the village since the previous century.

I myself was almost killed on three separate occasions during the 1980s. But that story, the story of my treasured years out of time spent serving the hierarchy, and how Yalur, our two little sons, and I navigated our dangerous journey taking the Village Heart to the United States, is the subject of a separate book.

By 1990 over seventy percent of our village had given up trying to keep the traditions alive against the tide of modernity that came on the heels of war. They were now members of one of nineteen evangelical Christian missions. The remaining villagers belonged to ritual sects of New Catholics, leaving only a persecuted and mocked vestige of traditionalists. The Christians moved quickly and opportunistically into the gaping cultural wounds caused by the so-called war.

These Christian churches forbade their congregations to aid or participate in any native rituals, marriage ceremonies, funeral customs, and especially hierarchy initiation feasts and giveaways. This extended to prohibiting their flocks from possessing, wearing, or weaving the beautiful ceremonial clothing of our people that represented the layers of initiation and remembrance. Because of this, most if not all of the real native ceremonial clothing and fabrics sold to collectors and museums in the United States, Japan, and Europe, was gathered by importers from Mayans converted by American Christian missionaries. The loss of ceremonial clothing and the subversion of the ancient language worked as effectively as shrapnel in the cultural devastation of the Highland Maya.

All forms of initiation for youth were suspended by 1992. The few officials, men and women, who tried to keep it all alive couldn't do so alone, because the initiation feasts and accompanying rituals require full village participation with goods and labor. On top of this, all adult Mayans who became well off had traditionally taken turns sponsoring the village chiefs or becoming chiefs themselves, distributing their abundance in sumptuous old rituals designed to bring them back eventually to a normal height again, but with increased village prestige.

The Christians refused to do this, told by their pastors and priests that their Lord wanted them to keep what He had given them in His church. This policy was in reality a concerted strategy to isolate the traditionalists and finish off the old village ways of generosity.

Through the 1980s, anywhere from three to eight hundred soldiers were continuously bivouacked at the southeastern edge of Santiago Atitlán. These troops were not fed by the government, but took their supplies directly from the villagers, who could barely feed themselves. The villagers were forced into poverty by this, and anyone who refused to feed or sleep with soldiers was killed in private and their fields burned.

On December 1, 1990, a famous massacre took place, killing twelve Tzutujils, children among them, disabling seventy villagers, and wounding hundreds. It started when frustrated villagers confronted the soldiers, asking them to return the mutilated body of a man who'd caught soldiers raiding his house. Soldiers fired into an unarmed crowd of four thousand Tzutujils of all genders and ages. I knew most of the wounded personally and had attended the births of almost all of the dead children.

This terrible tragedy followed on the heels of the assassination of two Holy Boy guards, who were gunned down by angry soldiers whom they had tried to stop from machine-gunning Holy Boy and his Sacred House. Holy Boy's priest was later shot during a ritual. Passing clean through his abdomen, the bullet exited through his back ribs while he carried Holy Boy successfully to the end of the ceremony. Miraculously, the man has survived to this day. He is my sons' great-uncle.

Nonetheless, by 1995 Holy Boy rituals were becoming more and more just tourist events, videotaped for a fee by foreign movie companies and tourists. Many of the traditionalist hierarchy were dead of old age or heartbreak, or had been killed. There were not enough fully initiated chiefs to take their places.

Most of the guns, rockets, grenades, ammunition, bombs, and helicopters used on us were purchased with support from foreign sources, some of which were American dollars. The village, while essentially held at gunpoint by the soldiers, was easily deculturated by the missionaries. Then merchandisers moved in through the cultural cracks. By 1995 in Santiago there were paved streets, cars, TVs, satellite dishes, thugs, gangs, rape, murder, guns, drug addiction, and overpopulation. Of course, on account of all that, every house now sported what there wasn't even a word for in the language: a door. Many people even had locking steel doors. All of these strange and dreadful things were the legacy of the developed and industrialized world we were supposed to aspire to.

As in a shamanic initiation, the soul of the village had in a few short years been dismembered, but because of the foreign nature of its fragmentation, the village, like the modern world, didn't have the memory rituals to reassemble itself. Because of greed and the missionaries and the verb "to be," not to be was now possible, and some things ceased "to be."

Shamed and pushed far away from the old ways, the villagers were unable to hear the sacred words calling them back to life. The village had forgotten how to re-member itself. It couldn't understand what it had forgotten from the old layered way. It had ceased to understand itself.

Called a civil war by other nations who sought to wash their hands of any responsibility, the violence we experienced in the 1980s was really a hideous string of senseless murders thinly disguised as a war funded by powerful entities to maintain their own political and business interests. Most villagers had little or no understanding of what was really happening to them. This was not a war between civilians, but a war between big powers, where mostly civilians died, and most of the civilians were Mayans.

There is still a large, beautiful town in Guatemala called Santiago Atitlán, with more than forty thousand people in it. But the Village Heart and its Gods have fled to higher ground. No longer the Canyon Village, the Twenties, or the people, the Atitecos have become Indians to the world. They are full citizens, now a fragment of a Republic that had once been a small distant part of their earth. Atitlán is no longer the Belly Button of the World, but an overpopulated village of rival Christians struggling for food and money to buy things they never before knew they needed.

Oddly enough, for all that, some Tzutujil shamanism has survived. This can be ascribed in part to the fact that Tzutujil shamans are anomalies whose business thrives on adversity. Another reason is that the shaman's vision of life and well-being did not depend on the rules and dogmas of any human institutions, native or European. It may be that real shamanism seeks a way to prevail in all ages. Hidden inside the hearts of certain individuals, artists and visionaries, shamanism's unique relationship with nature, with ancestors, and with the well-worn trails of antique tribal ways eroded into our souls has caused it to survive in fragmented forms into many ages of otherwise antipathetic cultural environments.

Even more startling to me was my discovery that the Mayan shamanic way of being, wired into my soul during my initiation, allowed me to live in non-Mayan culture with my spiritual direction intact, without bitterness, though I was scathed and harried by the modern rationalist inability to truly see or welcome spirit into everyday living.

Our shamans think that the way one individual goes, so goes a society of individuals. From that I realized that if I could be given life in an antipathetic setting, then possibly a whole culture could find its heart the same way. Perhaps the principles involved in some shamanism might be the cause for survival of the collective human spirit in the modern and postmodern era. I firsthand saw how the vision of an original but adaptable shamanism might help us through the self-devastation of culture caused by the immense spiritual fine levied against us humans by life for all the forgetful, unconscious wounding of nature and the wonderful naturalness of humans.

Ironically, many Tzutujil shamans must have understood all of this before the great cultural and spiritual demolition that crashed down upon us in the late twentieth century. We knew, too, that the whole world was spiritually endangered. Shamans knew this because we were shown during our training and initiation how the world is actually one big body. The world is also a sacred building called The House of the World, and our own individual bodies are made like it and are also called House of the World. Inside the other world of our bodies, everything that can be found in the outer world also exists. When the spirits see us, they see a beautiful house, a temple. When we see them, we see the world.

A shaman sees both. To the shaman, all the places, animals, weather, plants, and things outside in the world are also inside of you as your twin, and together everything makes an immense four-dimensional series of concentric cubes: the layers that stretch outside and inside simultaneously to create The House of the World, or World Body.

This structure is made by the Builders, certain Owners or Gods with their original sounds and words. These sounds and words become tangible meaning, made to live as they are spoken. Each God word builds the House of the World by echoing off the other words. These spirit world soundings, when made all at once, form the spiritual song of the world. This combined sound, when it gets here to this world, becomes vibrant and tangible, and grows the world in the form that we see and are. This song is the nervous system of the Universe.

When an individual falls ill, something in his World House–Earth Body is being attacked, gnawed away, eroded, shed, burnt, dismembered, or is beginning to fade away for neglect. The shaman assesses the destruction and, after dealing with the cause, begins to rebuild the World House of that person's body by remembering all its parts back to life—by making it echo off the Original Flowering Earth, what shamans call the creations, the Big Earth House Temple.

He does this by speaking or singing out a sacred map, following a natural order of holy words and magical sounds, in a rhythmic roll call. This is a miniature, or echo child, of the Original Big Sounds used by the Owners, the Gods, to make the entire World Body we live in. This map of holy sounds re-creates the concentric cubes of sacred places on the Earth that correspond to all the connecting planes in our bodies. Using the secret names of actual mountains, springs, caves, rivers, valleys, villages, ancestral wanderings, and the names of God families and their kingdoms for each of these places, the shaman remakes our spirit bodies in sound forms. If done right, our bodies then begin to echo and resound with the Original Earth from where all life takes its form. This is called remembering the Earth, and it makes us get well.

At the center of this renewed House of the Body is a person's twin souls of heart and gall bladder, where the moon and the fire sit respectively. The body is made around them, as they are the tenants of this house whose lease agreement with God is to die when it gets old. The heart, or moon, is the female, and the gall bladder is the fire, or the Old Grandpa; together they tie us together with stories, dreams, and rhythms.

As with the big ball of string that I formed as a little boy, the shaman winds a world of sacred God words and stories around our intangible spirits, giving them a house and a shape at the same time. This returns us home, making us visible in a new body or house, keeping us from fading away. This process is called "The fruit returns," or "Your face comes back," meaning that you have been healed.

The secret of village togetherness and happiness had always been the generosity of its people, but the secret to that generosity was village inefficiency and decay. The House of the World, like our village huts and our human bodies, no matter how magnificent, is not built to last very long. Because of this, all life must be regularly renewed. To do this, the villagers come together once a year at least, to work on putting back together somebody's hut, talking, laughing, feasting, and helping wherever they can in a gradual, graceful way. This way each family's place in the village is reestablished and remembered.

If a house is built too well, so efficiently that it is permanent and refuses to fall apart, then people have no reason to come together. Though the house stays together, the people fall apart, and nothing gets renewed. Smart people might be able to invent excuses to get together, but this is too abstract and hollow, and such contrivance insults the soul. People have a genuine need to make things with their ingenuity and with their hands.

This coming together to gather water by hand, to do communal tasks gracefully—tasks that a machine could do in an instant anonymously—or to repair rickety houses ensures the very smiley togetherness so missing in the pre-planned, alienated lives of modern civilization. When a Tzutujil says he needs to be healed, he asks the shaman to *chumij*, or replaster, him. When we begin to fade, the shaman plasters us with remembrance so that we can shine again.

Ironically, the great amount of unnatural violence, senseless killing, and mechanized warfare that we see these days signals an extreme fear in the face of natural death and decay. These difficult conditions come about when a people are not truly at home. Unable to re-create the House of the World as our shamans do, subscribers to modernity jettison all ideas of ritual life and the feeding of spirits. Instead they look for permanent solutions, such as nuclear bombs, war, concentration camps, laws, and ideals that must be then upheld and defended. All of this activity is a search for increased security to protect an uninitiated people from what they perceive as a hostile universe. Far removed from the humble familiarity of being at home, in a village, such people have forgotten their own natures and how to use these natures to speak a village back into life.

Not satisfied or confident that life can be renewed, unwilling and afraid to grow old, to gradually become magnificent, treelike elders, or die into cultural humus, the modern man or woman demands the permanence of steel cities and immortality. So sure they will never be remembered for having lived, such individuals struggle to stay permanently youthful, like cornered cats, frozen in the anxious void of modern communities.

Generosity of soul and tangible effort in the face of the constant pressure of decay are what give people purpose, fertile imaginations, vitality, a feeling of usefulness, and self-worth. When decay is "cured" instead of communally addressed, a culture becomes decadent. Then generosity becomes an advertising ploy or a dirty word. Violence is close behind when people won't come together to remake each others' houses.

Somewhere during the course of my initiation as a shaman, I came across a startling and troubling realization that every human being alive today, modern or tribal, primal or overdomesticated, has a soul that is original, natural, and, above all, indigenous in one way or another. And like all indigenous peoples today, that indigenous soul of the modern person has either been banished to some far reaches of the dream world or is under direct attack by the modern mind.

Since the human body is the world, every individual in the world, regardless of background or race, has an indigenous soul struggling to survive in an increasingly hostile environment created by that individual's mind, which subscribes to the mores of the machine age. Because of this, a modern person's body has become a battleground between the rationalist mind and the native soul. As a shaman, I saw this as the cause of a great deal of spiritual and physical illness.

Over the last two or three centuries, a heartless culture-crushing mentality has incremented its *progress* on the earth, devouring all peoples, nature, imagination, and spiritual knowledge. Like a big mechanized slug, it has left behind a flat, homogenized streak of civilization wherever it passed. Every human on this earth—African, Asian, European, Islanders, or from the Americas—has ancestors who at some point in their history had their stories, rituals, ingenuity, language, and lifeways taken away, enslaved, banned, exploited, twisted, or destroyed by this force.

Now what is indigenous, natural, subtle, hard to explain, generous, gradual, and village-oriented in each of us is being banished into the ghettos of our hearts, or hidden away from view onto reservations inside the spiritual landscape of the Earth Body. In shamanic terms, our minds are being taught to believe that whatever we can think is actually the center of a person's life, just like a conquering culture, or a modern culture which thinks with the mind, not with the ancestral soul.

Meanwhile, our natural souls, which are like Bushmen or rare waterbirds, know that our minds and our souls should be working together to maintain or replaster the crumbling hut of life. Instead, our indigenous souls are being utterly overlooked and pushed aside in the bustle of the minds' competitive activity, until our true beings feel just like a tribesman in a big, trafficky city: unwelcomed, lost, and homeless.

We Tzutujil shamans don't believe the primitive notion that human spirit resides in the brain or even in the mind, or that it is even human, for that matter. And memories, especially the most ancient, natural kind, definitely don't live in the head, but reside all over the place. Therefore, because this beautiful, dejected spirit is not given a home in a person's life anymore, the homeless soul has become a fugitive in the World House of our bodies, trying to hide somewhere so that our minds won't find it. It flees and hides because if our modern minds treat our personal indigenousness as viciously as the modern culture treats all the natural people of the world, then our personal spirits fear being discovered by their oppressors—our own thinking.

Though the modern world can appear somewhat soulless and its people numbed and asleep, I discovered that deep in the World House of their bodies live resourceful, intelligent, soulful refugees who, like myself, waited and wondered when they would ever be welcomed back home again.

When I divine the Earth Bodies of many people of today, their worlds look like a post-war country, bombed out, dry, flowerless, and tired. The flat devastation wreaked upon these people's Earth Body needs renewing. Their World House needs reassembling, replastering; it has to be remembered back to life, so that the faraway native souls, their natural indigenous beings, can return to their homes. Maybe this is why Chiviliu sent me away, to sing and speak these people's lives back together. After all, he said that the destruction was coming from them. Our world was being killed by people whose naturalness had been disenfranchised long ago. The violence they leveled upon us came from their soulless minds and angry, homeless souls, looking for permanence through violent business growth, killing, forgetting, and mocking everything that reminded them of their inadequacies.

For there to be a world at all, every indigenous, original, natural thing must start singing its song, dancing its dance, moving and breathing, each according to its own nature, saying its name, manifesting simultaneously its secret spiritual signature. Every Gypsy must be singing her ancient tune, every Bushman, Croat, Arab, Jew, Chukchee, Hmong,

Papuan, Celt, Yoruba, Saxon, Cree, Guarani, Sami, Inuit, Kazaki, Tahitian, Balinese, Han, Ainu, jaguar, honey creeper, anteater, shrike, beetle, butterfly, oak, birch, ceiba, baobab, dog, mosquito, shark, coral, lightning, tornado, mist, mountain, deer, desert, and so on forever, each must be making its magic sound. When any of these stops singing for being killed or destroyed, a piece of the World's House is lost. This in a village is the equivalent of losing a family. When this happens in the village, it's a call for all the people to come together to find or renew the family's lost tribe—or to grieve their gaping loss. Our grief, when deeply expressed communally, as it is in a village, sends the lost sound like an echo back to its home. This puts some mud back into the void left in the World House.

If done passionately, grief strengthens the World House, because the creative substance of our songs is perceived by the spirits as canoes to take the dead home. Our tears are jade beads to adorn the Face of Life, the Earth Fruit.

Shamans say the Village Heart can grow a brand-new World House if it is well-dressed in the layered clothing of each indigenous soul's magic sound, ancestral songs, and indigenous ingenuity. The wrecked landscape of our World House could sprout a renewed world, but a new language has to be found. We can't make the old world come alive again, but from its old seeds, the next layer could sprout.

This new language would have to grow from the indigenous hearts we all have hidden. It shouldn't be a language of oneness, not one language, not a computer tongue of homogenization, but a diverse, beautiful, badly made thing whose flimsiness and inefficiency force people to sing together to keep it well-spoken and sung into life over and over again, so that nobody forgets to remember. We need to find gorgeous, unsellable ritual words to reanimate, remeasure, rebuild, and replaster the ruined, depressed flatness left by the hollow failure of this mechanized, orphaned culture.

For this, we need all peoples: our poets, our shamans, our dreamers, our youth, our elders, our women, our men, our ancestors, and our real old memories from before we were people.

We live in a kind of dark age, craftily lit with synthetic light, so that no one can tell how dark it has really gotten. But our exiled spirits can tell. Deep in our bones resides an ancient, singing couple who just won't give up making their beautiful, wild noise. The world won't end if we can find them.

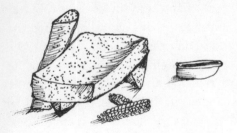

ABOUT THE AUTHOR

Martín Prechtel was raised on a Pueblo reservation in New Mexico before moving to Santiago Atitlán in Guatemala, where he apprenticed to Nicolas Chiviliu Tacaxoy, a Tzutujil Mayan shaman. Martín eventually rose to the office of *Nabey Mam*, first chief. Returning to the United States, Martín began working in New Mexico as a medicine man. He is now a nationally recognized healer, speaker, and artist who writes frequently for anthropological journals and university publications and is constantly on the road speaking and lecturing.